Religion and Political Theory

Religion and Political Theory

Secularism, Accommodation and the New Challenges of Religious Diversity

Edited by Jonathan Seglow and Andrew Shorten

ecpr PRESS

ROWMAN & LITTLEFIELD
INTERNATIONAL

London • New York

Published by Rowman & Littlefield International, Ltd.
6 Tinworth Street, London, SE11 5AL
www.rowmaninternational.com

In partnership with the European Consortium for Political Research, Harbour House, 6–8
Hythe Quay, Colchester, CO2 8JF, United Kingdom

Rowman & Littlefield International, Ltd. is an affiliate of
Rowman & Littlefield
4501 Forbes Boulevard, Suite 200, Lanham, Maryland 20706, USA
With additional offices in Boulder, New York, Toronto (Canada), and London (UK)
www.rowman.com

British Library Cataloguing in Publication Information
A catalogue record for this book is available from the British Library

ISBN: HB 978-1-78552-314-4
ISBN: PB 978-1-78552-315-1

Library of Congress Control Number: 2019949263

Contents

Acknowledgements

This edited collection arose from a workshop held at the Joint Sessions of the European Consortium of Political Research, which took place at the University of Nottingham in April 2017. Most of the chapters were first presented there and the editors would like to thank all of the participants at that event for their contributions. Additional thanks are due to Marcia Taylor and the other staff from the ECPR for organizing the Joint Sessions, to Madeleine Hatfield and Ian O'Flynn from the ECPR Press, and to Rebecca Anastasi and Dhara Snowden from Rowman & Littlefield International.

Acknowledgements

ONE

Introduction

Jonathan Seglow and Andrew Shorten

Religion has never been far away from political theorizing, especially in the liberal tradition. Indeed, much of the history of modern political thought, at least in the West, can be read as an attempt to grapple with religion's – and specifically Christianity's – claim to be a preemptory source of normative authority, rivalling that of the state, that is, not just a guide to life for the individual believer. The characteristically liberal solution to that puzzle – that religious adherents should be free to follow their beliefs in the private sphere, but that the public domain of law and state action should not draw its authority from any religious doctrine – finds its expression in the First Amendment to the US Constitution, as well as the more recent defence of political liberalism by the twentieth century's foremost political philosopher, John Rawls (1996). Of course, the public/private divide does not characterize only American constitutional theorizing. The French republican tradition of *laïcité* articulates a peculiarly strong version of a public realm that is free of religion, one explicitly invoked in France's 2011 law that outlawed the wearing of the burka or niqab in public places. The controversy that decision provoked – with similar bans following in Belgium and a number of other European states – illustrates too that contemporary discussion about the place of religion in the liberal democratic state does not just concern Christianity. The situation of Muslims in Europe raises other normative and practical concerns, such as the possible role for Sharia law alongside secular law, and shows too how contemporary thinking about religion and the political domain is affected by global trends such as large-scale immigration into Europe.

As far as the United States is concerned, the second clause of First Amendment explicitly forbids laws that would prohibit the exercise of religious liberty, just as the first clause rules out religious establishment. It is often said that these two clauses are somewhat in tension: the first clause grants special latitude to religious believers, *privileging* religion over nontheistic bodies of thought, while the nonestablishment clause peculiarly *disables* religion (in contrast to other, e.g., liberal, values). Reconciling the free exercise and the nonestablishment clauses has produced a lively, if slightly self-absorbed, body of work in American legal scholarship, much of it analysing the case law of the US Supreme Court. Political theorists are free of the constraints of legal interpretation, but they have grappled with the same issues. The ideal of nonestablishment has become generalized into the doctrine of liberal neutrality, popularized by Rawls, according to which the state should be neutral and is therefore disbarred from appealing to the value of any religious or nonreligious 'comprehensive doctrine' in the justification of its laws and policies. Liberty of conscience can also be developed along neutral lines. The European Charter on Human Rights (ECHR), to which almost every European state is a signatory, delineates in its Article 9 a right to manifest one's 'religion or belief', where the latter refers to an analogously weighty and serious doctrine. Article 14 of the ECHR also protects religious believers and bearers of other 'protected characteristics' from discrimination to which they may be subject, at least in the exercise of their other ECHR rights. Thus for example, a Christian Sabbatarian required by her employer to work on a Sunday could make a claim under both Article 9 (she cannot attend collective worship on Sundays) and Article 14 (she is treated less favourably than nonreligious employees). In the United States, nondiscrimination law has been theorized through the notion of 'disparate impact'.

Articles 9 and 14 have not only been interpreted by the European Court of Human Rights in various ways (with an accompanying legal commentary), the nature and basis of the interests they protect have also been explored by political theorists who have debated the vexed issue of religious (and nonreligious) accommodation, that is, when strong believers are exempted from otherwise universal laws or regulations or where these are interpreted with such latitude as to permit them to manifest their beliefs. In the United Kingdom, for example, Sikh men who want to ride motorbikes are exempted from the law mandating the wearing of crash helmets, and they are also permitted to wear their ceremonial dagger (kirpan) in public. Jews and Muslims also have special dispensation to slaughter animals in accordance with their religious rituals even though this would normally be contrary to animal welfare laws. Accommodating religious belief in the way that laws and regulations are applied and interpreted has raised a host of issues concerning religious dress (including, for example, the case of a Muslim woman who wished to wear the niqab at work), the permissibility of discrimination (where Christians have sometimes refused a service to a gay couple that they would extend to a heterosexual one), and even the right of a Hindu man to be cremated on an open funeral pyre.[1]

Crucial though they are for individual claimants, these issues may not seem so important in the larger scheme of things, compared to matters of social and economic policy, for instance. But particular debates over religious accommodation are important for symbolic reasons as they bring into focus questions about the place of religion in increasingly secular societies, of states' treatment of minority and in particular postmigration communities such as Muslims in Europe, thus spilling over into the debate on multiculturalism, as well as, at least in the British context, the place of an established church in multifaith societies. Moreover, the debate over religious accommodation and religious liberty more generally also raises questions for the very architecture of liberal theory. While classical liberal theorists such as John Locke urged the toleration of dissenting sects (in Locke's case, provided that they were Christian), Rawls and other contemporary liberals' doctrine of state neutrality is far more demanding. While Locke held that the coercive attempt to change a person's inner belief was irrational, Rawls sees it as illegitimate: citizens should not be subjected to laws whose rationale could not in principle enjoy their assent. Not everyone sees neutrality as even desirable, however. Writers sympathetic to religion see it, in practice if not in theory, as a movement for the secularization of the public sphere (as in *laïcité*). Allied to that is the now familiar charge that liberal freedom of conscience covertly privileges religious doctrines, such as Protestant Christianity, which emphasize individual belief, at the expense of others, such as Islam, whose practices suffuse the public as well as private spheres (Laborde 2017). Christian writers too, however, have attacked Rawls's principle of public reason by which legislators and public officials are prohibited from appealing to religious premises in political argument (e.g., Wolterstorff 2008).

The chapters in this book aim to provide a state of the art in political theorists' attempts to grapple with these issues, both philosophically and with regard to particular concrete disputes. Some of them provide a fresh perspective on longstanding problems of secularism, accommodation, and religious liberty, by a new generation of scholars of religion and political theory. Others raise an emerging issue where religious practice and political principle are on a collision course. The chapters in part 1 focus on secularism and on its relationship with liberalism. Those in part 2 consider the problem of accommodation, both in the narrow sense of exempting religious believers and institutions from generally applicable laws and in the broader sense of 'giving a break' to religious believers. Finally, those in part 3 sample a range of new challenges of religious diversity, in the workplace and society at large. In the remainder of this introduction we will elaborate on the themes raised above by way of introducing each part, and preview the arguments of the essays it contains.

1. SECULARISM AND LIBERALISM

'Secularism' is an ambiguous term. Sometimes it denotes a particular kind of worldview, typically an atheistic or antireligious outlook that defines the goals of human life and flourishing without reference to spiritual or otherworldly values. Meanwhile, it is also used to refer to a family of views that converge on the idea that a principled distance ought to be maintained between the state and religion. Rajeev Bhargava (1998) calls the first kind of view 'ethical secularism' and the second 'political secularism'. While ethical secularism can be contrasted with religion itself, political secularism is an alternative to both theocracy, where the state is governed by divine laws administered by a religiously ordained class of rulers, and establishment, in which the state recognizes (or 'establishes') one or more churches or religions as official.

The chapters in this section all concern the latter – political – form of secularism, and they explore various aspects of its relationship with liberal political theory. Although secularism has often been associated with the liberal tradition, it is not an exclusively liberal ideal. Indeed, scholars sometimes illustrate the breadth and flexibility of secularism by contrasting its republican and liberal variants. In its republican mode, secularism is an activist doctrine, requiring the state to control religion, for instance so as to preserve the freedom and equality of its citizens. Meanwhile, in its liberal mode, secularism merely insists that religious and political institutions be isolated from one another, as suggested by the characteristic image of a wall of separation.

Political secularism raises three difficult philosophical challenges for liberal political theory. The first concerns its relationship with ethical secularism. In its republican variant, political and ethical secularism seem to go hand-in-hand with one another. For example, republicanism in France was historically motivated by a form of ethical secularism, which regarded religion as an irrational and dangerous force requiring containment. Meanwhile, many liberal advocates of political secularism, following Rawls (1996), have been at pains to emphasize that support for their doctrine does not depend upon ethical secularism (e.g., Larmore 1999; Gaus 2011). This is crucial for them since, if political secularism is to be an acceptable mode of governance for diverse political communities, then its principles must be acceptable to as many people as possible, including religious believers as well as ethical secularists. Against this, critics regard the supposed inclusivity of liberal secularism as little more than a sleight of hand. For one thing, they point out that it is surely not coincidental that political secularism is more commonly found in secularized societies. This suggests that secular politics either depends upon, or perhaps hastens, the diminishing social and cultural significance of religion itself. Furthermore, critics also complain that liberal secularism is no less biased against religious beliefs and believers than republican secularism, since it requires the exclusion of religious reasons from political discourse and religious symbols from public life (Perry 2003; Wolterstorff 2008).

The second challenge raised by political secularism concerns the extent to which it is compatible with the various ways in which actually existing liberal democracies endorse or support particular religions, or religion in general. In public discourse at least, political secularism is often reduced to the narrow formula of separation of church and state, and this is typically understood to mean that the state must neither establish any particular religion as official nor publicly endorse or support any particular faith. For instance, and as noted earlier, this is what the First Amendment to the Constitution of the United States stipulates. However, if separation is interpreted strictly in this way, and if it is regarded as a necessary condition for political secularism, then many liberal democracies will not qualify as secular, since regimes of 'weak establishment' remain quite common. In response, some scholars have developed revisionist theories of secularism that relax the requirement of strict separation. For example, Cécile Laborde's (2017) theory of 'minimal' secularism permits state endorsement of religion under certain circumstances, while Tariq Modood's (2019) theory of 'moderate' or 'inclusive' secularism allows for an established church provided that equivalent forms of support are provided to minority faiths.

Finally, the third challenge raised by political secularism concerns its constitutive values. These are often obscured in public debates about secularism, since as already noted the doctrine is frequently reduced to the principle of separation. One reason to regret this is that separation – no less than its philosophically more respectable sibling neutrality – is not valuable in itself. Rather, if separation or neutrality are valuable they are so as means for realizing more basic values. Furthermore, as Jocelyn Maclure and Charles Taylor have observed, reducing political secularism to either separation or neutrality risks jeopardizing the basic values that secular political arrangements are supposed to protect. To illustrate this worry, they point to the tendency in French and Quebecker politics and public discourse to zealously defend the separation doctrine at the expense of freedom of conscience (Maclure and Taylor 2011, 28–29). On their reading, this is to fetishize the 'means' of secularism at the expense of its more fundamental 'ends'.

So, any theory of political secularism, including a liberal one, must identify its constitutive values, and liberal political theorists continue to disagree about the form and content of these values. Sune Lægaard's chapter takes a recent and distinctive answer to this puzzle as its point of departure, namely Laborde's 'disaggregation' of secularism into three dimensions (Laborde 2017). On Laborde's reading, the values underlying political secularism are public justifiability, civic equality, and personal freedom. Because her theory is a minimal one, Laborde allows that a variety of institutional arrangements might satisfy the requirements of liberalism's secular core. In particular, she believes that a state will qualify as minimally secular provided that, first, its institutions and representatives restrict themselves to accessible reasons when justifying laws; secondly, its laws and institutions include the followers of different faiths and none as equals; and thirdly, it respects the freedom of its citizens by refraining from imposing a comprehensive ethics upon them.

Of course, these dimensions of minimal secularism each require unpacking, and Lægaard sets himself the task of examining the second, egalitarian, principle, which he refers to as secularism as civic inclusiveness. He does so in order to address a general puzzle raised by political secularism, which is that it sometimes seems to require exclusionary policies in order to satisfy an egalitarian principle of inclusion. The kind of exclusionary policies Lægaard has in mind include things like bans on religious dress or symbols. Of course, whether such policies really are required in the name of secular equality is itself controversial, and Lægaard's analysis carefully sorts through the different ways in which an egalitarian principle of civic inclusiveness can be mobilized on both sides of the argument. Ultimately, Lægaard's analysis reveals some of the inner complexities and ambiguities of the secular ideal of inclusion, suggesting that any plausible theory of secularism which incorporates this ideal must specify when, how, and where it applies.

Alongside Laborde's theory, another recent attempt to identify the constitutive values of political secularism has been proposed by Maclure and Taylor (2011), and this theory provides the orientation for the next chapter, written by Sebastián Rudas. Maclure and Taylor believe that the fundamental values protected by political secularism are equal respect and freedom of conscience (and perhaps also fraternity, identified by Taylor in another essay; see Taylor 2011). As mentioned earlier, they arrive at this definition at least in part because they want to avoid reducing secularism to the separation of church and state. Furthermore, they also want to avoid defining secularism in such a way that it would be biased against religion, and it is crucial to them that the political ethic of a secular regime be acceptable to a diverse range of religious and nonreligious worldviews.

According to Rudas, however, Maclure and Taylor's approach to secularism is unhelpfully biased towards liberal versions of secularism, since defining secularism in terms of equal respect and freedom of conscience excludes regimes such as Ataturk's Turkey from the category. Furthermore, their theory also implies that only those states in which the separation doctrine is interpreted moderately, rather than strictly, qualify as genuinely secular. This is a problem, Rudas believes, because such a narrow and moralized definition of secularism is fitting only for societies that have already secularized. But in such places, political secularism is either optional or perhaps even redundant. Meanwhile, in other societies, containing religious institutions that have not internalized the values of liberal democracy, the most relevant version of secularism, argues Rudas against Maclure and Taylor, is the traditional doctrine of separation. In addition to revealing a possible shortcoming with dominant liberal egalitarian theories of secularism, Rudas's chapter also provides an interesting perspective on a long-standing problem for secularism, which concerns whether, given its European heritage, it can 'travel' beyond its original setting (Taylor 1998, 37; see also Bilgrami (ed.) 2016).

Paul Billingham's chapter also takes up the question of how liberal states ought to respond to groups and individuals whose beliefs or practices are at odds with liberal egalitarian norms, such as when religious organizations apply hierarchical or discriminatory rules internally or in their interactions with outsiders. Billingham asks whether liberal states are justified in using noncoercive powers to discourage practices like these, such as by withholding subsidies and tax exemptions or speaking out against them. This possibility is especially attractive to liberals, since the obvious alternatives – toleration or coercion – both seem unsatisfactory. Following Stephen Macedo (1998), Billingham labels this approach 'transformative liberalism', and his chapter strikes a sceptical note about it. On the one hand, he suggests that the case in favour of transformative liberalism is often based on mistaken assumptions, such as the beliefs that tax exemptions and subsidies for religious groups imply state endorsement of nonliberal beliefs and practices, or that members of nonliberal groups are likely to be bad citizens. On the other hand, he also argues that transformative liberalism may be too expansive a doctrine, since it seems to require state action on the basis of what will often be controversial judgments about religious practices. One reason why this should concern us, Billingham argues, is that the transformative state may impose an expressive harm on people whose practices it deems beyond the pale.

2. RELIGIOUS ACCOMMODATION

The contributions to the second section concern the idea of accommodation, which refers to 'giving religious people a "break" in some area' (Nussbaum 2008, 21), usually by applying regulations, policies, or laws in a sensitive way in order to avoid unnecessarily burdening people's conscientious convictions. Sometimes the term is used in a very broad sense, to refer to things like altering the way in which particular public services are provided so as to more effectively meet the distinctive needs of minority faith communities. Amongst political theorists, however, it is often used in a narrower sense, to refer to exemptions from generally applicable rules, such as the exemptions for Sikhs, Jews, and Muslims mentioned earlier.

Exemptions for religious minorities are long established in law. For example, the exemption permitting religious slaughter in the United Kingdom was formally provided for in the 1933 Slaughter of Animals Act (Poulter 1998, 134), and in the 1920s and 1930s, American Jews and Catholics were exempted from Prohibition laws to enable them to use wine for ceremonial purposes (Levy 1999, 128). However, it is only in the relatively recent past that political theorists have begun to discuss exemptions seriously. Initially they did so in the context of developing normative theories of multiculturalism (e.g., Kymlicka 1995; Parekh 2000). Here exemptions were usually characterized as rough-and-ready mechanisms to promote the inclusion or equality of marginalized minorities. Meanwhile, a subsequent generation of scholars developed a series of more refined normative arguments for exemptions, justifying them by appealing to values such as freedom (Eisgruber and Sager 2007; Nussbaum 2008) and integrity (Bou-Habib 2006; Maclure and Taylor 2011; Laborde 2017; Seglow 2017).

Exemptions have proven to be as controversial in theory as they have been in practice, and a number of philosophical objections have been levelled against them. In one influential critique, Brian Barry argued that almost any justification one might give for allowing a minority to do something will also be an argument for allowing everyone else to do that thing. So if Sikhs ought to be permitted to ride motorcycles without crash helmets then so should everyone else (Barry 2001). Others have argued that exemptions are incompatible with equal treatment and that the requirements of the latter should nearly always be overriding (Waldron 2002; Dworkin 2013). An important variant of this argument has been proposed by feminist scholars, who worry that at least some exemptions might be in tension with gender equality (Skjeie 2007). Still another line of criticism is that religious exemptions are unfair if they require nonreligious citizens to bear the costs of accommodating the beliefs of their religious compatriots (Jones 1994; Leiter 2012).

A particularly significant challenge for advocates of accommodation has been to identify the kinds of convictions, beliefs, or practices that deserve special consideration. For the most part, accommodation measures have been advanced on behalf of religious minorities, and some theorists believe that religious convictions are uniquely deserving of special consideration (Laycock 1990; Koppelman 2006). However, a number of philosophers have questioned this (Bedi 2007; Leiter 2012; Dworkin 2013) and, in response, liberal egalitarian political theorists have increasingly sought to identify grounds for exemptions that do not prioritize religious over other kinds of deeply held convictions. One of the most difficult challenges confronting these arguments is the threat of exemption proliferation, and this provides the subject matter for Nick Martin's chapter. The proliferation objection is a slippery slope argument, holding that exemptions are a risky form of accommodation since if too many are granted then both the authority of the law and social cohesion itself may be compromised.

Normative theories that allow exemptions for nonreligious practices as well as religious ones are especially vulnerable to the exemption proliferation objection, and advocates of such theories are often highly sensitive to this fact. For example, as Martin observes, leading theorists have variously felt it necessary to explain that although wearers of religious dress may be entitled to legal accommodations, consistency does not require extending comparable accommodations to the wearers of chicken suits, baseball caps, or clown hats (Nussbaum 2008, 169; Maclure and Taylor 2011, 77; Laborde 2017, 199–200). Focusing on arguments that connect the justification of exemptions to the protection of individual integrity, Martin proposes to counter the threat of proliferation by applying two tests. The first 'sincerity' test rules out exemptions for people with insincere commitments to the belief or practice in question, something which Martin thinks can usually be established by asking whether someone's conduct consistently meets the standards they declare themselves to have. For example, an employee seeking dietary accommodations on religious grounds would fail the sincerity test if they were known to regularly break the relevant dietary laws in their private life. Meanwhile, the second 'balancing' test compares the weight of an individual interest in a contested practice against the societal interest in upholding the relevant rule. Martin acknowledges that applying the second test in practice is bound to be controversial since we are prone to misestimating the relevant interests, for instance by exaggerating the importance of some laws or failing to appreciate the significance of a particular practice to a minority. Nevertheless, he concludes that it is the most effective means for integrity-based theories to avoid a proliferation of exemptions.

Until recently, political theorists who wrote about accommodation and exemptions were preoccupied with examples in which special treatment was sought by religious individuals. During the last decade, however, political theorists have expanded their repertoire of examples to also include ones in which religious associations or institutions have sought special treatment, typically in the form of exemptions from anti-discrimination laws. Examples of such accommodations range from the relatively uncontroversial, such as exemptions from employment laws permitting the Catholic Church to restrict the priesthood to men, to the fiercely contested, such as the decision in *Burwell v. Hobby Lobby* (2014) that allowed a firm owned by evangelical Christians to opt out of the requirement of providing emergency contraception insurance for its workers (Schwartzman, Flanders, and Robinson (eds.) 2016).

Two different frameworks have been employed by legal and political theorists to assess cases in which special treatment is sought by associations or collectives rather than individuals. One is a liberal rights-based framework, which asks whether religious associations have sufficiently weighty interests to justify special treatment (Shorten 2015; Laborde 2017). The other is a theory of jurisdictional autonomy or legal pluralism, which tends to be much more deferential towards religious associations, since it is based on the idea that the secular state lacks the authority to trespass on the internal governance of religious bodies (McConnell 1985; Muñiz-Fraticelli 2014; Smith 2016). Critics have mostly focused on the second framework, which says that religious associations ought to be treated as quasi-sovereign entities (Schragger and Schwartzman 2013; Cohen 2015). In her contribution, Andrea Baumeister draws upon and extends some of these objections, emphasizing that institutional autonomy might sometimes be contrary to the interests of vulnerable group members. In addition, she also argues that liberal rights-based theories are flawed, and develops a civic republican account of the limits of religious institutional accommodation.

Baumeister argues that advocates of institutional autonomy have mischaracterized the purposes of the separation of church and state. For them, separation is ultimately about insulating the church from the power of the state – hence their belief that religious authorities should have exclusive jurisdiction over what they regard as internal affairs. Meanwhile, Baumeister points out that separation also protects the state from religion, by protecting the political sphere from the sectarian claims of religion. This is crucial, since it reveals that separation is ultimately bound up with the idea that the state belongs to all its citizens as equals. Given this, civic republicans should be suspicious of calls for institutional autonomy, since they aim to remove matters from public contestation that would otherwise fall under the domain of popular sovereignty. Furthermore, a civic republican concern with the integrity of the public political sphere suggests that the freedom of religious collectives ought sometimes to be sharply curtailed in order to uphold the civic values of inclusivity and equality.

Christoph Baumgartner's contribution is concerned with accommodation in a broader rather than narrower sense, and his chapter addresses recent public controversies in Switzerland, the Netherlands, France, and Germany about the refusal of (some) Muslims to shake hands with members of the opposite sex. Such cases raise the issue of accommodation, since what has been sought is the modification of a certain range of social expectations. In his chapter, Baumgartner seeks to identify the relevant normative criteria for addressing this request by combining arguments about equality and culture from political theory with insights from anthropology, the latter of which explain some of the challenges faced by Muslims when negotiating the conflicting demands of society and religion. While advocates of the theory of transformative liberalism, as discussed in Billingham's chapter, might want the liberal state to encourage conformity with social norms about shaking hands, for instance in order to promote gender equality, Baumgartner instead argues that the preferences of those who refuse to shake hands with members of the opposite sex should be accommodated, for instance by encouraging the use of alternative greetings within public and professional settings.

3. THE NEW CHALLENGES OF RELIGIOUS DIVERSITY

The contributions to the final section cover the topics of compromise, the French burka ban and the Swiss referendum which led to a constitutional ban on the building of new minarets. Apart from the latter pair both involving Muslims in Europe, the chapters may not appear to have much in common. In fact, however, they highlight two different ways in which disputes over religious liberty and accommodation might be resolved, and this reflects a basic division of our political thinking. To see this, it is worth enquiring a little further into the logic of rights, whether human rights, as in the ECHR, or constitutional rights, as in the First Amendment to the US Constitution. Declarations of rights are generally rather short documents, notwithstanding their caveats. That is as it should be: rights are statements of principle. But seen from the perspective of conflict between religious custom and the demands of state (or indeed the interests of other citizens), the mere assertion of a right in any particular instance is usually uninformative, since what we need to know is how the right in question should be interpreted and, in particular, what its limits are. The issue is more vexatious still when one right clashes with another. For instance, in a recent case in the United States, *Phillips v. Craig and Mullins*, the Supreme Court dismissed the complaint of a gay couple about their being discriminated against by a baker who refused to make them a cake to celebrate their marriage.[2] Here, the baker's right to freedom of religion prevailed over the gay couple's interests. The Court was careful to state that their judgement should not be interpreted as the view that freedom of religion trumps nondiscrimination quite generally. To do so could have been seen as an admission of judicial overactivism; courts are meant to interpret law, not to make it. But a more charitable view of the Court's reticence in this case is simply that religious liberty, and nondiscrimination, vital though they are, are too broad and sweeping for the nitty gritty of judicial interpretation, which involves attending to contending parties' particular interests in specific circumstances. Declarations of rights are often drafted as moral rallying cries after revolutions (as in the United States) or catastrophes – the ECHR, like the UDHR a few years before it, championed the dignity of humankind amidst the ashes of the Second World War. But in the midst of the local issues of normal conflicts, the appeal to rights alone may not do much to help us.

Peter Jones asserts that resolving issues of accommodation are 'exercises in ad hockery', which he intends simply as a statement of fact, not a complaint (Jones 2017, 173). But when principles are involved, however vague, perhaps there is a little more we can say. The chapters in the third part of the book can be read as contributing to an alternative approach, one which emphasizes the horizontal relations between citizens, in contrast to the vertical image of judges issuing rulings from on high. In doing so, they have something in common with influential critics of judicial activism such as Jeremy Waldron (1999) and Richard Bellamy (2007), who complain of unelected judges illegitimately seizing political authority from its rightful owners, the citizen body. However, we need not endorse Waldron's appeal to democracy or Bellamy's championing of republicanism in order to see the merits of the horizontal approach. Such an approach reminds us that in a democratic state, sovereignty belongs to the people who remain the law's ultimate authors. So much, so obvious perhaps, but in fact the principle of popular sovereignty has been challenged by the legal pluralist school, mentioned above, who urge instead the division of sovereignty into separate spheres, civil matters are determined by the people, but questions of faith remain the province of the church. Seeing *all* law as issuing from the citizen body is to reject legal pluralism and also to assert instead citizens' ultimate authorship of society's rules (Cohen 2015). What that means in practice can vary, and the three chapters in this part of the book provide three different examples of the idea in practice.

Élise Rouméas's chapter on compromise begins by noting the apparent disparity between the world of negotiation and bargaining, on the one hand, and religious observance, on the other, at least insofar as the latter is thought to issue in apodictic demands, what one might call the 'intransigence thesis'. Though the intransigence thesis enjoys some support among philosophers, it arguably underplays the possibilities for creative solutions to apparently intractable conflicts between religious believers. Rouméas distinguishes between compromise and deliberation. The latter is an attractive but also demanding ideal as it urges the transformation of one's moral outlook in the light of others' reasoned argument, something not always possible or, from their point of view at least, desirable for religious believers. By contrast, parties to a compromise retain their deep-seated beliefs, they just leave them at the door of the negotiating room as they engage with the troublesome realities of a world composed of believers with views at sharp variance to their own. Rouméas goes on to explain three categories of compromise: dividing some resource, integrating elements of both sides' views, and finding an acceptable third way that is a second best for each party. The down-to-earth nature of compromise shifts attention away from contending propositional truths and 'the war of gods', though care must be taken not to exclude minority voices. Compromise is one way that laws and rules can be returned to the people; and in contexts such as employment is often a pragmatically superior alternative to the use of tribunals.

Simon Thompson's chapter reconstructs the arguments for and against the legal ban of the Muslim burka in France, a decision that enjoyed considerable popular support. In the recent case of *SAS v. France* (2014), the European Court of Human Rights considered the issue from the perspective of Articles 9 and 14, and in upholding the French ban effectively invented a new legal interest in 'living together'. Departing from a rights-based perspective, Thompson instead makes use of the framework developed by David Miller (2013) whereby diverse citizens should enjoy equal opportunities to realize their cultural or religious commitments, provided that doing so does not cause harm to others or undermine the basis for important public goods. As Thompson notes, however, the opportunity to wear the burka made use of by some Muslim women was not about engaging in some private act, but rather about appearance in public. Thus, the debate involves how different interests may be combined in public space. Rejecting the view that wearing the burka causes anyone harm, or that it undermines the good of 'living together' in public space, or causes inequalities in opportunities, Thompson argues that the French and other bans should be repealed. Unlike the rights-based approach which pits the interests of some citizens against those of others, Thompson appeals to Miller's call for democratic deliberation and wonders whether a blanket approach to questions of accommodation could really enjoy widespread legitimacy. In this instance, the democratic approach seems preferable to the rights-based one in the way it is sensitive to the interests of all affected parties.

Esma Baycan and Matteo Gianni's chapter considers the decision of the Swiss populace in their referendum of 2009 to ban the construction of new minarets on mosques. Though the Muslim population of Switzerland is small, and few extant mosques there in fact have minarets, the vote attracted international comment, much of it condemnatory, as it was seen as singling out Islam for specially disabling treatment. As Baycan and Gianni point out, political theorists' treatment of the episode has focused on the substantive outcome of the referendum. The consensus is that the decision was an unjust one insofar as Islam was discriminated against and thus not treated impartially with other religions. While not rejecting that conclusion, Baycan and Gianni examine instead the process of the referendum, and in particular its democratic pedigree. Though referenda at both the federal and cantonal levels are an established part of Swiss politics, the minaret decision was, they argue, democratically deficient on a number of levels: the discourse leading up to the vote constructed Swiss Muslims as an alien 'other' who had not properly assimilated into Swiss society; there was little appreciation of their point of view, and practically speaking as most Muslim residents of Switzerland were not naturalized citizens, the decision was foisted upon them in terms they couldn't contest. Baycan and Gianni's contribution raises larger issues, not just about the place of Muslims in majority Christian states, but also, more theoretically, about the relationship between justice and democracy. On one view, if minarets can be defended through the right to religious freedom, then it is unclear whether democratic majorities have the authority to ban them. As we suggested above, however, exactly what the contours of that right involve is a substantive question. Given that, it seems fitting for the people to resolve the issue since they are the ones who have to live with the results.

REFERENCES

Barry, Brian. 2001. *Culture and Equality: An Egalitarian Critique of Multiculturalism.* Cambridge: Polity Press.

Bedi, Sonu. 2007. 'What Is So Special About Religion? The Dilemma of the Religious Exemption'. *Journal of Political Philosophy* 15 (2): 235–49.

Bellamy, Richard. 2007. *Political Constitutionalism: A Republican Defence of the Constitutionality of Democracy.* Cambridge: Cambridge University Press.

Bhargava, Rajeev. 1998. 'Giving Secularism Its Due'. In *Secularism and Its Critics,* edited by Rajeev Bhargava, 486–511. New Delhi: Oxford University Press.

Bilgrami, Akeel, ed. 2016. *Beyond the Secular West.* New York: Columbia University Press.

Bou-Habib, Paul. 2006. 'A Theory of Religious Accommodation'. *Journal of Applied Philosophy* 23 (1): 109–26.

Cohen, Jean. 2015. 'Freedom of Religion, Inc. Whose Sovereignty?' *Netherlands Journal of Legal Philosophy* 44 (3).

Dworkin, Ronald. 2013. *Religion without God.* Cambridge, MA: Harvard University Press.

Eisgruber, Christopher L., and Lawrence G. Sager. 2007. *Religious Freedom and the Constitution.* Cambridge, MA: Harvard University Press.

Gaus, Gerald. 2011. *The Order of Public Reason: A Theory of Freedom and Morality in a Diverse and Bounded World.* Cambridge: Cambridge University Press.

Jones, Peter. 1994. 'Bearing the Consequences of Belief'. *Journal of Political Philosophy* 2 (1): 24–43.

———. 2017. 'Religious Exemptions and Distributive Justice'. In *Religion in Liberal Political Philosophy,* edited by Cécile Laborde and Aurelia Bardon, 163–76. Oxford: Oxford University Press.

Koppelman, Andrew. 2006. 'Is It Fair to Give Religion Special Treatment?' *University of Illinois Law Review* 2006: 571–604.

Kymlicka, Will. 1995. *Multicultural Citizenship.* Oxford: Oxford University Press.

Laborde, Cécile. 2017. *Liberalism's Religion.* Cambridge, MA: Harvard University Press.

Larmore, Charles. 1999. 'The Moral Basis of Political Liberalism'. *The Journal of Philosophy* 96 (12): 599–625.

Laycock, Douglas. 1990. 'The Remnants of Free Exercise'. *The Supreme Court Review* 1990: 1–68.

Leiter, Brian. 2012. *Why Tolerate Religion?* Princeton, NJ: Princeton University Press.

Levy, Jacob. 1999. *The Multiculturalism of Fear.* Oxford: Oxford University Press.

Macedo, Stephen. 1998. 'Transformative Constitutionalism and the Case of Religion: Defending the Moderate Hegemony of Liberalism'. *Political Theory* 26 (1): 56–80.

Maclure, Jocelyn, and Charles Taylor. 2011. *Secularism and Freedom of Conscience.* Translated by Jane Marie Todd. Cambridge, MA: Harvard University Press.

McConnell, Michael W. 1985. 'Accommodation of Religion'. *The Supreme Court Review* 1985: 1–59.

Miller, David. 2013. 'Liberalism, Equal Opportunities and Cultural Commitments'. In *Justice for Earthlings: Essays in Political Philosophy,* 93–114. Cambridge: Cambridge University Press.

Modood, Tariq. 2019. *Essays on Secularism and Multiculturalism.* London: Rowman & Littlefield.

Muñiz-Fraticelli, Victor. 2014. *The Structure of Pluralism: On the Authority of Association.* Oxford: Oxford University Press.

Nussbaum, Martha. 2008. *Liberty of Conscience: In Defence of America's Tradition of Religious Equality.* New York: Basic Books.

Parekh, Bhikhu. 2000. *Rethinking Multiculturalism.* Basingstoke: Macmillan.

Perry, Michael. 2003. *Under God?* Cambridge: Cambridge University Press.

Poulter, Sebastian. 1998. *Ethnicity, Law and Human Rights: The English Experience.* Oxford: Clarendon Press.

Rawls, John. 1996. *Political Liberalism.* New York: Columbia University Press.

Schragger, Richard, and Micah Schwartzman. 2013. 'Against Religious Institutionalism'. *Virginia Law Review* 99 (5): 917–86.

Schwartzman, Micah, Chad Flanders, and Zoë Robinson (eds.). 2016. *The Rise of Corporate Religious Liberty.* Oxford: Oxford University Press.

Seglow, Jonathan. 2017. 'Religious Accommodation: Agency, Integrity, and Self-Respect'. In *Religion in Liberal Political Philosophy,* edited by Cécile Laborde and Aurelia Bardon, 177–90. Oxford: Oxford University Press.

Shorten, Andrew. 2015. 'Are There Rights To Institutional Exemptions?' *Journal of Social Philosophy* 46 (2): 242–63.

Skjeie, Hege. 2007. 'Religious Exemptions to Equality'. *Critical Review of International Social and Political Philosophy* 10 (4): 471–90.

Smith, Steven D. 2016. 'The Jurisdictional Conception of Church Autonomy'. In *The Rise of Corporate Religious Liberty,* edited by Micah Schwartzman, Chad Flanders, and Zoë Robinson, 19–37. Oxford: Oxford University Press.

Taylor, Charles. 1998. 'Modes of Secularism'. In *Secularism and Its Critics,* edited by Rajeev Bhargava, 31–53. New Delhi: Oxford University Press.

———. 2011. 'Why We Need a Radical Redefinition of Secularism'. In *The Power of Religion in the Public Sphere,* edited by Eduardo Mendieta and Jonathan VanAntwerpen, 34–59. New York: Columbia University Press.

Waldron, Jeremy. 1999. *Law and Disagreement.* Oxford: Oxford University Press.

———. 2002. 'One Law for All: The Logic of Cultural Accommodation'. *Washington & Lee Law Review* 59 (1): 3–34.

Wolterstorff, Nicholas. 2008. *Justice: Rights and Wrongs.* Princeton, NJ: Princeton University Press.

NOTES

1. The first case is *Azmi v. Kirklees Metropolitan Borough Council* IRLR 434 (EAT) (2007). Examples of the second include *Bull v. Hall* and *Preddy* EWCA Civ 83 (2012), and the third is *Ghai v. Newcastle City Council* EWCA Civ 59 (2010).

2. *Phillips v. Craig and Mullins* 584 U.S. (2018).

Part I

Secularism and Liberalism

TWO

Inclusion or Exclusion of Religion

What Does Secularism Require?

Sune Lægaard

In debates about religion and politics, it is often said that liberal states should be secular and separate politics and religion. Such claims are widespread in liberal theories and are often invoked in specific controversies over religion. Secularism has for instance been taken to justify claims that liberal states cannot have established churches or otherwise support organized religion, and to support bans on religious symbols and religious dress. Call these *exclusion claims*, since they demand that religion should not be part of public institutions or public space.

Secularism is invoked to justify such exclusion claims. But the meaning and nature of 'secularism' is just as controversial and contested as these claims. The term denotes different things to different people. But the same people also often invoke several different senses of secularism. Cécile Laborde (2017) elucidates this complexity by disaggregating the concept of religion in three dimensions relevant to understanding secularism as a minimal normative requirement of liberal legitimacy. According to Laborde, liberalism should indeed be neutral about religion in some respects but there are different reasons for this, which require different kinds of neutrality. A liberal state has to be *justifiable, inclusive*, and *limited*. These aspects of legitimacy reflect liberal values of respect, equality, and liberty, respectively, and imply requirements that states abstain from invoking inaccessible truth claims, treat citizens equally, and refrain from imposing controversial personal ethics on people. These requirements pick out specific aspects of religion, namely nonaccessibility, vulnerability, and comprehensiveness (Laborde 2017, 117–18). Insofar as religion is inaccessible, vulnerable, or comprehensive, liberal states should separate politics and religion. However, when religion does not have these features, liberal states are not required to do so.

In this chapter, I follow Laborde's disaggregation approach. I focus on the dimension of secularism concerned with civic inclusiveness. For ease of reference, I will term principles regarding this dimension 'Secularism as Civic Inclusiveness' (SCI). I am concerned with this general type of view, of which Laborde merely sketches one version. One reason for this focus is that there has already been extensive debates in the public reason literature on the dimension of justifiability and on the dimension of individual freedom in the literature on exemptions, whereas the dimension of inclusion is less frequently discussed. Another reason is that this dimension seems to capture many of the debates on religion that attract most attention in Europe as well as in the United States, namely issues about religious signs in public spaces and state endorsement of religion. A third reason turns on an apparent tension, which should be evident now: this dimension of secularism is supposedly concerned with civic *inclusion*. This is the underlying liberal value driving this form of secularism. However, the main outputs or policy implications flowing from this concern take the form of claims of *exclusion*. Why does inclusion require exclusion? This seems to capture a broader tension in debates about religion, which are not simply about being for or against religion, but which often involve contradictory pulls towards inclusion and exclusion.

I will use this apparent tension to organize my discussion of SCI, both to get a better understanding of such views and of the further questions they occasion. My claim is not that there is a paradox in secularism, but that the apparent tension between inclusion and exclusion shows the complexity of such views and how they require quite a lot of specification in order to determine when they require exclusion and when they require inclusion. Section 1 introduces some distinctions to qualify the notion of secularism, explaining how a concern with civic inclusiveness can be a form of secularism. Section 2 discusses how we should understand SCI at the level of theory and section 3 examines SCI in practice. I reconstruct the reasoning in relation to two cases commented on by Laborde, namely the *Lautsi* case about mandatory crucifixes in Italian public schools and the Swiss ban on constructions of minarets. I use these cases to illustrate and qualify the initial puzzle about secularism as inclusion and exclusion, which I discuss in section 4. Here I show how the underlying concern with civic equality requires specification in order to determine when it results in exclusion claims and inclusion claims, respectively. I consider various ways of settling when secularism requires one or the other type of claim, including versions of the public/private distinction. I argue, however, that the tension between inclusion and exclusion cannot easily be handled by way of such simple distinctions. One reason for this is that the same underlying concern with civic equality can in some cases provide reasons both for inclusion and for exclusion claims. Section 5 concludes by summing up the tension and complexities in SCI.

1. SENSES OF SECULARISM

All versions of secularism are concerned with religion. The term 'secular' derives from Christian distinctions between worldly and godly matters, between sacred and profane, between the Church and the world outside the Church, and between eternal and temporal time (Bilgrami 2014). There are, however, different ways in which a view can be concerned with religion. One is *intensional*: a view is about religion if it is *defined* in a way explicitly referring to religion. Another is *extensional*: a view is a view about religion if it has *implications* for religion. If a view is defined with reference to religion, full understanding of it requires a definition of religion as well. This raises a number of well-known problems, for example, about most definitions being over- or underinclusive (Laborde 2017, 20–22). If a view is only extensionally about religion, however, a full understanding of it does not require a definition of religion — it is then an open question whether the groups and practices for which the view has implications which count as religious or not.

There is, furthermore, an important difference between forms of secularism. *Antireligious* forms of secularism, that is, versions of so-called 'new atheism', claim that religion is false and bad or dangerous. Purely *political* forms of secularism abstain from claims about the truth or value of religion as such and only concern the regulation of the relationship between religion and state.[1] While antireligious attitudes can underlie some demands for separation of church and state, separation claims are not necessarily antireligious – they might even be motivated by a concern with protecting religion. Political principles of secularism are independent of the religion–atheism debate. Antireligious forms of secularism are almost by definition concerned with exclusion of religion. Therefore, the tension between inclusion and exclusion mainly arises for political forms of secularism. I focus on political secularism, since the controversies over religion I want to discuss are not about the truth or value of religion but about how it should be handled politically. Laborde's theory is one view about this.

We further need to distinguish between political secularism as specific *institutional measures*, for example, legal rights protection and institutional separation, and *theoretical principles*, for example, doctrines of public reason (Lægaard 2013). The term 'secularism' is often used as a label of both measures and of principles. This causes confusion since the latter are supposed to justify the former. If we distinguish between secularism as a label of political measures and secularism as a label for the underlying principles that justify these measures *as* secularist measures (Lægaard 2017a), we can see why the initial puzzle about inclusion and exclusion is not a paradox. This is because the exclusion claims are at the policy level and the ideal of civic inclusion is at the underlying level of principle. So 'inclusion' and 'exclusion' are not contradictory in a strict sense, since the conceptual pair inclusion/exclusion has different meanings at different levels. Nevertheless, this leaves a broader question about when and why inclusion (at the level of principle) requires exclusion (at the level of policy).

Secularism as a political principle is not only distinct from specific institutional measures; secularism as a political principle itself stands in need of justification. So secularism is a *mid-level principle* (one that is more fundamental than specific institutional measures, but which itself is justified on the basis of more fundamental premises). This means that there can be different versions of secularism as a political principle, depending on what the more fundamental concerns are. There can be both liberal and nonliberal forms of secularism (Lægaard 2017a). As Laborde's disaggregation approach argues, there are even several distinct types of reasons for secularism within liberalism. I now turn to one of these.

2. CIVIC INCLUSIVENESS AS A THEORETICAL PRINCIPLE

Laborde formulates her version of what I call SCI as this:

> When a social identity is a marker of vulnerability and domination, it should not be symbolically endorsed and promoted by the state. (Laborde 2017, 137)

It is a political principle in the noted sense, since it gives directives about how states should act but does not provide an evaluation of, nor say anything about social identities in other respects. 'Social identities' includes religion but covers much else, for example, race, culture or ethnic identities (Laborde 2017, 137). The principle is accordingly not an intensional form of secularism, since it is not formulated with reference to religion. It is rather an extensional form of secularism, insofar as religious identities are often markers of vulnerability and domination.

The Underlying Concern with Civic Equality

Laborde's principle appeals to vulnerability and domination as the normatively relevant characteristics. However, these are actually expressions of a more fundamental concern:

> Symbolic religious establishment is wrong when it communicates that religious identity is a component of civic identity—of what it means to be a citizen of that state—and thereby denies civic status to those who

do not endorse that identity, who are then treated as second-class citizens. (Laborde 2017, 135)

The kind of wrong Laborde is concerned with is *communicative*: it is about the message sent by the state. The relevant messages are those about *civic status*. The relevant kind of assessment in this respect is *comparative* with the normative standard doing the work being one of equality. This makes the inclusiveness aspect of minimal secularism a 'symbolic equality account', according to which symbolic establishment is problematic if it sends the message that nonadherents of the established church are not equal citizens (Lægaard 2017b, 124; for criticism of such claims, see Seglow 2017).

The crucial questions for such accounts is how one determines when a state act in fact communicates such a message, and what the standard of equal civic status is against which this has to be assessed? Laborde touches on this in her elaboration of the view:

> The thought is that when the state associates itself too closely with the symbols of the majority, non-adherents are rejected outside the imagined community of citizens. Symbolic establishment is wrong, on this account, when it constitutes and perpetuates social relations of hierarchy, subordination, and domination. (2017, 136)

Here, 'hierarchy, subordination, and domination' denote specific kinds of deviations from the ideal of equal civic status; something only counts as domination if it violates civic equality. Therefore, the guiding criterion is a standard of civic equality. 'Domination' is a label for a specific kind of deviation from this standard.

Laborde's principle has to be understood against her other remarks. Although the principle itself does not refer explicitly to civic equality, this is what really provides its normative force and what gives content to the notions of 'vulnerability and domination'. This shows that Laborde's principle is a mid-level principle in the sense characteristic of secularism noted above: the principle is itself based on more fundamental and more general normative liberal concerns with civic equality.

3. CIVIC INCLUSIVENESS IN PRACTICE

To address the issue of inclusion and exclusion, it is not enough to know that SCI is a mid-level principle involving a concern with civic equality. It is not clear from the abstractly formulated idea of equal citizenship and inclusion what SCI requires or prohibits. Laborde does, however, illustrate her principle in relation to two main cases, namely the Swiss minaret ban and the *Lautsi* case. I now analyze her remarks about these two cases in order to understand how the principle might underlie her judgments.

Laborde on the Lautsi *Case*

In the 2011 *Lautsi* case, the Grand Chamber of the European Court of Human Rights ruled that obligatory crucifixes in public schools did not violate the right to freedom of religion because crucifixes were not religious indoctrination (Pierik 2012). Before the Court, the Italian government had attempted to describe crucifixes as cultural and traditional rather than *religious* symbols. In criticism of this, Laborde asserts, 'What matters is whether state-enforced symbols are markers of social vulnerability; and culture is not intrinsically more inclusive than religion' (2017, 140).

We can reconstruct her implicit argument regarding the *Lautsi* case like this:

1. When a social identity is a marker of vulnerability and domination, it should not be symbolically endorsed and promoted by the state;
2. Christian identity is a marker of vulnerability and domination (here, in the sense that non-Christian identities are vulnerable and subject to domination);
3. When the Italian state makes crucifixes mandatory in classrooms of public schools, it symbolically endorses Christian identity;
4. Therefore, the Italian state should not make crucifixes mandatory in public schools.

This argument is not explicit in Laborde's text. Her brief remarks on *Lautsi* only pertain to the Italian government's attempt to redescribe crucifixes as nonreligious symbols, supposed to undermine charges of failure to respect freedom of religion. Her remarks point out that there is nothing in the implicit argument reconstructed above that turns on whether Christianity is a religious or cultural identity. What does all the work is rather the claim that the state symbolically endorses Christian identity by making crucifixes mandatory (premise 3) and that the state thereby communicates that Christian identity is a component of civic identity. The Italian state therefore fails to respect the equal civic status of non-Christians by making their minority status relevant – negatively – to their civic status.

Laborde's brief remarks about the *Lautsi* case shows that this is a central example of the *kind* of cases to which the principle is supposed to apply and that, in this particular case, Laborde takes the principle to imply that the Italian state acted *contrary* to the principle (and, accordingly, that the Court's decision was morally wrong). The Italian government could, however, respond either that Christian identity is not in fact a marker of vulnerability and domination (i.e., by denying premise 2) or that it does not endorse Christian identity by making crucifixes mandatory (i.e., by denying premise 3). My reconstruction of the reasoning re-

quired to connect the principle with the case in a way yielding this implication accordingly shows the need for:

- an account of *which* social identities are markers of vulnerability
  and domination in a given context (to support the necessary second
  premise), and
- an *account of the expressive meaning* of state acts (to support the necessary third premise).

These are necessary requirements for the *application* of the principle to a
given case.[2] Finally, the resulting argument has to be valid, which requires 'vulnerability and domination' to have the same meaning in all the
premises (explicitly in the principle itself (first premise) and the second
premise, but implicitly in the account of expressive meaning needed to
support the third premise as well). To secure this, the principle has to be
specified in a way providing:

- a *criterion of vulnerability and domination*. Since vulnerability and
  domination should be understood in relation to equal civic status,
  the required criterion is exactly the criterion of civic inclusiveness
  that Laborde refers to herself (2017, 138) but does not spell out.[3]

Laborde on the Swiss Minaret Ban

The other case to which Laborde applies her principle is the one concerning the Swiss ban on all future construction of Islamic minarets, decided
in a national referendum in November 2009 (Miller 2016). Against the
point raised by defenders of the ban that it is not a violation of freedom of
religion, since minarets are not required for Muslims to practice their
religion, Laborde responds that

> Whether or not Muslims value minarets, a public ban on minarets un-
> ambiguously sends a message of exclusion to Muslims. What is wrong
> with the ban is that it places minarets—and, by analogy, Muslims—at
> the outer border of the imagined national community. (2017, 139)

This can be reconstructed as an argument with a similar structure as the
one above, the difference merely being that this time the argument concerns a state ban rather than a legal requirement:

1. When a social identity is a marker of vulnerability and domination,
   it should not be symbolically endorsed and promoted by the state;
2. Christian identity is a marker of vulnerability and domination
   (here, in the sense that non-Christian identities are vulnerable and
   subject to domination);
3. When the Swiss state bans the construction of minarets while still
   allowing church buildings or crucifixes in public, it symbolically

endorses Christian identity [and thereby subjects non-Christians and specifically Muslims to domination];

4. Therefore, the Swiss state should not ban minarets while still allowing church buildings and public crucifixes.

Even though this argument is about a ban rather than an endorsement, the problematic aspect of the state's action is the same. According to Laborde, by banning minarets, but not Christian church buildings or public crucifixes, the Swiss state communicates that Christian identity is a component of civic identity whereas Muslim identity is not. The Swiss state thereby fails to respect the equal civic status of Muslims, by making their minority status relevant – negatively – to their civic status.

The reconstruction illustrates the comparative nature of the argument – the ban on minarets is wrong, because the Swiss state does not at the same time ban other religious symbols in public spaces. Muslims are wronged because they are treated worse than, in this case, Christians.

Since the argument regarding the minaret ban has the same structure as the one about *Lautsi*, the same questions can be asked about why we should accept the premises. To answer these questions, we again need an account of the expressive meaning of the state act in question and an account of the socially vulnerable identities in the case, as well as a criterion of inclusiveness that links these together.

4. SCI AS INCLUSION AND EXCLUSION

The initial puzzle motivating the chapter was that secularism on the one hand draws on a concern with civic inclusion, and on the other hand yields requirements of exclusion. The two cases show that this is not the entire picture. SCI does imply exclusion claims – as in the *Lautsi* case – but it also implies inclusion claims – as in the minaret case. So while the initial tension was earlier resolved by distinguishing between secularism as a principle and secularism at the level of policy, it now reappears at the level of policy.[4] In this section, I will examine this tension at the level of policy implications. I will do this by focusing on three questions that are crucial in specifying and applying SCI:

1. The *scope* of SCI: to what kinds of targets does the principle apply?
2. The *valence* of SCI: what does it provide reasons for and/or against?
3. The *strength* of SCI: how weighty are these reasons?

I focus on the first two questions but touch on the third in the subsequent discussion.

Regarding the first question about scope, we need to consider whether the principle of civic equality underlying SCI only applies to *institutions* or also to *individuals*. Laborde's two cases concern legal regulation of public schools and private religious associations, respectively.[5] The actors affected by the principle are therefore institutional or collective actors. These examples accordingly tell us that Laborde takes her principle to apply to state regulation of such institutional actors but not whether (and, if so, how) it also applies to direct state regulation of individual citizens.

Regarding the second question about valence, the two cases considered by Laborde are apparently different. Regarding *Lautsi*, Laborde takes her principle to justify rejection of the legal requirement of mandatory crucifixes. However, the same reasoning reconstructed above could plausible be extended to all acts on the part of state institutions expressing endorsement of religion. So regarding these kinds of cases, Laborde's principle justifies *exclusion* of religious symbols from state *institutions*.

In the case of the Swiss minaret ban, to the contrary, Laborde takes her principle to justify rejection of a legal ban on construction of minarets. So regarding these kinds of cases, Laborde's principle justifies *inclusion* of religious symbols in *public space*.[6]

Therefore, the valence of the principle can be both exclusionary and inclusionary and the target could be both institutional and individual. These two distinctions together yield four kinds of claims that the principle could justify:

	Exclusionary valence	**Inclusionary valence**
Institutional target	Institutional exclusion claim	Institutional inclusion claim
Individual target	Individual exclusion claim	Individual inclusion claim

We can now articulate the inclusion/exclusion issue as a series of questions concerning when and why SCI yields these different kinds of claims. I will now discuss these questions and the further issues they give rise to. The aim of this discussion is not to determine the specific implications of a particular version of SCI for specific cases, let alone to argue for or against these in normative terms, but to draw out the general issues about inclusion and exclusion raised by these kinds of secularism, including what 'inclusion' and 'exclusion' might mean.

Individual as Well as Institutional Scope?

While Laborde's two cases concern institutional actors, there are plenty of other cases about inclusion or exclusion of religious symbols that pertain to individuals. The prototypical individual exclusion claims are bans against Islamic headscarves, the discussion of which in Europe started out in relation to public schools in the Paris suburb Creil in 1989 and culminated in the 2004 French law against religious clothing in public schools (Laborde 2008). Subsequently, similar cases have been discussed in many other European countries and new and more extensive bans have been added, for example, the 2010 French law against clothing covering the face in public spaces, which was effectively about Muslim burqas and niqabs (Laborde 2012).

Individual exclusion claims have regularly been justified with reference to secularism. In the classic French headscarf cases, the claim was that public schools should be secular. Therefore, pupils could not wear Islamic headscarves. In the more recent burqa ban case, the claim was rather that it is a duty of civility to appear before one's cocitizens in public space with one's face uncovered (Lægaard 2015).

There are also, however, individual inclusion claims. This would be the case if one thinks that civic equality requires permission of headscarves in a given context. Obvious examples of this are the various cases where headscarves, or similar religious forms of dress like the Sikh turban, have been incorporated into official uniforms of, for example, police officers, such as has been the case in both Britain and Canada. Civic inclusion would seem to provide an immediately obvious rationale for such policies (cf. Modood 2007 on multiculturalism as a civic idea).[7]

All of these claims take SCI to apply not only to institutions but also to individual persons. This is not surprising. If the underlying concern is one of civic equality, one would expect it to have implications for individual citizens and not only for institutions or collectives.

Inclusionary or Exclusionary Valence?

What relevant difference can explain the contrary valences in the institutional cases? A possible explanation of the difference in Laborde's two cases is that *Lautsi* concerns *public institutions* whereas the Swiss case concerns *private institutional actors in public space* more generally. Not only does this public/private distinction fit with Laborde's judgements in the institutional cases, it also provides a plausible justification relative to the normative concern with state endorsement central to the principle. Given this concern, it should make a difference whether an institution is public or not.[8]

If this is the explanation of the difference in valence in institutional cases, and if the principle applies at the individual level as well, then it might also justify some forms of headscarf bans in the individual case. If what matters is state endorsement, one would expect the principle to imply exclusion claims for individuals in *public* functions (see Maclure and Taylor 2011, 42–48). In that case, inclusion of Sikh turbans for public officials would go against the principle of civic inclusion.

Conversely, one would expect the principle to imply individual inclusion claims in public spaces more generally. Just as it yields a rejection of the Swiss minaret ban, it would also reject policies like the more recent French burqa ban (as Laborde 2012 indeed does, although on other grounds).

The apparent implication of this extension of Laborde's principle to individual cases therefore is that it implies individual *exclusion* claims for persons in *public* functions and individual *inclusion* claims for persons in *nonpublic* functions.

Public Functions

We then need a precise specification of what the relevant sense of 'public function' is. According to the proposed specification, it is the fact that individuals occupy public functions that triggers individual exclusion claims. One specification might say that what matters is the mere *presence* of individual citizens *in public institutions*. This is the reasoning informing the French headscarf law, according to which pupils have to appear only as citizens and should therefore not display their private religious identity as long as they are in a public school (Laborde 2008). The examples at the institutional level do not force us to accept this expansive reading, however, insofar as we can come up with a less expansive reading that fits just as well. If what is driving exclusion claims is the concern with state endorsement, then the relevant specification arguably should track those functions where individuals in some sense *represent* the state. On this reading, it is not the fact that an individual is present within a public institution that triggers exclusion claims. It is rather that an individual *occupies a public function* where they *represent* the state.

While this might place pupils in public schools and ordinary citizens claiming public services outside the scope of exclusion claims, it still leaves a number of things open. Is public employment, for instance, sufficient to trigger an exclusion claim? This again seems unwarranted if what matters is the message sent. The fact that publicly employed cleaning staff displays religious dress, for instance, does not seem to express state endorsement of the religion in question. If so, representation has to involve more than mere employment. At the opposite extreme, it seems plausible that the head of state wearing religious dress while performing official functions would express state endorsement of the religion in question. Between these two extremes there is a broad spectrum of different cases, ranging from nurses and doctors in public hospitals, over teachers in public schools, to police officers and judges, whom we can understand as representing the state in different ways and to different degrees.

One possibility here is to say that the relevant difference is whether a public employee has a *public-facing* function. If it is the case that the cleaner, unlike the schoolteacher, does not have a public-facing role, even if she is a public employee, this might be used as an explanation why the schoolteacher should be excluded from wearing religious dress while the cleaner should not. The reasoning would be that no public endorsement is signalled if the cleaner wears religious dress, whereas such a message is sent if the teacher does. The problem here is that cleaners often do have a public-facing function in the banal sense that they clean while others are around – cleaners might actually meet more members of the public than a teacher, who only faces particular classes. So, this solution seems to presuppose what has to be shown, namely that there is a difference in kind between the way publicly employed cleaners and teachers represent the state.

Alternatively, rather than thinking that there has to be a specific point on this spectrum where public employees suddenly start to represent the state, which then triggers individual exclusion claims, one might think that the case for exclusion claims becomes gradually stronger when one moves from one end of the spectrum towards the other. Here the question about the strength of the reasons provided by the principle becomes relevant. If the reason is gradual in the sense noted above, it seems most natural to understand it as a *pro tanto* reason that we may weigh against other reasons. In that case, the *all things considered* case for an exclusion claim depends on both reasons based on civic equality and other relevant reasons as well as their relative weight.

Contradictory Valence

The inclusion/exclusion issue is not settled, however, once we have found a place on this spectrum where the concern with state endorsement of religion becomes sufficiently strong to *pro tanto* justify an individual exclusion claim. If this holds, for instance, for police officers, perhaps because they represent the state as a coercive authority, this gives rise to the further question whether such an individual exclusion claim might undermine the civic equality of religious persons *employed* in the given public function. Would individual exclusion claims for police officers, which would, for instance, disallow Sikh men from wearing turbans while on duty as police officers, symbolically express that visible members of religious minority groups cannot represent the state and would this signal that they are therefore not equal citizens? If so, this would then provide a reason *against* individual exclusion claims in public functions based on the principle of civic equality. It is then the *same* principle of civic inclusion that provides reasons both *for* and *against* exclusion claims.

This would be different from cases where there are other kinds of reasons against individual exclusion claims. Laborde for instance discusses religious exemptions as justified on the basis of a concern with what she calls 'integrity protecting commitments' (IPCs) (Laborde 2017, chap. 6). If liberals are concerned with integrity, and insofar as religious practices such as wearing religious forms of dress are an important IPC for some people, this provides a distinct reason for exempting individuals from requirements that interfere with their opportunity for wearing such religious dress. Appeal to Mill's harm principle might be another distinct reason for opposing such claims. However, the justification in both cases comes from a separate principle (of integrity or no-harm). The argument from integrity furthermore takes the form of reasons for granting exemptions from otherwise justified rules.

What I am considering now is different, because it is not a concern based on integrity and does not take the form of an argument for exemptions. It is rather a concern based on civic equality. The concern is that civic equality might require that all citizens are equal when it comes to whether they can represent the state. Even if the principle of civic equality provides *pro tanto* reasons for individual exclusion claims to the effect that police officers *cannot* wear religious forms of dress, because this might express state endorsement of the religion, the exact same concern with civic equality might provide *pro tanto* reasons for the opposite claim, namely that police officers *should* be able to wear religious dress, because this signals inclusion of all religious groups as equal citizens. Because this is a concern with civic equality, it does not take the form of an argument for an exemption (and criticisms of equality-based arguments for exemptions, e.g., Shorten 2010, do then not apply). Exemptions presuppose that there is a general rule that is justified as such, but which can be set aside for certain groups because there are special considerations that outweigh the justification for the rule in these cases without undermining the general justification of the rule. However, if individual exclusion claims are problematic on grounds of civic equality, this precisely challenges the general rule.

A principle of civic equality then leads to an apparent dilemma, since the same value can provide reasons for and against the same policy. This is yet another version of the general inclusion/exclusion puzzle, which is now not only that a principle of inclusion can require exclusion, or require inclusion in some cases and exclusion in other; now the worry is that it might provide reasons for both inclusion and exclusion in the exact same cases. This new problem cannot be explained away by reference to the possibility that the inclusion/exclusion conceptual pair might have different meanings, for in this case it is the exact same concept that is in play on both sides, merely with contradictory valence. The specification of the principle therefore not only has to spell it out in sufficient detail to locate the point where individual exclusion claims are justified. It also has to articulate the concern with civic equality in a way that makes it possible to justify why one rather than the other of the horns of this apparent dilemma is the right one to choose.

State Endorsement and Civic Equality

One way of doing this might be to consider whether there is a relevant difference in terms of state endorsement between public *institutions* and *individuals* in public functions. The worry driving both inclusion and exclusion claims is one concerning state endorsement of religion. In the institutional case, the worry concerns the institution as such, for example, the public crucifixes in *Lautsi* or religious curriculum or ceremonies in schools, whereas the latter option also focuses on the individual people staffing the institution, for example, cases about dress. Therefore, when we extend this concern from the institutional to the individual level, the question is whether allowing individuals in public functions to wear religious dress really expresses state endorsement of the religion in question. If not, then the apparent dilemma dissolves in favor of individual inclusion claims – but then there is *no* reason from civic equality for excluding religious forms of dress in *any* public functions. If, on the other hand, the concern with state endorsement is still strong enough to settle the dilemma in favor of individual exclusion claims, then the question is whether the reason is so strong that it justifies individual exclusion claims for a *broader* class of people.

Another issue might arise regarding those public employees for whom the concern with state endorsement does not justify individual exclusion claims, namely whether the resulting individual inclusion in public functions undermines the civic equality of *other citizens* using the public institutions in question? If some public officials are allowed to wear, for example, Muslim headscarves, does this undermine the civic equality of non-Muslim citizens using the public institutions, for example, patients treated by nurses or doctors, children taught by schoolteachers, or citizens having a civil marriage conducted by a registrar? One might think this because ordinary citizens may have to engage with public officials and might then take the fact that officials wear religious dress as a sign of public endorsement of the religion in question. Does civic equality require that you do not have to engage with public officials with visible religious signs? The question is whether this kind of concern is an expression of a concern with civic equality or whether opposition to individual inclusion is based on some other kind of principle. If this kind of opposition is based, for instance, on the assumption that people have a right, not only to freedom of religion, but also to freedom from religion, then it would be an expression of a distinct principle. In that case, civic equality might provide reasons for one claim and this distinct principle (if there indeed is such an independent right to freedom from religion) for the opposite claim, and we would then have to weigh the two against each other. What is more problematic, however, is if civic equality itself directly provides a reason for why ordinary citizens engaging with the state or claiming public services should not be met by representatives of the state wearing religious forms of dress. In that case, we would again have an example where the same principle of civic equality provides both reasons for and reasons against individual exclusion claims. So the specification of the principle of civic equality will have to take a stand, not only on what might express state endorsement at both the institutional and individual level, but also whether the concern with civic equality furthermore translates into claim rights for individual citizens engaging with representatives of the state – and, if so, what these citizens have a claim to.

Civic Equality and Nondiscrimination

The general argument is that civic equality provides reasons for exclusion claims in state institutions and certain representative public functions, because these raise issues of state endorsement of religion. The flip side of this argument seems to be that civic equality provides reasons for *inclusion* in cases *not* involving state institutions or public officials. This raises another set of questions that a specification of the principle of civic equality has to address, namely what (if anything) this implies for cases of *private* employment. If civic equality requires that religious symbols should be allowed in the public sphere in general, as Laborde's claim in the Swiss minaret case suggests, and if civic equality also applies at the individual level, would this mean that *private* employers violate civil equality if they require their employees not to carry visible religious forms of dress at work?

This would then give rise to a clash between the right of employers to decide issues such as dress code at work and the principle of civic equality. One might think, however, that this clash is already well described and largely solved, because this falls within the remit of ordinary discrimination law. Discrimination law in all European jurisdictions already applies to private employment and there are a number of decisions both at national levels and at the European Court of Human Rights indicating how the balance should be struck (see, e.g., Vickers 2008). So to the extent that courts have upheld requirements of nondiscrimination, this might be taken as an indication that considerations of civic equality apply to private employers, and to the extent that claims about discrimination have not been upheld, this might be taken to show the limits of these requirements.

This answer assumes that established nondiscrimination law implements moral requirements of civic equality in the public sphere outside state institutions. If so, this has implications for the general understanding of civic equality as a moral principle. Established discrimination legislation allows bans against religious dress provided they are part of a general dress code (and so not direct discrimination) and if it is a proportionate means to a legitimate aim (so that ostensible neutral rules that happen to burden specific groups are not indirect discrimination). If nondiscrimination laws express the moral concern with civic equality, this then means that civic equality does not apply or can be outweighed in such cases. This on the one hand means that requirements of civic equality will not impose additional burdens beyond those already holding on private employers. On the other hand, it also means that the value of civic equality either has a narrow scope that does not expand to the entire public sphere or that it is not very weighty.

Both of these implications might have repercussions for the application and weight of the principle of civic equality in other domains, unless we can point to relevant differences between these domains that explains why the principle applies and is weighty in some domains and does not apply at all or has little weight in other domains. One relevant difference might be that civic equality *only* applies to state institutions and public officials because it is only concerned with *state* endorsement. The question is whether this proposal fits with the assumed implication for the Swiss minaret case, where civic equality applied to the regulation of *private* entities. Here, one might argue that the Swiss case involved *state interference* and that the principle kicked in because of this. That is clearly correct. However, this leaves it unclear what the principle might imply at the individual level of private employment, which the state is *already* actively regulating. One might argue that the analogy between the institutional and individual cases would only hold if the state suddenly decided to impose a ban on Muslim headscarves in private businesses. That would not only be problematic from the point of view of the presumed right of employers to decide over their own businesses, it would also clearly send the same kind of problematic message as the minaret ban. But if the principle rules out state interference of this kind, because it would undermine the civic equality of Muslims, why would it not also apply to the existing state regulation of differential treatment, which allows bans on Muslim headscarves if this is a proportionate means to a legitimate end? The exclusion claims permitted by this legislation is something *the state* has *actively* allowed as part of the existing discrimination law, so why does this not similarly undermine the civic equality of Muslims, if a sudden imposition of a ban would do so?

One might avoid the implications of linking the principle of civic equality as applied to individuals outside state institutions to existing nondiscrimination regulations by separating civic equality from other kinds of concerns about equal treatment. In that case, nothing follows about the strength or scope of the moral principle of civic equality from existing nondiscrimination law, since the latter is not an implementation of the former. The question then remains whether the principle of civic equality applies to private employers in another form. The importance of civic equality and the considerations about state endorsement canvassed above about why it might also apply to private businesses are relevant here as well. If these considerations imply that the principle does apply to and have some weight in state regulation of private businesses, this means that there are a set of distinct demands on private employers in addition to those already imposed by existing nondiscrimination regulation. A specification of the principle then has to explain what these additional requirements are.

The question whether the principle of civic equality applies to individuals outside public institutions accordingly raises two dilemmas. If it does apply, the dilemma is that either civic equality *just is* ordinary non-discrimination, in which case it is a weak consideration relatively easily overridden, which might weaken claims based on the principle in other domains. If civic equality is *distinct* from existing nondiscrimination regulation, then the requirements on private employers are more exacting, which might show the principle to be unduly burdensome. To avoid this dilemma, one might argue that the principle does *not* apply to individuals outside public institutions. Then one has to explain why state non-intervention in an already regulated area does not express anything in terms of state endorsement, which might also undermine claims about the expressive meaning of state acts in other domains.

5. CONCLUSION

This chapter started out with the apparent puzzle that secularism based on civic inclusion leads to claims for exclusion. By distinguishing between secularism as a political principle and secular policies, this puzzle was transformed to a question about when and why principles of inclusion justify policies of exclusion. I further qualified this by noting that Laborde's illustrations of her version of SCI include both claims of inclusion and exclusion. This gave rise to a number of issues that any specification of a version of SCI would have to take a stand on. This raised the further possibility that the same principle of inclusion might provide reasons both for and against inclusion in the same cases. The chapter has not attempted to solve the inclusion/exclusion puzzle. I have rather tried to use the puzzle to qualify and deepen the understanding of SCI with respect to what kind of view it is, in which sense it is a form of secularism, and what it might mean in practice.

One outcome of this examination is that the complications and issues noted above arise for any specification of SCI, no matter what understanding of equality one assumes at the more fundamental level. Any conception of equality can seemingly imply inclusion claims in one case and exclusion claims in others. If so, the inclusion/exclusion tension is not a contingent effect of a very specific conception of equality, but a feature of any version of SCI.

Another lesson is that we cannot discuss the noted issues in isolation. How we handle claims of inclusion and exclusion in one case has repercussions for what a principle of civic equality might imply in other cases. So there is a methodological reason not only to focus, for instance, on exemptions (or individual inclusion claims more generally), or on institutional establishment, since what we say about some types of cases will have consequences for other types of issues.

So although secularism is a mid-level principle and thus not foundational, it is not only a premise in arguments for specific policies. Secularism also connects debates about policies of quite different kinds in what might initially seem quite different areas.

REFERENCES

Bilgrami, Akeel. 2014. 'Secularism: Its Content and Context'. *Journal of Social Philosophy* 45 (1): 25–48.

Garrau, Marie, and Cécile Laborde. 2015. 'Relational Equality, Non-Domination, and Vulnerability'. In *Social Equality, on What It Means to Be Equals*, edited by Carina Fourie, Fabian Schuppert, and Ivo Wallimann-Helmer, 45–64. Oxford: Oxford University Press.

Laborde, Cécile. 2008. *Critical Republicanism*. Oxford: Oxford University Press.

———. 2012. 'State Paternalism and Religious Dress'. *International Journal of Constitutional Law* 10: 398–410.

———. 2017. *Liberalism's Religion*. Cambridge, MA: Harvard University Press.

Lægaard, Sune. 2013. 'Secular Religious Establishment: A Framework for Discussing the Compatibility of Institutional Religious Establishment with Political Secularism'. *Philosophy and Public Issues* 3 (2): 119–57.

———. 2015. 'Burqa Ban, Freedom of Religion and "Living Together"'. *Human Rights Review* 16 (3): 203–19.

———. 2017a. 'Multiculturalism and Secularism: Theoretical Understandings and Possible Conflicts'. *Ethnicities* 17 (2): 154–71.

———. 2017b. 'What's the Problem with Symbolic Religious Establishment? The Alienation and Symbolic Equality Accounts'. In *Religion in Liberal Political Philosophy*, edited by Cécile Laborde and Aurélia Bardon, 118–31. Oxford: Oxford University Press.

Maclure, Jocelyn, and Charles Taylor. 2011. *Secularism and Freedom of Conscience*. Cambridge, MA: Harvard University Press.

Miller, David. 2016. 'Majorities and Minarets: Religious Freedom and Public Space'. *British Journal of Political Science* 46 (2): 437–56.

Modood, Tariq. 2007. *Multiculturalism: A Civic Idea*. Cambridge: Polity.

Pierik, Roland. 2012. 'State Neutrality and the Limits of Religious Symbolism'. In *The Lautsi Papers*, edited by Jeroen Temperman, 201–18. Leiden: Martin Nijhoff.

Rawls, John. 1993. *Political Liberalism*. New York: Columbia University Press.

Schwartzman, Micah. 2012. 'What if Religion Is Not Special?' *University of Chicago Law Review* 79:1351–427.

Seglow, Jonathan. 2017. 'What's Wrong with Establishment?' *Ethnicities* 17 (2): 189–204.

Shorten, Andrew. 2010. 'Cultural Exemptions, Equality and Basic Interests'. *Ethnicities* 10 (1): 100–26.

Vickers, Lucy. 2008. *Religious Freedom, Religious Discrimination, and the Workplace*. Oxford: Hart.

NOTES

1. This distinction is drawn from Rawls's idea of political liberalism, according to which a view is political if (a) it only concerns the basic structure of society and (b)

only relies on a freestanding political conception of justice (Rawls 1993). But the distinction can be applied without assuming political liberalism.

2. Both of these kinds of support involve contextual empirical facts about the specific cases. The question is which contextual facts are relevant, which requires a view about how to interpret state acts, and what counts as vulnerability. One might of course question whether state acts in fact have harmful expressive meanings in specific cases (as Seglow 2017 does). But here I am not assessing or applying Laborde's view but rather analyzing what it involves.

3. Here one option would be simply to plug in a generic notion of vulnerability, which in Laborde's case might be connected to her republican commitments, e.g., as discussed in Garrau and Laborde (2015). Here I am not, however, interested in a specific, e.g., republican, version of SCI, but with general features of the view.

4. One objection might be that this is again only an apparent tension, since the inclusion/exclusion conceptual pair might mean different things even at the level of policy. This is true. But it would still require an elucidation of the different meanings of the conceptual pair at this level and an explanation of why it has different meanings in different cases. This is what I try to consider the prospects for in the remainder of the chapter.

5. The Swiss Muslims in the minaret case are of course also individual citizens. However, building permissions for minarets (and mosques, etc.) are usually granted to religious associations. This focus on associations does not imply anything about whether they have rights of associational self-governance (which Laborde discusses later in her book).

6. My distinction between inclusion claims and exclusion claims resembles but is importantly different from the one employed by Micah Schwartzman (2012, 1358). He distinguishes between inclusion and exclusion at the level of reasons for policies and between accommodation and nonaccommodation at the level of exemptions for religious practices from generally valid laws. The former concerns the aspect of secularism as a matter of justifiability covered by Laborde's first principle, the latter concerns the aspect of secularism as a matter of liberty covered by Laborde's third principle. However, neither directly concern the aspect of secularism as civic inclusiveness covered by Laborde's second principle, which is my focus. My suggestion is that the terminology of inclusion and exclusion can be fruitfully transposed from the issue of justifiability and reasons to the issue of civic inclusion and equality. The latter partly concerns practices like those of concern to the exemption/accommodation debate, but the normative rationale is different, namely one deriving from civic equality rather than individual liberty. Inclusion and exclusion has analogous meaning regarding symbols and practices as it has regarding reasons, namely a matter of whether these are permitted in a certain context. In addition to using the inclusion/exclusion dichotomy in another context, I also depart from Schwartzman in not focusing on whether religion is special. I take Laborde's disaggregation approach for granted as an answer to this question. So inclusion/exclusion is primarily related to symbols and practices linked to social identities, and only secondarily to religious symbols and practices, insofar as they are social identities that might be markers of vulnerability and domination.

7. What I call individual inclusion claims may take the form of what has often been discussed as cultural or religious *exemptions* (see, e.g., Shorten 2010). To say that allowing religious dress is a cultural exemption presupposes an existing rule that would prohibit such clothing, which is legitimate and kept in place for others. Inclusion does not need, however, to take the form of exemptions; it can also be secured by revising existing rules.

8. A terminological complication here is that 'public' is used is different senses, e.g., 'public institution' and 'public space'. If the concern is with state endorsement, then the relevant sense is the one where 'public' denotes state institutions. The rationale is that individuals have religious liberty, but the liberal state does not have religious liberty.

THREE

The Paradox of Political Secularism

Sebastián Rudas

Debates about what secularism requires tend to be contradictory. In discussions about sexual and reproductive rights, secularism is invoked to prevent conservative religious groups from influencing decision-making processes and public deliberation. Initiatives that intend to restrict individuals from wearing visible religious symbols within state institutions – and in some cases even in the public sphere, as shown by attempts to ban the use of burkinis in some European cities and the burqa bans in several European countries – are sometimes supported by appeals to the idea of the secularity of the state. Secularism is also used to justify the restriction of public officials' public expression of their faith, to deny state subsidies to religious organizations, and in general to keep religion separated from what is broadly constructed as 'the political'. On the other hand, references to secularism also appear in defence of the presence of religion in the public and political spheres. The principle of secularism has been invoked in order to defend the diversification of religious establishment, the inclusion of religious education in state schools, the permission of religious symbols within state institutions, or allowing public officials publicly to express faith.[1] In sum, 'secularism' is invoked to both restrict and permit the public appearance of religion.

Within contemporary liberal political philosophy, a version of the second use of the term 'secularism' has become widely accepted. This is, for instance, the case of the influential view of political secularism defended by Charles Taylor and Jocelyn Maclure, who in recent years have defended the 'overlapping consensus' definition of secularism. A fundamental characteristic of their view is that it is not presented as a form of regulation of religion, more specifically, as a form of giving content to the idea of separation of church and state. According to them, in a liberal and democratic society religion can occupy a visible position in the public and political spheres (some versions of religious establishment might be permissible and financial funding for religious-based initiatives might be justified) and can also justify legislation (for instance, the reasonable accommodations on religious grounds).

In this chapter, I analyse this influential view on political secularism. I argue that it leads to a paradoxical conclusion, namely that regimes which we tend to characterize as being very secular – even *secularist* – are not captured by this definition of political secularism, while regimes that display the typical features of secularism in a very modest fashion are those that better satisfy Taylor and Maclure's account of it. This paradoxical conclusion is generated by the attempt to provide a definition that is neither focused on religion nor based on the idea of the institutional separation of church and state. Although the motive leading to frame secularism in such a way is valid (i.e., to avoid reproducing conceptions of secularism that are biased against religion and which are therefore illiberal), I argue that it is not necessary to abandon the traditional understanding of secularism *as separation of church and state*, because this understanding is not inescapably at odds with the principles liberal egalitarians want to preserve.

I proceed as follows: in section 1, I present Taylor and Maclure's account of secularism. In sections 2 and 3, I argue that this account is paradoxical and that it fails to demonstrate the relevance of secularism for contemporary politics. In sections 4 and 5, I argue that secularism can be understood in terms of the institutional separation of church and state and I show in which circumstances secularism can be relevant today. Section 6 shows that my proposal does not pose a serious problem for Taylor and Maclure's liberal egalitarian project, although an implication of my argument is that, strictly speaking, their conception of secularism is not a conception of secularism at all.

1. THE OVERLAPPING CONSENSUS MODE OF SECULARISM

According to the overlapping consensus mode of secularism, a secular state must be grounded on 'political principles [such as] human rights, equality, the rule of law, democracy' (Taylor 2011, 37). These principles constitute the political ethic of the state, which can be shared by individuals endorsing very different moral worldviews. Citizens can 'concur in the principles, but differ in the deeper reasons for holding to this ethic' (Taylor 2011, 37). The fact that they embrace diverging and even mutually incompatible moral worldviews is no reason to think that they cannot also embrace the political morality of the state. The possibility of an overlapping consensus relies on the fact that the reasons supporting the political ethic of the state are superficial, while the ones supporting each individual's moral worldview are 'deeper'. The secular state embraces the former while refraining 'from favouring any of the deeper reasons' (Taylor 2011, 37).

The 'overlapping consensus' definition puts forward an important distinction between political secularism's moral values and its institutional principles. The former constitute the political ethic of secularism, while the latter are the institutional arrangements necessary to realize the political ethic. Importantly, the moral values of political secularism are its fundamental ends and they should be associated with the values of freedom, equality, and fraternity.[2] The institutional principles are the means conductive to the realization of the moral values of the secular state. The relationship between the moral ends and the institutional principles is thus one of conditionality of the latter in virtue of their capacity to promote the former. Separation of church and state and state neutrality are not intrinsic goods, but merely means towards the moral ideal of freedom of conscience, equal respect, and fraternity. Consequently, a law or policy that seems to be contrary to either one of them – for instance the presence of religious symbols within state institutions – might be approved if it promotes freedom, equality, or fraternity.

This is an attractive definition of secularism because it avoids two common problems that appear when secularism is discussed. First, it does not fall into the practice of the 'fetishism of means' of secularism (Taylor 2011, 41; Maclure and Taylor 2011, 29). Second, it does not reproduce 'our fixation on religion as [a] problem' (Taylor 2011, 48). The fetishism of means of secularism consists of conceiving state neutrality or (especially) church–state separation as the ends of secularism rather than as its means. This is a common attitude in public debates about whether religious symbols can be displayed within state institutions.[3] Accordingly, such displays must be restricted because they are at odds with the separation of church and state, which is conceived as a constitutive element of the secularity of the state.[4] Debates about whether pupils and teachers in public schools should be permitted to wear religious symbols are thus decided on the grounds of whether they honour the separation of church and state instead of whether the values of equality, freedom, and fraternity are fostered by such restrictions. The institutional design of church–state separation is therefore fetishized as it is given intrinsic value. This is an outcome Taylor and Maclure want to avoid. In their view, the value given to the separation of church and state is 'derived rather than intrinsic', which emphasizes its nature as a means to realize secularism's 'properly moral ends' (Maclure and Taylor 2011, 24).

On the other hand, the fixation on religion as a problem consists of developing institutions and policies under the assumption that the real purpose of secularism is to avoid religious domination (Taylor 2011, 48). According to Taylor, secularism has traditionally been conceived in opposition to the permanent threat of domination by one (or several) religious traditions. In this regard, he thinks of the early justifications of the separation of church and state in the United States as being primarily a strategy guaranteeing that no Christian denomination uses state power to impose its doctrine to the detriment of the other denominations. Similarly, French separation, Taylor argues, was sought as a strategy to prevent the Catholic Church's effective opposition to the promotion of the ideal of a modern republican state in France. Although these might have been legitimate purposes in their respective historical contexts, Taylor maintains, in contemporary societies religion should not be seen as a problem from which the secular state has to be protected. At least in the Western world, religious institutions have privatized their faiths in ways that are compatible with liberal and democratic politics, and most individuals demonstrate a fairly high level of social secularization that reduces the likelihood of intractable conflicts between their faiths and the requirements of the liberal and democratic states of which they are citizens.[5] Taylor's conclusion is that the secular state must not be built up around an identifiable challenge or threat posed by a particular religion. Therefore, he thinks, debates on secularism should not be about how to understand the institutional separation of church and state. In contrast, the secular state must be conceived in relation to *diversity*: the overlapping consensus on the political ethic of the state must be wide enough as to be able to gain the support of individuals embracing the widest possible array of moral worldviews, both religious and nonreligious (Taylor 2011, 36).[6]

A conception of secularism in these terms is intended to provide responses to critics of secularism coming from opposite camps. On the one hand, some critics have argued that secularism is unavoidably biased against religion, as it usually requires that religion plays a restricted role in the public life of a society (Eberle 2002; Wolterstorff 1996). On the other hand, it has also been argued that the liberal tradition of religious freedom has given primacy to religion over nonreligious moral worldviews. One of the purposes of egalitarian theories of religious freedom has been to demonstrate that nonreligious worldviews should be given the same treatment that religious worldviews have historically received; that there is not valid reason to single out religion as worthy of special protection (Maclure and Taylor 2011; Leiter 2012; Eisgruber and Sager 2007; Schwartzman 2012).[7] By emphasizing the ends-means distinction and the fact that it is diversity, not religion, which grounds the secularity of the state, the overlapping consensus mode of secularism presumably provides satisfactory responses to both kinds of criticisms. Religion can have broad presence in a liberal democratic public sphere, but religion is not granted a special status: moral worldviews that are analogous to religious ones enjoy the same treatment by the state.

2. THE PARADOX OF POLITICAL SECULARISM

Taylor identifies a further advantage that derives from his definition of political secularism; he says:

> One of the ways of demonstrating the superiority of the three-principle model [equality, liberty, and fraternity], over that which is fixated on religion, is that *it would never allow one to misrecognize the regime founded by Ataturk as genuinely secular.* (Taylor 2011, 37, emphasis added)

Taylor is probably referring to the fact that under Ataturk's regime, state-promoted religious persecution was widespread. Inspired by a particular understanding of French *laïcité*, the regime promoted modernization and intervened on religious issues, and policed practices, beliefs, and traditions with the purpose of turning Turkey's religious landscape into one that suited the state's political ideology. Why, according to the overlapping consensus definition of secularism, would it be a mischaracterization to say that Ataturk's Turkey was a genuinely secular regime? Taylor's claim seems to be based on the premise that the moral values of freedom of conscience, equal respect, and fraternity are constitutive of any definition of secularism. Being a regime in which religious freedom was not protected and citizens embracing diverging moral worldviews were not treated as equals (probably nonobservant Muslims were treated as second-class citizens *vis à vis* observant Muslims and secular citizens), Ataturk's regime could not be described as a regime of secularism.

This conclusion leads to a paradox, for paradigmatic secular regimes – such as Ataturk's – do not qualify as being considered realizations of political secularism, and the ones that *modestly* exhibit features typically associated to secularism are labelled as the exemplars of what secularism entails. Consider the communist *dictum* that religion is the opium of the people, or states in which the ideals of the Enlightenment were interpreted as promoting freedom from religion. Despite being typically presented as regimes of secularism – or, what is more telling, as being *secularist* – portraying them as genuine exhibits of secularism would be a mischaracterization under the overlapping consensus definition. On the other hand, those which would qualify as regimes of political secularism under this definition would be those that display more modestly the institutional means of secularism as they favour protection of equality, freedom, and fraternity. The overlapping consensus definition suggests that political secularism is not primarily focused on preserving state neutrality and (especially) church–state separation. Instead, it focuses on the promotion of their moral ideals while replacing the language of *religious pluralism* with the language of *diversity*, thereby refraining to make references to the requirement of the institutional arrangement of separation of church and state in the justification of public policy.

The paradox is thus the following: in order to be considered a regime of secularism, a state must display the historically salient features of secularism (i.e., separation of church and state) *in a very modest manner* – for instance, by not adopting a regime of nonestablishment, while states that most visibly display such features are more likely to be discarded as genuine expressions of secularism – for instance, by labelling them as secularist instead of as secular.[8] This paradoxical consequence is problematic to Taylor's claim that 'a radical definition of secularism is needed' (Taylor 2011), as the explanatory power of his newly proposed definition is too narrow: only a very restricted set of regimes of secularism, namely those that are committed to liberal and democratic values, can be genuinely identified as such.

It could be objected that the paradox can be avoided if secularism is understood as a second-order doctrine about how first-order worldviews, including religion, can be treated fairly by the state.[9] The secularisms espoused by Ataturk's ideology, the communist view of religion as the opium of the people, or the Enlightenment conception of freedom from religion would then be first-order moral worldviews that, in different periods of history and in different contexts, were taken as political ideologies. Since they do not attempt to treat religions fairly, they cannot be considered as genuine conceptions of political secularism and no paradox would follow.

The paradox follows, however, if it is made explicit that defining secularism as a second-order normative category can trace a distinction between political and moral secularism. The former is the normative view about how the state relates to first-order worldviews, including religion. The latter is a normative view about how an individual leads her life. A characteristic feature of political secularism could be that it requires fair treatment of all first-order worldviews. Notice that, so stated, political secularism still does not unveil what counts as *fair treatment*. This would be determined in relation to the preferred political morality implemented by the state at hand. Consider, for instance, a political morality that accepts the importance of treating first-order worldviews fairly but that identifies a subset of them, among which the major religions, as highly harmful for the people. A state inspired by this political morality would set institutions that seek to keep its citizens away from the alleged harms of religion, while at the same time would attempt to institutionalize its fair relationships with nonharmful first-order worldviews. In such a case, *it could* be argued that political secularism promotes hostility towards the major religions. If assessed from a liberal perspective, however, this state would be objectionable. According to the overlapping consensus definition, the incompatibility of this state with liberal values disqualifies it from being considered a materialization of a conception of secularism.

3. THE IRRELEVANCE OF SECULARISM

The paradox might be avoided if it is argued that the real purpose of a definition like the overlapping consensus mode of secularism is to show that only liberal and democratic regimes should be considered as genuinely secular. In this case, Maclure and Taylor's position could be interpreted as arguing that debates about secularism should not be presented in terms of what separation of church and state entails – and whether it should be fostered – but in terms of how best to protect the values of equality, freedom, and fraternity in contexts of moral diversity. I think this is a plausible possibility, to which I return in section 6. In this section, I show the consequence that follows from it – and, more broadly, from Maclure and Taylor's proposal to focus on diversity rather than on religion.

The consequence of this strategy is that the relevancy of the category 'secularism' becomes blurred. This can lead to proposals of discarding it from our political vocabulary, as the vocabulary available to us within the liberal and democratic tradition can provide with any normative role that could be ascribed to secularism (Bader 2012, 2007, chap. 3). Furthermore, it is in stark contrast with Taylor's philosophy on political secularism, which is explicit in arguing that secularism is a *relevant* concept for contemporary politics. After all, his quest for a 'radical redefinition of secularism' (2011) and his questions about whether secularism 'can travel' (2016)[10] suggest that he believes there is something within the language of secularism that makes it relevant for addressing some of the most pressing challenges contemporary societies face nowadays. Yet the proposal to replace religion with diversity fails to show that secularism is a relevant political category.

In order to see why the proposal to replace religion with diversity fails to preserve secularism as a relevant normative political category, it is useful to revise Taylor's conceptualization of the 'two modes of secularism' that have historically appeared in the Western world. These are the 'independent ethics' and the 'common ground' (Taylor 1998). The former is characterized by identifying a secular ethics the normative force of which is derived by reason alone, independently of religious metaphysics. The latter is characterized by what is minimally shared by the diversity of religious worldviews. In this case, the state does not embrace a secular ethics but a minimally religious one. These modes are associated with the early experiences of secularism in France and the United States respectively. In Taylor's description, these two modes come with a justification of their relevance in their own contexts: in France, an intransigent Catholic Church used its political power to oppose the development of the modern republican state. *Laïcité* was thus advanced as an attempt to tame such political power and ultimately to consolidate the French state as a republic. On the other hand, the society of the United States was characterized by religious pluralism and by the urge to protect freedom of religion, as the experience of religious persecution in Europe was still fresh among US settlers. The search for a common ground among all religious denominations – at the time only Protestant denominations were acknowledged – led to the separation of church and state: no religion would be established and free exercise of religion would thereby be guaranteed. In either case, secularism, that is, *separation of church and state*, seemed to be the answer to the challenges posed both by the fact that religion might be in tension with the project of the state and by the fact that religious pluralism might impede the consolidation of a unitary form of government.

Neither of these modes of secularism, Taylor argues, is relevant for addressing the challenges contemporary societies face. The irrelevance of the independent ethic is showed by the fact that most religious institutions have already internalized the requirement of political secularization,[11] thereby accepting that they are not authorized to seek primacy over the political authority of the state.[12] In other words, political clericalism of the French Catholic Church ceased to be a threat to the stability of the republic. Additionally, Taylor claims that in pluralistic societies the independent ethic mode is unstable, because it situates atheists and religious believers in a '*Kulturkampf*, in which "secularists" slug it out with believers on issues about the fundamentals of their society' (Taylor 1998, 36). On the other hand, the irrelevance of the common-ground mode of secularism is showed by Taylor by pointing out that it is not reasonable to expect all members of a society to embrace the common ground of all religions. Contemporary societies are more diverse than what this mode can support and therefore would lead to unjust exclusions (Taylor 1998, 35–36).

From this diagnosis, it could be concluded that secularism is irrelevant (or outdated), for neither of its two most representative expressions offer an attractive alternative for contemporary societies, given their great moral diversity and their high degree of social secularization. This is a logical conclusion of the criticism advanced by Taylor of the two modes of secularism. However, from these criticisms Taylor does not conclude that secularism is necessarily irrelevant (or outdated) in order to address the challenges of contemporary societies. He defends instead the need to redefine secularism through the idea of an overlapping consensus.

The redefinition of secularism in terms of an overlapping consensus obeys to the acknowledgement of the great diversification of contemporary Western societies. Processes of social secularization and global migrations have radically changed the religious composition of these societies, which therefore forces a redefinition of political secularism that responds to such transformation. Hence the main motivation behind the overlapping consensus definition of secularism is to emphasize on diversity instead of on religion. An important consequence of this is that secularism cannot be defined as 'separation of church and state'. However, if this is taken to be the main motivation for defining secularism in terms of the overlapping consensus, then the objection that secularism is irrelevant kicks in again. Replacing religion with diversity is justified by the recognition that the secular age is also – and probably mostly – composed by nonreligious moral worldviews, the political claims of which raise similar challenges to the ones advanced by religious individuals, communities, or institutions. The problem with this definition of political secularism is that it leaves open the possibility that political secularism has nothing to do with religion. Political secularism would not be relevant in societies – though as of today improbable – where religion plays an insignificant role in their public life.[13] Think, for instance, of a hypothetical society of nonreligious people. In such a society, dilemmas, conflicts, and disagreements will no doubt be pervasive, yet they would not be about the role and place of religion in the public sphere. Taylor's view is that secularism would be the adequate strategy to implement in order to settle disagreements in a society of nonreligious individuals. This, however, seems unnecessarily counterintuitive. In this case, dispensing of the concept of secularism would appear to be a more plausible conceptualization of the practical challenges this society needs to address.

4. SECULARISM AS SEPARATION OF CHURCH AND STATE

I have argued that the overlapping consensus definition of secularism is problematic because it leads to the paradox according to which the less paradigmatically secular a regime is, the more secular it becomes. I have also argued that the attempt to provide a definition that focuses on diversity instead of on religion is problematic because it fails to show the relevance of secularism in contemporary societies. In this section, I show that a definition of secularism in terms of the institutional separation of church and state does not entail an illiberal relationship with religion, as it is implied by Taylor's and Maclure's description of the fetishism of the means of secularism.

An advantage of defining secularism in terms of the institutional separation of church and state is that it is consistent both with the history of secularism described by Taylor in his analysis of the common ground and independent ethics modes of secularism, and with a fairly generalized usage of the term 'secularism' in the public sphere. According to this generalized use, the two traditional modes of secularism are called modes *of secularism* because they are understood as institutional arrangements that define the conditions in which the separation of religion and politics is supposed to be advanced. Similarly, a regime is labelled secularist because it aggressively pursues the separation of politics and religion. Our usage of the term 'secularism' shows that we do not necessarily intend to communicate that a regime is just when it is labelled as a secular regime. We use the term 'secularism' in order to identify both liberal egalitarian democracies and atheist dictatorships as regimes of secularism – because of their respective commitment to separation of church and state. Everyday intuitions might also identify only the first one as a potentially just regime.

The advantage of a definition of secularism in terms of the institutional separation of church and state is not merely that it fits easily with our usage of the term in the public sphere. It also helps to clarify questions about the reasons that motivate initiatives seeking secularism (or initiatives aiming at its removal). If defined as an institutional arrangement of separation of church and state, secularism cannot be taken as an end in itself. This implies that its promotion (or removal) requires justifications, which would ultimately refer to the moral and political goals pursued by defenders of the promotion (or removal) of secularism – otherwise secularism is not properly justified. If the goals exposed in the justification of a position that promotes the institutional separation of church and state are morally compelling and legitimately accepted, then the requirements of secularism are likely to be morally acceptable. Secularism appears in different fashions and their respective moral acceptability varies accordingly: conceptions of secularism internal to a liberal and democratic regime might be more appealing than the ones internal to an atheist dictatorship. This difference is not due to whether secularism is conceived as separation or as something else; it is due to the moral and political goals that are pursued by the institutional separation of church and state.

Conceiving secularism in terms of the separation of church and state does not substantively affect the main reason motivating the overlapping consensus mode of secularism, namely the interest to guarantee that citizens of contemporary liberal democracies are treated in such a way that they can live according to their core commitments of conscience.[14] This means that they are not compelled to believe or to behave in ways that violate their deepest commitments of conscience (unless compelling justifications are provided) and that, in this respect, they are treated as equals. According to overlapping consensus secularism, if secularism is intended to fulfil such purposes, it cannot be conceived as institutional separation of church and state. Nonetheless, the reason to be sceptical of this definition is not compelling – secularism can refer to the institutional separation of church and state and still be subjected to moral evaluation in relationship to the values it intends to promote.

The main reason Taylor and Maclure offer for being sceptical of conceiving secularism as separation is that they believe it necessarily leads to the fetishism of the separation of church and state, which is directly connected to violations of freedom of religion. In this respect, a good example is the ban on public officials displaying religious symbols while exercising their official tasks. The idea of separation of church and state, when fetishized, is taken to entail that public officials, in virtue of being members of the state, should incarnate the values of the state and therefore appear to the public honouring separation. If secularism as separation of church and state is conceived in these terms, then it is plausible to aim at disentangling secularism from separation.

It is possible, however, to interpret the ban as not being an instance of the fetishization of the means of secularism, while still maintaining the critical stand towards it. There are at least two alternatives in this regard. First, it is possible that the ban be a genuine requirement of secularism. If emancipation from religious belief is assumed as one of the fundamental goals of the state, then the form of separation of church and state at work in the ban will be a way of promoting such emancipation. In this case, the problem is not with the institutions and the policies, but with the ideals they are assumed to advance. What is at stake is not the fetishization of the institutional separation of church and state, but the promotion of an ideology that is incompatible with religiosity in general. Second, the ban could be interpreted as a poor implementation of the requirements of secularism. In this case, it might be that the political ideals pursued by the state are morally sound but that their institutionalization deviates from them – secularism would be the institutionalization of such ideals in issues in which religion is involved. If secularism is interpreted as in the example above, then it would be the case in which the political ideals are sound, yet their institutionalization is not. The argument that shows that, in liberal states, it is permissible that public officials sometimes carry religious symbols while on duty entails that secularism (as separation of church and state) has to be constrained by what the political values of freedom and equality (and fraternity) entail in matters of religion and politics. Conceiving secularism as the institutional separation of church and state does not necessarily imply that separation needs to be pursued as if it were a good in itself. It merely implies that a differentiation between the realms of politics and religion must be preserved—that some degree of separation needs to be protected.

A possible consequence of the definition of secularism just advanced is that liberal states where there is religious establishment, such as England, Scotland, or Denmark, would not be considered secular. I think this does not follow from my account. The reason is that secularism is not an all-or-nothing feature of states. There are degrees of separation and consequently liberal democratic states vary in their degrees of secularism. Mexico, France, or the United States are *more secular* states than England, Scotland, or Denmark. Although it is true that they do not share the property separating church and state at the constitutional level, they are all secular states in the sense that in all of them there is a degree of institutional separation of church and state. Indeed, it could be argued, following Laborde (2017, chap. 4), that all liberal states are at least minimally secular. In the next two sections, I present some examples that illustrate some conditions that could trigger the promotion of a higher degree of secularism.

5. THE RELEVANCE OF SECULARISM

I have demonstrated that defining secularism in terms of the institutional separation of church and state does not necessarily entail reproducing the vices associated with the fetishism of the means. It remains to be shown that secularism is relevant for contemporary societies – for it might be the case that religion does not pose any sort of challenge within the polity. Taylor believes secularism is relevant, yet I have argued that he fails in demonstrating why. The claim that diversity, instead of religion, should be the main focus of reflections about secularism could be interpreted as meaning that contemporary societies are not in need of secularism. Instead, they would be in need of other kinds of institutional arrangements that address the challenges which diversity poses to the realizations of their political values. On this view, the contemporary social world is interpreted as having reached a degree of social secularization such that religious and nonreligious worldviews are equal alternatives in the quest for meaning in life. This implies that religions are conceived as having adjusted themselves to the demands of liberal and democratic institutions.[15] In contexts where this is an accurate description, secularism (as separation) is not relevant because it is already consolidated both at the social and political levels. Arguably, the contexts Taylor has in mind when he reflects on secularism – the North Atlantic world – display the sort of features that might encourage us to think that the most urgent task is not to consolidate the secular state or to protect secular institutions, but to guarantee that all citizens, regardless of their membership, are effective recipients of their liberal-democratic rights.

There are, however, other contexts in which the features that characterize North Atlantic societies are not apparent and which might prompt the pursuit of separation of church and state. These are contexts in which, despite their liberal and democratic political institutions, organized religion has not internalized the political values that sustain the liberal and democratic state – in other words, where religion has not embraced the conception of justice that liberal and democratic states adopt. In these cases, the relevance of political secularism is apparent: it is necessary that the state is at least minimally secular in order for everybody to enjoy the status of free and equal citizenship. Falling short of such minimal separation, the state would be unable to guarantee fair treatment to all its citizens. In these contexts, disestablishment of religion might be the only way to go if liberal and democratic values are to be protected.

Some examples in which secularism is relevant can be mentioned. Think, for instance, of cases in which a historical dominant religious institution can impede access to state-subsidized contraceptives; or of instances in which a high percentage of physicians are conscientious objectors and refuse, on religious grounds, to perform abortions, with the consequence that women see their rights curtailed. In these cases, if the historically dominant religious institution receives official recognition, then liberal egalitarian political actors – that is, progressive-minded actors – have a good reason to disestablish it. They have an incentive to pursue secularism given that the official religious institution is using its position within state institutions to guarantee that political power is exercised in a way that does not contradict its moral precepts. Secularism is also relevant in instances in which religious and national identities are conflated in such a way that nonconforming minorities are excluded: in these cases, it is important to insist on the reasons that support the necessity of keeping religion and politics (at least minimally) separated. Secularism is also relevant as a political project to be pursued in political deliberation in the public sphere of liberal democracies. In this scenario, political activists might have as their goal the promotion of a *starker* separation of church and state (or of religion and politics). Consider, for instance, a liberal state where there is religious establishment and in which a conservative-religious ethos influences public policy, such as in Laborde's *Divinitia* (Laborde 2017, 151). In such a context, secularism might be defended as an institutional mechanism to reverse policies that are morally conservative and religiously inspired – even if they are legitimate. Political advocates of secularism would embrace a political view that includes the promotion of separation between church and state as one of their most pressing goals. On their view, a truly egalitarian society is achieved by the promotion of the secularity of the state: given that morally conservative public policy is religiously inspired, separation of religion and politics would prevent it. Finally, secularism can also be relevant in contexts in which religious minorities are excluded by religious establishment, or in which these minorities have theological reasons to oppose establishment (for instance, because they do not believe in a God that is involved with politics, or that has a 'chosen' people) (Nussbaum 2009, 309). On their view, separation of church and state is how the state treats with equal respect all moral worldviews.

I have not attempted to provide an exhaustive list of cases in which secularism, understood as the institutional separation of church and state, is relevant in contemporary liberal societies. Yet the list of examples is sufficient to think that it can make sense to understand and to pursue secularism in the terms that Taylor rejects. Secularism can be understood as the institutional separation of church and state, and it can be pursued as the main political goal to be reached. Importantly, it is possible to do so in terms that are permissible according to the moral standards of a liberal and democratic political morality, that is, in terms that are compatible with religious freedom or that are not biased against religion.

6. CONCLUSION

In this chapter, I have argued that the attempt to provide a definition of secularism that avoids references to religion, and more specifically to the institutional separation of church and state, leads to the paradox that secularism ends up being defined in a way that paradigmatic regimes of secularism cannot be labelled as being genuine regimes of secularism, while those that loosely exhibit features traditionally associated to secularism end up being the most authentic secular regimes. In order to avoid this paradox, I have suggested we interpret secularism in the terms that proponents of the overlapping consensus reject, namely as the institutional separation of church and state. A consequence of my proposal is that the overlapping consensus mode of secularism is not a conception of secularism at all. In this concluding section I show why this conceptual clarification is not a serious problem for Taylor and Maclure's liberal egalitarian project.

The claim that the overlapping consensus definition of secularism is not really offering a definition of secularism must not be understood as implying that this view does not have anything to say about the nature of secularism. It contains a conception of political secularism in the sense that it *presupposes* a degree of institutional separation of church and state. Liberal egalitarians who have embraced some version of Rawls's approach to the question of religion in liberal politics – through the idea of an overlapping consensus and of public reason – generally agree that there must be at least some minimal separation between religion and politics. This means that liberal states have, as Laborde has called it, a 'secular core' (Laborde 2008, 32), or a minimal degree of separation of religion and politics. The disagreement among liberal egalitarians is about how minimal such core can be in order to guarantee a fair treatment to all citizens.

In an overlapping consensus, the state embraces a political ethic that can be supported by reasons that are acceptable to all citizens. They, however, disagree about the deeper considerations of the nature and normative source of political morality. Such state is secular because the political ethic that can be embraced by disagreeing citizens is likely one that presupposes separation of church and state. The origins of this presupposition are contextual: the idea of an overlapping consensus emerges in Western political thought as a development of the history of European religious intolerance.[16] Liberal and democratic states need to be at least minimally secular, and in cases in which the secular core of the state is threatened, it is important to defend the relevance of pursuing (or consolidating) separation of church and state. From the fact that such a secular core is not threatened in several Western democracies right now – arguably, in the North Atlantic world – it must not be concluded that it will never be or that it is not being threatened in other liberal democracies, in which the institutional separation of church and state is a timely project to be pursued and consolidated. It might well be the case that in several Western contexts it is important to stop thinking about secularism and start thinking about diversity. This is especially valid in contexts in which secularism is used as a proxy to discriminate against minority religions. Yet this does not exclude the fact that there are contexts in which secularism is relevant and in which the transition towards a debate that focuses on diversity rather than on the cleavages created by the presence of religion in politics might obstruct an adequate diagnosis of the challenges faced in these contexts.

ACKNOWLEDGEMENTS

Research for this work was supported by the São Paulo Research Foundation (FAPESP), grant number 15/12948-4. I benefited from comments by Ali Emre Benli, Tim Heysse, Laura Iozzelli, Sune Lægaard, Jocelyn Maclure, Jonathan Seglow, Andrew Shorten, and audiences at the 2017 ECPR Joint Sessions and RIPPLE's Justice Seminar at KU Leuven.

REFERENCES

Bader, Veit. 2007. *Secularism or Democracy? Associational Governance of Religious Diversity*. Amsterdam: Amsterdam University Press.

———. 2012. 'Post-Secularism or Liberal-Democratic Constitutionalism?' *Erasmus Law Review* 5 (1): 6–26.

Bardon, Aurélia. 2015. 'Render unto Caesar the Things Which Are God's: The Requirement of Political Profound Secularization in Liberal Democracy'. *Constellations*, March, 1–11. https://doi.org/10.1111/1467-8675.12145.

Casanova, José. 1994. *Public Religions in the Modern World*. First edition. Chicago: University of Chicago Press.

Eberle, Christopher J. 2002. *Religious Conviction in Liberal Politics*. First edition. Cambridge: Cambridge University Press.

Eisgruber, Christopher L., and Lawrence G. Sager. 2007. *Religious Freedom and the Constitution*. Cambridge, MA: Harvard University Press.

Habermas, Jürgen. 2006. 'Religion in the Public Sphere'. *European Journal of Philosophy* 14 (1): 1–25. https://doi.org/10.1111/j.1468-0378.2006.00241.x.

Laborde, Cécile. 2008. *Critical Republicanism: The Hijab Controversy and Political Philosophy*. Oxford: Oxford University Press.

———. 2013. 'Equal Liberty, Non-Establishment and Religious Freedom'. *Legal Theory*.

———. 2017. *Liberalism's Religion*. Cambridge, MA: Harvard University Press.

Leiter, Brian. 2012. *Why Tolerate Religion?* Princeton, NJ: Princeton University Press.

Maclure, Jocelyn, and Charles Taylor. 2011. *Secularism and Freedom of Conscience*. Translated by Jane Marie Todd. Cambridge, MA: Harvard University Press.

Modood, Tariq. 2013. *Multiculturalism*. Second edition. Cambridge: Polity.

Nussbaum, Martha. 2009. *Liberty of Conscience: In Defense of America's Tradition of Religious Equality*. New York: Basic Books.

Rawls, John. 2005. *Political Liberalism: Expanded Edition*. Second edition. New York: Columbia University Press.

Schwartzman, Micah. 2012. 'What If Religion Isn't Special?' *The University of Chicago Law Review* 79 (4): 1351–427.

Taylor, Charles. 1998. 'Modes of Secularism'. In *Secularism and Its Critics*, edited by Rajeev Bhargava, 31–53. New Delhi: Oxford University Press.

———. 2007. *A Secular Age*. Cambridge, MA: Harvard University Press.

———. 2011. 'Why We Need a Radical Redefinition of Secularism?' In *The Power of Religion in the Public Sphere*, edited by Eduardo Mendieta and Jonathan VanAntwerpen, 34–59. New York: Columbia University Press.

———. 2016. 'Can Secularism Travel?' In *Beyond the Secular West*, edited by Akeel Bilgrami. New York: Columbia University Press.

Wolterstorff, Nicholas. 1996. 'The Role of Religion in Decision and Discussion of Political Issues'. In *Religion in the Public Square: The Place of Religious Convictions in Political Debate*, edited by Robert Audi and Nicholas Wolterstorff, 67–120. Lanham, MD: Rowman & Littlefield.

Zucca, Lorenzo. 2012. *A Secular Europe: Law and Religion in the European Constitutional Landscape*. Oxford: Oxford University Press.

NOTES

1. Tariq Modood's 'moderate secularism,' which defends the diversification of religious establishment, is presented and defended in these terms (Modood 2013, chap. 4).

2. Taylor and Maclure do not include fraternity as a moral value of secularism. Taylor, however, has done so in other writings (Taylor 2011, 34–35). This modification might be because fraternity is a value that is ideologically too close to French republicanism and which might jeopardize the values of equality and freedom in the promotion of social unity or integration—two common interpretations of what fraternity entails. Maclure and Taylor do not completely discard the importance of these goals in politics, yet they situate it in a secondary position with regards to equality and liberty (Maclure and Taylor 2011, 32).

3. Martha Nussbaum (2009, 10) uses the term 'arrogant secularism' to refer to a similar idea.

4. Here it is useful to introduce Taylor's three senses of 'secularity'. Secularity 1 refers to the nonpresence of religion in public spaces, for instance the state. Secularity 2 refers to the 'decline of belief and practice' (Taylor 2007, 20). Secularity 3 refers to new conditions of belief, which are characterized by the fact that religion does not occupy the most prominent role in the life of a given society and of its individuals. Instead, religion is seen as one moral worldview among many others, and probably not the easiest to embrace. Secularity 3 can also be referred to as social secularization (Taylor 2007, 3).

5. Maclure and Taylor believe in the empirical fact that contemporary western societies have reached an overlapping consensus about the 'basic public values' of the polity (Maclure and Taylor 2011, 11–12). In his important book *Public Religions in the Modern World*, José Casanova considers to have offered 'adequate empirical evidence' in support of the claim that public religions, including the reticent Catholic Church, have finally embraced religious freedom and the constitutional separation of church and state—at least in the 'Western Christendom and its colonial outposts' (Casanova 1994, 213).

6. For a similar switch of religion for diversity, see Zucca (2012).

7. For a critical engagement with this theory, see Laborde (2013, 2017, chaps. 2, 3).

8. This use of the term 'secularist' is common among authors such as Jürgen Habermas (2006, 3, 6, 15–16, 18).

9. I thank the editors of the book for pressing me on this point.

10. In 1998, Taylor said, 'in this form [independent ethics mode of secularism], indeed, Western secularism may not "travel" very well outside its heartland; or only in the form of an authoritarian programme designed to diminish the hold of religion on the masses, as in Turkey under Atatürk or China under Mao' (Taylor 1998, 37).

11. On the requirements of political secularization in liberal democracies, see Aurélia Bardon (2015).

12. Laborde's analysis of 'religious institutionalism' suggests that the authority of the secular state over religious institutions is still contested, see Laborde (2017, chap. 5).

13. Nussbaum seems to have this in mind when she claims that 'public, governmental references to faith, or even to a particular faith' might be permissible if 'toleration and protection of minorities' are ensured. This scenario, she claims, would be possible 'only in a country where people do not care very much about religion or the values that divide people along religious lines' (Nussbaum 2009, 13). Laborde might be on the same track when she argues that religious establishment can be permissible in contexts where religion is not a marker of social vulnerability and domination (Laborde 2017, 132–43).

14. 'Core' or 'meaning giving convictions' are those that 'allow people to structure their moral identity and to exercise their faculty of judgment in a world where potential values and life plans are multiple and often compete with one another' (Maclure and Taylor 2011, 76).

15. Maclure and Taylor talk of the 'individualization' of religious belief, which makes religion more suitable for responding to the demands derived from inhabiting a liberal and democratic polity (Maclure and Taylor 2011, 83). José Casanova shows that despite the fact that religions remain active in the public and political spheres, they have reformed themselves in such a way that they are not in conflict with liberal democracies (Casanova 1994).

16. This is, for instance, Rawls's view (Rawls 2005, xxv–xxvi).

FOUR

Shaping Religion

The Limits of Transformative Liberalism

Paul Billingham

1. THE QUESTION OF INCONGRUENCE

How should the liberal state respond to individuals and groups whose religious beliefs or practices (seemingly) do not cohere with liberal egalitarian norms and principles? There are two points of agreement here among liberal theorists.

First, toleration of religious diversity is at the heart of liberalism. A core conviction of liberal political theory is that agents ought to be free to form, revise, and pursue a conception of the good. The capacity to do this is one of the two fundamental moral powers within John Rawls's political conception of the person, and is central to the ideal of autonomy celebrated by comprehensive liberals.[1] Furthermore, individuals exercising this capacity under conditions of freedom will come to hold a variety of different, and indeed incompatible, conceptions of the good, including diverse religious conceptions. Respect for citizens' use of their moral powers therefore requires tolerance of a wide range of religious beliefs and practices. Thus, freedom of religion – in both its internal dimension as freedom of belief and its external dimension as freedom of religious expression, worship, and association – is a basic liberal right.

Second, religion cannot be an excuse for grave injustice or direct violations of fundamental rights. No one should be permitted to murder, assault, or enslave others. Such conduct being religiously motivated does not exempt it from coercive prevention or punishment.

This common ground leaves a large space of difficult cases: those in which individuals engage in practices grounded in their religious beliefs that (arguably) run counter to liberal egalitarian norms, but cannot (uncontroversially) be said to violate fundamental rights. Here are some examples.

First, individuals might structure their domestic lives on the basis of religious beliefs that diverge from liberal egalitarian principles. For example, a couple might arrange their home life based on traditional gender norms, according to which wives ought to be primary caregivers for children, while husbands have primary responsibility for earning an income to support the family.

Second, the internal organization of some religious groups deviates from liberal egalitarian norms. Religious groups can be hierarchical. Some have discriminatory leadership policies. For example, only men can be priests within the Catholic Church, and its hierarchical nature means that this can be changed only by papal decision, even if a majority of Catholics personally endorsed female priesthood.[2]

Third, some religious groups have discriminatory membership policies. For example, they might only admit members who share their doctrinal and ethical beliefs, and thus exclude those whose behaviour they consider immoral, and expel individuals who deviate from the religion's teaching.[3]

Fourth, some religious service-providers wish to refrain from providing their services in certain contexts, in order to avoid expressing support for certain lifestyles or behaviour. This includes Catholic adoption agencies that refuse to place children with gay couples and the infamous 'gay cake' cases.[4]

Fifth, some religious requirements with regard to dress or other features of one's (public) appearance might be in tension with liberal egalitarian norms, for example due to reflecting patriarchal norms. The most familiar example here is the controversy over the Islamic veil.[5]

Finally, there are various cases involving children. These include traditional religious practices such as circumcision, questions about the transmission of nonliberal norms, and parents wishing to withdraw their children from public education, or certain lessons, due to religiously grounded objections to its content.[6]

These cases vary widely, but all involve the kind of tensions and conflicts that I am interested in. They all raise the question of how far the state should tolerate or accommodate religious practices[7] that are *incongruent* with liberal egalitarian norms and principles. The answer to this is likely to vary between the cases I have mentioned, given their variety.[8] I will not directly address or provide judgments on each case. Instead, in the next section I will identify three kinds of response that a liberal theorist might offer. Providing this conceptual framework is one of aims of this chapter. The other aim is to critically assess an increasingly popular response: 'transformative liberalism'. I will argue that our use of this response should be much more limited than its advocates propose.

2. RESPONSES TO INCONGRUENCE

This section will sketch three possible responses to incongruence. But some terminological and conceptual clarifications are required first. Thus far I have used the term 'liberal egalitarian norms and principles' fairly vaguely, and I will continue to do so. There are many accounts of liberal egalitarianism, which I want largely to remain neutral between. Suffice to say that I have in mind a substantive form of liberal egalitarianism, based on values of equality, freedom, and fairness, rather than a thinner, more libertarian, view. The relevant norms and principles thus include nondiscrimination, democracy, gender equality, and so on.

I use the term 'incongruence' broadly to refer to any practice that is in tension or conflict with liberal egalitarian norms, in the sense that it fails to reflect or apply those norms. While it is not only religious individuals or groups who engage in such practices, I will focus exclusively on those cases here: cases where the incongruent practice is endorsed on the basis of religious beliefs and values. To the extent that religious beliefs entail such practices, we might say that those beliefs are themselves incongruent; holding those beliefs leads ones to endorse and engage in actions that diverge from liberal egalitarian norms.

To be clear, a practice being incongruent does not mean that liberal egalitarians must believe that it ought to be legally regulated. For example, Rawls holds that his principles of justice only apply to the basic structure, and not to private associations. Unequal relationships outside the basic structure are permitted. Nonetheless, we can say that such relationships are incongruent because they involve the internal life and organization of families or associations failing to mirror or instantiate the norms and principles applied to public institutions.

Not all liberal egalitarians are so sanguine about such incongruence. Indeed, the three views that I will presently sketch disagree over the existence, nature, and scope of 'incongruence rights': rights to engage in incongruent practices.[9] Incongruence rights are claim-rights: rights with correlative duties held by others, particularly the state, to permit, and to refrain from interfering with, a practice. Incongruence rights are part of more general, largely content-independent, claim-rights of expression, religion, and association, which provide a protected sphere of autonomy in which we are able to pursue our chosen conduct free from others' interference.[10] Some of the conduct within this sphere of autonomy can be wrongful, such that we lack Hohfeldian liberty-rights, or moral permissions, with respect to it. We have a moral duty not to act in this way, but that duty is one that others are not permitted to enforce – hence the claim-right. Not all incongruence is necessarily wrongful, however. Individuals and groups might be morally permitted to deviate in various ways from liberal egalitarian norms within their home and associational lives. Indeed, one might argue that part of the point of liberal egalitarian laws and norms is to protect and permit individuals and groups to structure their private lives based on a variety of different norms. Individuals and groups are morally permitted to act in various ways that it would be impermissible for the state or public institutions to act.[11] Nonetheless, I refer to all deviations from liberal egalitarian norms as cases of incongruence, and use the term 'nonliberal groups' to refer to those exhibiting incongruence.[12] If a group has a claim-right to engage in such a practice, then this is an incongruence right. The dispute between the three views I will now sketch concerns these rights.

The first response denies the existence of incongruence rights in a particular case. Liberal egalitarian principles should thus be coercively imposed. Individuals' and groups' protected sphere of autonomy does not include the claim-right to engage in this particular conduct – conduct that is patriarchal, discriminatory, harmful to children, or violative of others' dignity – and thus it ought to be prohibited.

A view that offered this response to *every* example of nonliberal religion would deny that there are *any* incongruence rights. This does not amount to a denial of the existence of rights of freedom of expression, religion, or association. But it says that those rights are thoroughly constrained by liberal egalitarian norms, such that they are rights only to act in ways that cohere with those norms. Few theorists would hold such a view.[13] Indeed, it not clear that a theory could remain a *liberal* theory while holding that even decisions solely involving consenting individuals, such as the internal structure of the home, must display full congruence with liberal egalitarian norms.[14]

Nonetheless, some theorists would apply this approach to many cases. Some have argued that the Catholic Church should not be permitted to maintain its male-only priesthood (e.g., Conly 2016, 34–35), various European countries have banned the burqa and niqab in public places,[15] and many theorists hold that service-providers should not be permitted to withhold services on religious grounds. This approach embodies what Nancy Rosenblum (1998a, 36–41; 1998b; 2010) has labelled 'the logic of congruence': individuals and groups are required to conform to liberal egalitarian public norms in their practices and conduct. It is 'imperative that the internal life and organization of associations mirror liberal democratic principles and practices' (Rosenblum 1998, 36).

I think that this approach is usually mistaken. The value of freedom of religion is weighty enough to justify toleration of various incongruent practices. In other words, the scope of freedom of religion should not be defined as extending only as far as avoiding any kind of conflict with (other) liberal egalitarian principles. Such conflicts should be acknowledged, and incongruent conduct should often be permitted. We should often recognize incongruence rights. This is most clearly the case when it comes to groups' internal structures. Groups should have extensive – although not unlimited – autonomy to decide their own membership policies and internal structures of leadership, organization, hierarchy, and so on.[16] Matters are of course more complicated when groups are providing outward-focused services, but even here there are liberal grounds for permitting religious groups to provide these services on their own terms, at least within certain limits.

These comments point to the second response: granting incongruence rights. The most expansive version of this approach would hold that all religious practices that do not violate fundamental rights should be immune from state intervention, no matter how far they might deviate from liberal egalitarian norms.

Of course, part of the disagreement between these two approaches concerns the scope of fundamental rights themselves. For example, theorists disagree about whether rights against facing various kinds of discrimination are fundamental rights that must never be violated and whether children's right to bodily integrity includes a right against circumcision. The distance between the first and second approaches will be small if one adopts a very capacious understanding of fundamental rights, which rules out much of the conduct I have mentioned as violative of those rights, and thus not within the sphere of incongruence rights on either approach. But most understandings of fundamental rights will leave many cases where the two approaches diverge.

The third response, which is something of a middle way, is 'transformative liberalism'.[17] This approach involves permitting a practice, on grounds of religious freedom, but also using the state's noncoercive powers to push groups towards congruence. While the state should not prohibit, or otherwise coercively prevent, the practice, it should use tools such as literal speech (by officials and representatives), symbolic speech (e.g., statues and road names), and funding and subsidy (or their withdrawal) to promulgate liberal egalitarian norms and principles, oppose practices that conflict with those norms and principles, and encourage religious individuals and groups to reform their incongruent practices and beliefs. In other words, transformative liberalism acknowledges incongruence rights, but denies that such rights necessarily prevent the state from publicly criticizing the incongruent conduct and imposing pressure upon it. It is a response focused on the kinds of interference that incongruence rights do and do not protect against.

For example, the state might make congruence a requirement for charitable or tax-exempt status. Groups might be permitted to discriminate in their membership or leadership decisions, but only at the cost of no longer being eligible for tax exemptions. Similarly, Catholic adoption agencies might be permitted to only place children with heterosexual couples, but would not be eligible for public funding or participation in public adoption programs. State officials might permit the Islamic veil, but also speak out against it, explaining why they consider it incompatible with equality. While I will not say much about these in this chapter, states can also promote liberal egalitarian principles using 'positive' transformative policies, such as civic education and various kinds of symbolic expression – public memorials, statues, street names, and national holidays that celebrate figures or events that reflect ideals and principles that the state wishes to promulgate.

As with the other approaches, one might endorse transformative policies with regard to some cases of incongruence but not others. Transformative liberals endorse those policies in cases where they deem a practice to conflict with liberal egalitarian norms to a sufficient extent to justify the state exerting pressure towards congruence, but not to violate fundamental rights in a way that would justify prohibition. There is thus an incongruence right to engage in the practice, but a right that does not protect against noncoercive forms of state interference. When such policies are deemed appropriate will depend on one's view of the scope both of fundamental rights and of (relatively) benign forms of incongruence, where even noncoercive state interference is unjustified.

Transformative liberalism has become increasingly popular (for example, see Cohen 2012; Corbin 2012; Balint 2017, 37). One reason for this is that theorists have developed increasingly demanding accounts of relational and civic equality, and thus become more attentive to various kinds of exclusion, discrimination, and inequality within civil society. At the same time, liberals maintain a scepticism of coercive state power and belief in an expansive private sphere and individual rights – including incongruence rights. They are thus wary of using the state's coercive power to force people to conform with liberal egalitarian norms. Yet a lack of conformity threatens to perpetuate social inequality and cause dignitary harms. From this perspective, both the first and second approaches will often look inadequate. Transformative liberalism appears an attractive third option, combining the liberties granted by the second approach with the public disapprobation and state action involved in the first. The transformative state actively promotes liberal egalitarian norms and principles, and opposes beliefs and practice that conflict with them, while still giving wide scope for personal, including religious, freedom.

Despite these attractions, I believe that our enthusiasm for transformative liberalism should be tempered, and our endorsement severely constrained. Those who endorse the first approach will see transformative liberalism as failing to do enough to prevent discriminatory, inegalitarian, or nondemocratic practices. My argument comes from the other direction. The normative limits on the state's authority should lead us to reject expansive versions of transformative liberalism.

Of course, the most plausible liberal theory will likely contain examples of all three responses. It will deny the existence of incongruence rights that would permit citizens to violate fundamental rights, but admit some range of incongruence rights, some but not all of which include protection against transformative policies. My basic claim is that incongruence rights usually protect individuals and groups against even non-coercive, transformative state interference. While transformative policies are appropriate in some extreme cases, their use should be much more limited than transformative liberals propose. Liberal rights generally include the freedom to make use of those rights based on one's own values and commitments without being penalized by the state. For example, if (as I believe) freedom of association includes the right to form groups that discriminate in certain ways in their membership or leadership decisions, then groups that do so should not face additional burdens or pressures from the state than those whose internal structures are congruent with liberal egalitarian norms. This means, for example, that tax exemptions should be available to both kinds of group on the same terms. The state should thus not use the threat of removing tax exemptions as a way of pressuring such groups to liberalize – even if this threat is noncoercive.[18]

The rest of this chapter defends this view. First, I will argue that several possible motivations for transformative liberalism are mistaken, such that the view must rest on a direct claim that the state is obligated to promote congruence. I will then argue that we often have strong reasons to resist this claim, given the force of the official approbation involved in transformative policies, the contestable judgments required in deciding when to endorse such policies, and the proper limits on the state's authority.

3. MISTAKEN TRANSFORMATIVE LIBERAL MOTIVATIONS

This section argues that three possible motivations for transformative liberalism are mistaken. The first is believing that transformative policies are necessary in order to avoid the protection of incongruence rights implying endorsement of the protected individual or group. This is clearly a mistake when applied to the mere protection of liberal rights of free expression, association, and religion. Liberal states protect these rights for all, and do not thereby express endorsement of the way that citizens make use of those rights. As Rosenblum (1998b, 90) writes, 'freedom of association is no stamp of public approval of the internal life of an association in a liberal democracy.'

Less obviously, tax-exempt status also does not imply endorsement of its recipients – or at least endorsement of their beliefs, values, or practices. Tax-exempt status is granted to organizations that do not function for profit and seek to advance the interests (as they see them) of some group or category of people, beyond those who work for the organization. While the justification for such status is disputed, all plausible justifications hold that it is granted based on groups' nature or purpose, not their practices or beliefs. It is thus not a mark of state approval for, or granted in order to advance, the latter. We can see this by briefly reviewing four common justifications.

First, some hold that nonprofit organizations simply do not belong within the tax base. The purposes of corporate income taxation, such as indirectly taxing shareholders' income and regulating managers, do not apply to nonprofits (Herzig and Brunson 2017, especially 1134–37). Such organizations do not pay dividends and are regulated in other ways, so their nature and structure make them inappropriate targets for such taxation. Tax-exempt status is thus a baseline situation for these groups, not a sign of government approval.

Second, an argument for tax exemptions for religious groups in particular is that they reinforce the separation between church and state, by avoiding regulatory processes involved in taxation (Berg 2009, 186; *Walz v. Tax Commission of New York*, 674–75). Here, then, the argument turns on groups' religious nature and a doctrine of separation.

Third, some argue that tax exemptions are justified as a way for the state to support and facilitate an active, pluralistic, civil society. According to Jeff Spinner-Halev (2011, 778), 'a vibrant democracy has a wide variety of charitable and volunteer organizations within it' which increase trust among citizens, give a diverse range of choices, allow citizens to choose to support different causes and charities, and ensure important sites of dissent. Tax-exempt status is a way for the state to encourage this kind of 'rich associational life' (Spinner-Halev 2011, 778). Again, this justification does not imply endorsement of all exempted groups' practices or values. Its advocates hold that decisions about tax exemptions should not be based on ideological constraints, but should be consciously pluralistic, making exemptions available to groups with a diversity of viewpoints (Inazu 2015, 608, 611). In Justice Brennan's words, 'each group contributes to the diversity of association, viewpoint, and enterprise essential to a vigorous, pluralistic society' (*Walz v. Tax Commission of New York*, 689 [Brennan J concurring]).

A final argument for tax exemptions is that they are a means by which the state encourages charitable activity that benefits the public, and increases the public benefits produced.[19] Exemptions from income taxes leave charities with more resources with which to pursue their purposes, while charitable donations being tax deductible encourages individuals to donate. This justification does involve some kind of state approval for charities' activities.[20] But the approval is for the organization's charitable purpose or mission, not for every aspect of its beliefs, values, or practices. The state can judge an organization to be charitable without thereby endorsing its internal organization, membership decisions, values, or even all the means by which it advances its charitable purpose.

Tax exemptions therefore do not involve endorsement. Things are obviously somewhat different when it comes to direct government funding. Here, the state is providing money to a group in order to fulfil a task or project, so its agency is more directly implicated in groups' actions. Nonetheless, funding is provided in order to achieve a *particular* task, without necessarily implying endorsement of everything the funded group stands for. There is space for groups to fulfil the relevant task without displaying full congruence, since funding need not imply endorsement for the incongruence.[21]

Overall, then, arguments for transformative liberalism that claim they are needed in order for the state to avoid endorsing incongruent practices fail.[22]

The second mistaken motivation for transformative liberalism is the assumption that congruence is necessary if individuals are to be good democratic citizens. Rosenblum (1998b, 88) notes that advocates of congruence often assume that 'social habits and moral dispositions cultivated and expressed in voluntary associations are carried over willy-nilly to public life', such that nonliberal practices within civil society will produce (endorsement of) nonliberal political practices or policies. But moral psychology is more complex than this. Groups whose internal lives and practices do not conform to democratic principles do not necessarily cultivate beliefs and practices that undermine democracy. Similarly, groups that discriminate within their membership or leadership policies do not necessarily foster support for discrimination, or any form of second-class citizenship, within political life. People can 'discriminate discriminatingly' (Rosenblum 1998b, 89; see also Rosenblum 1998a, 47–50). Individuals can believe that certain kinds of people should not be permitted as members or leaders within their religious group while nonetheless supporting equality of citizenship and access to political influence. Catholics who endorse male-only priesthood do not thereby commit themselves to endorsing male-only political representation, less-than-equal opportunity for women in public life, or rejecting female leadership in all domains. 'Prized democratic dispositions do not have to be cultivated or exhibited everywhere to be practiced in political life.' Indeed, 'incongruent groups do often cultivate democratic dispositions indirectly and do shape members who are also good citizens' (Rosenblum 2010, 392).

Even if transformative liberalism cannot rest on concerns with state endorsement of incongruence or the creation of bad citizens, one might argue that it is justified simply due to reducing the occurrence of wrongful uses of incongruence rights. Some versions of this argument involve a third mistake that liberals should be sensitive to: the impulse to call upon the state to resolve all social problems or wrongs. Liberals have always been sceptical of state power and prized individual rights of dissent. Yet contemporary liberals are often quick to turn to the state's actions as the means by which wrongs should be prevented and society reshaped. There are certainly good reasons for this; the modern state has brought much positive change and contains great potential for advancing justice. Nonetheless, it is not the solution to everything. Some issues – and even some wrongs – are beyond its capacity and authority. When we consider how religious or cultural groups might be reformed, there are many reasons to favour change that originates from within over change that is imposed, or even pressured, by the state. Ironically, religious groups themselves have often learned these lessons better than transformative liberals. Many such groups recognise the limits of politics to confront things they consider immoral, and believe that much immorality should not be subject to state interference.[23] Liberals should be willing to admit this too.

If this is right, then the justification for transformative liberalism must be that there are *particular* kinds of violations of liberal egalitarian norms – and harms arising from those violations – that do require a response from the state. The state should not seek to right all wrongs, but has a duty to promote congruence to a certain degree. For example, Corey Brettschneider (2012) argues that transformative policies are justified when aimed at practices that are incompatible with the basic liberal ideal of 'free and equal citizenship', and the norms and principles that it generates. Citizens and associations whose practices violate this ideal can rightly be opposed by the state using its expressive capacities, while other forms of incongruence should remain unopposed. Alternatively, a transformative liberal might focus on specific practices that they believe *will* undermine vital civic virtues or democratic dispositions, even taking Rosenblum's arguments on board. The next section argues that there are good reasons to limit even these transformative aspirations.

4. AGAINST TRANSFORMATION

The central reason for opposing transformation is to place appropriate limits on the state's authority, in particular its power to shape civil society. Liberals have long been concerned with restricting the power of the state in this domain – partly due to general scepticism about extensive state power and partly due to the particular role that civil society groups play as 'mediating institutions' between individuals and the state, which provide both a check on state power and a central location for individual flourishing. Transformative liberalism expands the state's power over civil society, by permitting (or requiring) it to oppose groups it deems insufficiently liberal and place pressure on them to reform.

Some reasons for wariness here come from the risk of abuse of power. Officials might conflate opposition to their policies with opposition to liberal egalitarian ideals, and direct transformative pressures at political opponents rather than nonliberal groups (Calabresi 2014; Herzig and Brunson 2017, 159).[24] Transformative liberalism might encourage what Robin West (2014, 1037–39) calls the 'hypocritical state', which uses engagement in transformation as cover for its own failures to live up to standards of equality and fairness.

Even setting these considerations aside, we must recognize the *force* of transformative policies. They involve the state declaring a particular practice, and the beliefs underlying it, to be unacceptable from the perspective of the political community – one that merits official public opposition. The state, speaking in the name of political community, expresses disapprobation towards the practice. While the practice is tolerated, it is also officially declared to be incompatible with good citizenship. In this sense, it is publicly presented as beyond the pale. The strength of this message of official public condemnation gives strong reason for caution.

Of course, transformative liberals would argue that we *should* condemn sexism, homophobia, and other illiberal viewpoints. Those who reject norms of gender equality and nondiscrimination should be opposed. The question, however, is whether the *state*, specifically, ought to engage in this opposition. If we accept incongruence rights in relation to a particular practice, based on our commitment to freedom of expression, religion, and association (as transformative liberals do), then we should be wary of drawing upon the state's authority to declare that practice to nonetheless be beyond the pale. We should not require individuals or groups to be thoroughgoing liberal egalitarians throughout their public and private lives in order to be citizens in good standing, and this includes not directing the weight of state condemnation against most incongruence. Freedom to engage in incongruent practices, and to hold incongruent beliefs, should include being treated equally to congruent individuals and groups by the state. This is an important part of the liberal concern for limiting state power and permitting individuals to form and act upon their own beliefs, even when they are not fully aligned with liberal egalitarian public norms.

Some transformative liberals accept this argument in general, but hold that a particular class of practices, and the beliefs underlying them, should be officially publicly condemned, due to opposing liberal democracy's most fundamental ideals. Brettschneider offers the most fully developed such view. As I mentioned above, he endorses extensive incongruence rights, but argues that they should not extend so far as freedom from state opposition in cases of conflicts with free and equal citizenship (FEC), the core ideal of liberal democracy. 'Beliefs and practices that conflict with the ideal of free and equal citizenship can be of public concern, and should be changed to make them compatible with democratic values' (Brettschneider 2012, 24). The state should use its expressive capacities in order to promote this change, and thus 'should intentionally seek to transform some religious beliefs [and practices] that are at odds with the underlying values of democracy' (Brettschneider 2012, 99).

The ideal of FEC can be defined in various ways. A minimal conception would focus on accepting that all citizens have an equal public standing that entitles them to a range of basic rights – including both liberal freedoms and political rights. One rejects this ideal if one denies some citizens' basic moral worth, entitlement to vote, freedom of expression, and so on, or endorses state discrimination against those citizens. Some do reject this ideal; indeed, there is growing concern about the rise of far-right groups that do so. Most incongruent groups do not reject this minimal conception, however. Very few conservative or nonliberal religious groups believe that some citizens should be denied basic liberal and political rights or treated as inferior by the state.

The ideal can be thickened in various ways. Most relevant here, one might view certain inegalitarian or discriminatory practices within voluntary associations or individuals' private lives to be incompatible with supporting FEC. Perhaps endorsing traditional gender roles within the home, denying group membership to those who reject a conservative sexual morality, or holding that only men can be priests constitute denials of the equal public standing of women or gay citizens.

The thickest conception of FEC would conflict with all incongruence, since any failure to apply liberal egalitarian norms to one's private and associational life would be seen as a denial of all citizens' status as free and equal. All liberal justice is ultimately grounded in the idea of fair cooperation among free and equals, and arguments for particular policies invariably involve claims about the demands of freedom and equality. So it is not surprising that one could hold that all forms of incongruence constitute violations of FEC.[25]

Transformative liberals do not tend to adopt the maximally thick conception. Brettschneider (2012, 135) argues that the Catholic Church's policy of male-only priesthood does not deny women's equal citizenship, in the light of the Church's general attitude towards women in public life and restriction of inegalitarianism to the specific role of priest. But Brettschneider also does not adopt the minimal conception. He argues that groups denying membership based on a conservative sexual morality should face transformative policies, and hints at this for groups that oppose same-sex marriage (Brettschneider 2012, 134–37, 117–20).

The judgments involved in specifying a conception of FEC, and determining whether particular examples of incongruence conflict with it, are often complicated and controversial, for (at least) two reasons,[26] which provide considerations against transformative liberalism.

First, there are often plausible arguments on both sides concerning whether a practice conflicts with FEC. Take a group that requires members to endorse central aspects of its religious views, including a conservative sexual morality, such that it denies (or rescinds) membership to those who engage in sexual activity outside of heterosexual marriage. Brettschneider (2012, 117–20) argues that this constitutes a denial of the equal status of gay citizens, since it bars them from membership based on an unchosen aspect of their identity. But one might argue that the group is discriminating based on individuals' beliefs and practices, not their status or identity. Membership is not denied simply on the basis of being gay, but of endorsing or engaging in homosexual conduct – and any other sexual practices outside of heterosexual marriage (Garnett 2012, 219–21). Michael McConnell (2000, 472) argues that 'it is not invidiously discriminatory for a private association committed to certain beliefs and values to limit itself to persons who share those beliefs and values.' Of course, this would be invidious if the beliefs in question themselves denied the basic moral status or civic equality of the excluded. But this does not seem true in this case. The group here might violate a thick conception of FEC, but plausibly does not violate a thin one. This kind of contentious line-drawing is inherent in determining whether a belief or practice conflicts with whatever conception of FEC one adopts as the basis for transformative policies.

Transformative liberals might argue that the state regularly makes complicated and contentious judgments, in all policy areas. It often must act in the face of reasonable disagreement. For example, reasonable disagreement about distributive justice does not mean the state lacks the authority to implement Rawls's difference principle. The criticism here thus cannot simply be that the state can never make controversial judgments or engage in reasonably disputable actions. But there is something importantly distinct about the message of transformative liberal policies. They declare a belief or practice to be beyond the pale – incompatible with society's fundamental values. The state can implement the difference principle without declaring that sufficientarianism is an unacceptable position, or that its advocates are not decent citizens. Transformative liberal policies make precisely this statement; they involve official disapprobation. This is why they raise a special normative concern, and why the contestable nature of the judgments involved is important. Goodwilled people committed to core liberal democratic ideals, including the minimal conception of FEC, can disagree about cases like male-only priesthood and the exclusion of individuals who reject conservative sexual morality. This should give us pause before calling upon the state to officially declare such practices inconsistent with fundamental liberal democratic ideals.

Furthermore, the state cannot avoid acting in the domain of distributive justice – it must enact some kind of tax and spend policy. But it often can avoid making the judgments and statements involved in transformative policies. This would not be true if protecting liberal rights expressed endorsement for how those rights are used, or granting tax-exempt status expressed endorsement for a group's beliefs and practices. But since this is not the case (as I argued above), the message behind transformative liberal polices can usually be avoided. We often have good reason to avoid it, given the force of that message and the contestable nature of the judgments involved.

Second, matters are further complicated when the relevant practice is grounded in theological doctrines. As Kevin Vallier (2016, 13–16) notes, this is the case for many religious practices that are potential transformative targets. They are rooted in theological conceptions of personal identity, natural law, God's creative ordering, the role of intentions in moral evaluation, the nature of salvation, the authority and interpretation of tradition, Scriptural hermeneutics, and so on. Judging the compatibility of a practice with FEC requires understanding its meaning, which unavoidably requires evaluation of theological material. For example, whether the exclusion of those violating a conservative sexual morality constitutes a denial of their equal status partly depends on the group's theological understanding of sexual identity, the distinction between status and behaviour, and the grounding of the relevant sexual morality. Similarly, whether the burqa is an affront to women's equal citizenship partly depends on its meaning within Islam. Transformative liberalism thus requires the state to make judgments that involve a kind of substantive theological interpretation and adjudication for which it is ill-equipped and that make the state an arbiter of religious beliefs and activities in a way that runs against the liberal commitment to freedom of religion. It asks the state to adjudicate on the meaning of theologically embedded practices at the bar of liberal egalitarian ideals – including making judgments that contradict groups' own understanding of their theological and political morality. Liberals have good reason to reject this expansion of the state's interpretative authority.

A transformative liberal might argue that the state cannot avoid some adjudication of theologically grounded claims. If discrimination in hiring on religious grounds is permissible for religious organizations – as in UK law (Equality Act 2010, Schedule 9, paras 2–3) – then courts have to decide whether a particular decision was made for genuine religious reasons. Similarly, some examination of religious beliefs is required when decisions are made about whether exemptions should be granted, for example under Article 9 of the European Convention of Human Rights.[27] Even in these contexts, however, courts seek to avoid substantive theological adjudication, and distinguish the question of what parties' religious beliefs and practices are from the question of their validity or acceptability. These are difficult lines to draw, of course. But transformative liberalism is different in kind. It directly requires the kinds of adjudication that courts have tried to avoid: interpreting the meaning of religious doctrines and proclaiming upon their acceptability in the light of liberal egalitarian ideals. Again, reasons of both state ability and authority speak against this.

As a final critical point, we should also note the potentially far-reaching consequences of transformative liberalism. Groups with beliefs and practices that are in some way incongruent with liberal egalitarian norms include many organizations that provide important charitable services, often within poor and marginalized communities. Under transformative liberalism, they face the threat of losing tax-exempt status and access to public funding. Some might be forced to shut down. Individual citizens can also face large costs. Brettschneider argues that the state should fire individuals whose viewpoints oppose FEC. The cost of exercising incongruence rights might be losing one's job. While incongruence rights are still formally recognized, the costs imposed upon their exercise can be extensive, limiting the substantive freedom to hold and act upon incongruent beliefs.[28]

Three clarifications regarding my view of incongruence rights are required here.

First, I have implicitly endorsed transformative liberal policies in relation to violations of the minimal conception of FEC. For example, speech that directly denies that some citizens should enjoy equal status or be granted fundamental rights should face official public disapprobation. Much speech in this category would be legally prohibited hate speech in most European jurisdictions. But not all actions violating the minimal conception should be legally prohibited, and this makes room for transformative policies. For example, a neo-Nazi rally should be permitted, but state officials ought to speak out against it, condemning it as representing ideas that contravene the most fundamental liberal democratic principles.

Second, I have focused on 'negative' transformative policies—condemnatory state speech, tax exemptions being revoked, and so on. As I noted above, the state can also enact 'positive' transformative policies, such as symbolic expression. Some of these policies raise distinct normative concerns, such as that their influence on citizens is subliminal or manipulative (Tsai 2016). But assuming that they can be legitimate, I think that they too ought to be based on the minimal conception of FEC. While I lack space to defend this view, it is based on similar considerations as those discussed above.

Finally, we should note the difference between official state speech – speech by officials or representatives uttered in the name of the state – and representative speech – all other speech by politicians and representatives.[29] The latter need not be as constrained as the former. Even if transformative policies undertaken through official state speech should be limited to the minimal conception of FEC, representative speech can go much further in articulating a thick conception and criticizing beliefs or practices that the representative considers incompatible with that conception. Politicians are free to oppose forms of incongruence that those

speaking in the name of the state should not express public disapprobation towards.

5. CONCLUSION

Opposing transformative liberalism carries risk. Incongruent voluntary
associations might cause various kinds of harms, and might shape citizens in ways that lead them to support less just outcomes, or vote against
laws that instantiate a full understanding of FEC. But we must live with
this risk, for the sake of liberal values themselves. In this sense, liberal
democracy is always a risk. Citizens might vote for unjust laws or politicians who are unfit for office. And liberalism requires that we grant freedoms that could lead to the rejection of liberalism. The fate of the liberal
democratic state ultimately rests on the conduct of individuals and
groups who are to a significant extent outside of its control – not simply
for practical capacity-based reasons, but for normative reasons provided
by liberalism itself.

Those alert to incongruence and sceptical of civil society might be
resistant to this; hence the attraction of transformative liberalism. En-
trusting citizens' moral formation to a civil society containing racist, sex-
ist, and homophobic groups might seem unacceptably risky.

But we must be careful not to contrast a nonideal picture of civil
society with an idealized state. The state itself has great potential for
abuse of power. Liberals limit it partly for this reason. If we fear corrupt
civil society then we have just as much, if not more, reason to fear the
corruption of the state.

Furthermore, even within ideal theory, there are important reasons to
limit the state's transformative authority and resist the expansive kind of
transformative liberalism that has become increasingly popular, as we
have seen. This does involve placing some trust and hope in civil society.
Liberalism demands that we do this – just as we do for the state itself. But
this is not wishful thinking or blind faith. We have good reason to hope
that protections of liberal rights will themselves lead citizens to form an
allegiance to liberal institutions, as all enjoy the benefits of living in a free
society.

We should also note that nonliberal groups within liberal societies
will always face some, usually fairly strong, pressure to reform. This
includes the pressure that comes from liberal egalitarian law itself. Those
who oppose same-sex marriage or endorse male-only priesthood already
know they are outside of the mainstream. It also includes pressure within
civil society, from citizens who engage nonliberals in dialogue or debate.[30]

Nonetheless, a critic might claim that transformative policies are particularly necessary *now*, at a time when liberal democracy appears less

stable and far-right and antisystem parties and movements are making headway. My reply to this is twofold. First, my view permits transformative policies targeted at those who clearly reject even the most fundamental liberal democratic ideals, embodied in the minimal conception of FEC. There are question of effectiveness here. As West (2016, 1036–37) notes, those who find the liberal state hateful are likely to have their views reinforced by state attempts to persuade them of liberalism. But there are no principled objections to public officials speaking out against neo-Nazis or reaffirming first-class citizenship for all. Second, the current situation actually *strengthens* the reasons against extending transformative policies beyond the minimal conception. Policies based on a thicker conception would portray a greater variety of beliefs and practices as incompatible with liberal democracy, which risks marginalizing many who consider themselves genuine supporters of liberal democracy. If individuals who defend liberal rights and endorse all citizens' equal status are publicly portrayed as holding religious (or other) views that fall outside the bounds of acceptable pluralism, then they will likely feel alienated, and could become disillusioned with the liberal democratic political project. Christian law professor Stephen Carter rejects transformative liberalism on grounds of freedom of religion and the importance of dissent and difference within democracy. I think he is largely right about these deontological limits on the state's legitimate authority to shape religion. But he also comments that 'liberal theorists seem to believe that deep faith commitments pose serious threats to the order they are trying to create. I hope they are wrong. If they are right, then the order is not worth preserving' (Carter 2001, 43). The present moment gives us reason against expansive transformative policies precisely because the kind of renewal of liberal democracy that we need cannot be achieved by alienating citizens like Carter. So, there are also powerful instrumental reasons against transformative liberalism.

ACKNOWLEDGEMENTS

I owe thanks to Jonathan Seglow, Andrew Shorten, and Kevin Vallier for helpful comments on earlier drafts of this chapter.

REFERENCES

Badano, Gabriele, and Alasia Nuti. 2018. 'Under Pressure: Political Liberalism, the Rise of Unreasonableness, and the Complexity of Containment'. *The Journal of Political Philosophy* 26 (2): 145–68.

Balint, Peter. 2017. *Respecting Toleration: Traditional Liberalism and Contemporary Diversity*. New York: Oxford University Press.

BBC News. 2018. 'The Islamic Veil Across Europe'. May 31, 2018. http://www.bbc.co.uk/news/world-europe-13038095.

Berg, Thomas C. 2009. 'Religious Organizational Freedom and Conditions on Government Benefits'. *Georgetown Journal of Law and Public Policy* 7 (1): 165–215.

Billingham, Paul. 2017. 'How Should Claims for Religious Exemptions Be Weighed?' *Oxford Journal of Law and Religion* 6 (1): 1–23.

———. 2019a. 'Exemptions for Religious Groups and the Problem of Internal Dissent'. In *Religious Beliefs and Conscientious Exemptions in a Liberal State*, edited by John Adenitire, 51–69. London: Hart Publishing.

———. 2019b. 'State Speech as a Response to Hate Speech: Assessing "Transformative Liberalism"'. *Ethical Theory and Moral Practice*, online first. doi: 10.1007/s10677-019-10001-1.

———. Working paper. 'The Scope of Religious Group Autonomy: Varieties of Judicial Examination of Church Employment Decisions'.

Brettschneider, Corey. 2012. *When the State Speaks, What Should It Say? How Democracies Can Protect Expression and Promote Equality*. Princeton, NJ: Princeton University Press.

Brownlee, Kimberley. 2015. 'Freedom of Association: It's Not What You Think'. *Oxford Journal of Legal Studies* 35 (2): 267–82.

Calabresi, Steven G. 2014. 'Freedom of Expression and the Golden Mean'. *Brooklyn Law Review* 79 (3): 1005–14.

Carter, Stephen L. 2001. 'Liberal Hegemony and Religious Resistance: An Essay on Legal Theory'. In *Christian Perspectives on Legal Thought*, edited by Michael W. McConnell, Robert F. Cochran, and Angela C. Carmella, 25–53. New Haven, CT: Yale University Press.

Chaplin, Jonathan. 2012. 'Law, Religion and Public Reasoning'. *Oxford Journal of Law and Religion* 1 (2): 319–37.

Clayton, Matthew, and David Stevens. 2014. 'When God Commands Disobedience: Political Liberalism and Unreasonable Religions'. *Res Publica* 20 (1): 65–84.

Cohen, Jean L. 2012. 'The Politics and Risks of the New Legal Pluralism in the Domain of Intimacy'. *International Journal of Constitutional Law* 10 (2): 380–97.

Conly, Sarah. 2016. 'In Defense of the (Somewhat More) Invasive State'. *Philosophy & Public Issues (New Series)* 6 (1): 25–37.

Corbin, Caroline Mala. 2012. 'Expanding the *Bob Jones* Compromise'. In *Legal Responses to Religious Practices in the United States: Accommodation and Its Limits*, edited by Austin Sarat, 123–67. Cambridge: Cambridge University Press.

Ekeli, Kristian Skagen. 2012. 'Liberalism and Permissible Suppression of Illiberal Ideas'. *Inquiry* 55 (2): 171–93.

Fergusson, David. 1998. *Community, Liberalism and Christian Ethics*. Cambridge: Cambridge University Press.

Garnett, Richard W. 2012. 'Religious Freedom and the Nondiscrimination Norm'. In *Legal Responses to Religious Practices in the United States: Accommodation and Its Limits*, edited by Austin Sarat, 194–227. Cambridge: Cambridge University Press.

Goldfarb, Zachary A., and Karen Tumulty. 2013. 'IRS Admits Targeting Conservatives for Tax Scrutiny in 2012 Election'. *Washington Post*, May 10, 2013. https://www.washingtonpost.com/business/economy/irs-admits-targetingconservatives-for-tax-scrutiny-in-2012-election/2013/05/10/3b6a0ada-b987-11e2-92f3-f291801936b8_story.html.

Herzig, David J., and Samuel D. Brunson. 2017. 'Let Prophets Be (Non) Profits'. *Wake Forest Law Review* 52 (2): 1111–61.

Hollenbach, David. 2002. *The Common Good and Christian Ethics*. Cambridge: Cambridge University Press.

Inazu, John D. 2015. 'A Confident Pluralism'. *Southern California Law Review* 88 (3): 587–617.

Insole, Christopher J. 2004. *The Politics of Human Frailty: A Theological Defence of Political Liberalism*. London: SCM Press.

Leigh, Ian. 2012. 'Balancing Religious Autonomy and Other Human Rights under the European Convention'. *Oxford Journal of Law and Religion* 1 (1): 109–25.

Macedo, Stephen, 1998. 'Transformative Constitutionalism and the Case of Religion: Defending the Moderate Hegemony of Liberalism'. *Political Theory* 26 (1): 56–80.

Martin, Nick. 2012. 'Liberal Neutrality and Charitable Purposes'. *Political Studies* 60 (4): 936–52.

McConnell, Michael W. 2000. 'The New Establishmentarianism'. *Chicago-Kent Law Review* 75 (2): 453–75.

Meilaender, Peter C. 2003. 'The Problem of Having Only One City: An Augustinian Response to Rawls'. *Faith and Philosophy* 20 (2): 170–88.

Pew Research Center. 2015. 'US Catholics Open to Non-Traditional Families'. September 2. http://assets.pewresearch.org/wp-content/uploads/sites/11/2015/09/Catholics-and-Family-Life-09-01-2015.pdf.

Rawls, John. 2005. *Political Liberalism*. Expanded edition. New York: Columbia University Press.

Raz, Joseph. 1986. *The Morality of Freedom*. Oxford: Clarendon Press.

Rosenblum, Nancy L. 1998a. *Membership and Morals: The Personal Uses of Pluralism in America*. Princeton, NJ: Princeton University Press.

———. 1998b. 'Compelled Association: Public Standing, Self-Respect, and the Dynamic of Exclusion'. In *Freedom of Association*, edited by Amy Gutmann, 75–108. Princeton, NJ: Princeton University Press.

———. 2010. 'Faith in America: Political Theory's Logic of Autonomy and Logic of Congruence'. In *Religion and Democracy in the United States: Danger or Opportunity?*, edited by Alan Wolfe and Ira Katznelson, 382–410. Princeton, NJ: Princeton University Press.

Spinner-Halev, Jeff. 2011. 'A Restrained View of Transformation'. *Political Theory* 39 (6): 777–84.

Tsai, George. 2016. 'The Morality of State Symbolic Power'. *Social Theory and Practice* 42 (2): 318–42.

Univision. 2014. 'Global Survey of Roman Catholics'. https://maryofmagdala-mke.org/documents/Vatican%20questionnaire%20results%202.2014.pdf.

Vallier, Kevin. 2016. 'Religious Freedom and the Reasons for Rights'. *Philosophy & Public Issues (New Series)* 6 (1): 9–24.

West, Robin. 2014. 'Liberty, Equality, and State Responsibilities'. *Brooklyn Law Review* 79 (3): 1031–45.

Legal Cases Cited

Walz v. Tax Commission of New York 397 U.S. 664 (1970).

Wisconsin v. Yoder 406 U.S. 205 (1972).

Mozert v. Hawkins 827 F.2d 1058 (6th Cir. 1987).

Christian Legal Society v. Martinez 561 U.S. 661 (2011).

S.A.S. v. France [2014] ECHR 695.

Masterpiece Cakeshop v. Colorado Civil Rights Commission 584 U.S. ___ (2018).

NOTES

1. See Rawls (2005, 19, 103–4); Raz (1986, 369–78).

2. According to a 2015 Pew Survey, 59 per cent of American Catholics believe the Church ought to allow women to become priests. See Pew Research Centre (2015, 73–5). A 2014 poll of twelve thousand Catholics from twelve countries put this figure at 64 per cent for Europe, and 45 per cent worldwide. See Univision (2014, 10–11).

3. For a legal case of this kind, see *Christian Legal Society v. Martinez* 561 U.S. 661 (2011).

4. In Northern Ireland, Ashers bakery refused to make a cake with the slogan 'support gay marriage'. The bakery was found guilty of unlawful discrimination

based on sexual orientation by the Northern Irish courts, but this ruling was over-turned on appeal by the UK Supreme Court, in *Lee v. Ashers Baking Company Ltd. and others* (2018) UKSC 49, on the grounds that the 'less favourable treatment was afforded to the message, not to the man' (paragraph 47). The bakery could not refuse to serve Mr. Lee 'because he was a gay man or because he supported gay marriage', but they could refuse 'to supply a cake iced with a message with which they profoundly dis-agreed' (55). Mr. Lee announced in August 2019 that he would challenge the Supreme Court decision at the European Court of Human Rights. In the United States, in *Mas-terpiece Cakeshop v. Colorado Civil Rights Commission* 584 U.S. __ (2018), a bakery refused to make a cake for a same-sex wedding. The US Supreme Court ruled in the bakery's favor, but on very narrow grounds regarding the way that this specific case was handled by the Colorado Civil Rights Commission.

5. For a helpful overview of policies towards the veil across Europe, see BBC News (2018).

6. The most famous legal cases of this kind are *Wisconsin v. Yoder* 406 U.S. 205 (1972) and *Mozert v. Hawkins* 827 F.2d 1058 (6th Cir. 1987).

7. By 'religious practices' I simply mean practices grounded in religious beliefs.

8. For example, one obvious difference involves the levels of consent given by the parties engaged in, or affected by, the practices.

9. While her topic is different to mine (she is discussing freedom of intimate asso-ciation), my conceptual analysis in this paragraph draws on that in Brownlee (2015).

10. 'Incongruence rights' are therefore not a separate category of rights for nonliber-al groups. 'Incongruence rights' is a label used to refer to cases where general liberal rights enjoyed by everyone are used to engage in an incongruent practice, and the general right includes the right to engage in that practice. This specific right to engage in that practice is the incongruence right.

11. For example, Garnett (2012, 194–227) argues that certain kinds of discrimination are not wrongful, even though they would be wrongful if the state practised them.

12. I use this term rather than 'illiberal' because 'illiberal' might imply a negative judgment, whereas 'nonliberal' is more neutral.

13. Levy (2015, 51, fn. 15) cites Russell Hardin as someone who might endorse this view.

14. Of course, there is scope for disagreement about what policies are required in order to ensure that consent is adequately informed or autonomous.

15. Furthermore, in *S.A.S. v. France* [2014] ECHR 695, France's prohibition of the concealment of one's face in public places was ruled by the Grand Chamber of the European Court of Human Rights (ECtHR) not to violate Articles 8 (right to privacy) and 9 (right to religious freedom) of the European Convention on Human Rights.

16. For discussion of how ECtHR has balanced such claims against other European Convention rights, see Leigh (2012). I develop some of my own views on these matters in Billingham (2019a); Billingham (working paper).

17. My use of this term is based on Macedo (1998). Brettschneider (2012, 1–21) presents his transformative liberal view as a middle way between 'militant democra-cy' and minimal liberalism, which enables liberal democracies to avoid both of two dystopias: the 'invasive state' and the 'hateful society'.

18. I argue that such threats are in fact coercive in Billingham (2019b). I set this issue aside here.

19. This justification seems to lie behind UK charity law. The Charities Act 2006 lists thirteen categories of eligible charitable purposes (including advancing religion) and requires charities to function for public benefit.

20. It also raises controversial questions regarding the definition of 'charitable pur-poses' and the compatibility of this approach with liberal neutrality. See Martin (2012).

21. I think this can be true even if the state funds an organization whose service-provision is (from the state's perspective) incomplete – such as adoption agencies that will not place children with gay couples. Even this need not imply endorsement for the incongruence itself, especially since the state will also ensure that all who have the

right to the service have access to it, via alternative providers. To be clear, I am not claiming that such funding is justifiable, merely that the objection to it should not be endorsement-based. Clearly more argument would be needed to properly defend even this claim.

22. An implication of this is that Brettschneider's (2012, 43–45) complicity-based argument fails, since his understanding of complicity appeals to (the appearance of) endorsement of incongruence.

23. For example, many Christian theologians argue that Christianity 'desacralizes' politics, revealing limits on what can be achieved through earthly political authority. Hollenbach (2002, 55) writes that Christians 'are required by their faith to reject any attempt to achieve the full common good, as it is understood theologically, by political means.' See also Fergusson (1998, 158); Insole (2004, 59); Meilaender (2003).

24. For a recent real-life case, see Goldfarb and Tumulty (2013).

25. This means that endorsing a 'political', as opposed to 'comprehensive', conception of transformative liberalism, as Brettschneider (2012, 30–37) does, does not necessarily prevent a thoroughgoing transformative program.

26. Similar questions apply to the characterization of 'fundamental liberal values' offered in Ekeli (2012).

27. For an argument concerning how such judgments should be made, see Billingham (2017). The United States' Religious Freedom Restoration Act (1993) also requires such judgments.

28. For further critique of the implications of Brettschneider's view, see Billingham (2019b).

29. Chaplin (2012, 330–37) uses this distinction in the context of debates over public reason.

30. For arguments that citizens have *duties* to seek to persuade certain nonliberal compatriots of liberal egalitarian values, see Clayton and Stevens (2014); Badano and Nuti (2018).

Part II

Religious Accommodation

FIVE

Exemption Proliferation

Nick Martin

An exemption permits some to act contrary to a law or rule that others are expected to follow. For many philosophers and jurists, exemptions are a necessary instrument of justice. An exemption, so the argument goes, relieves those that suffer unintended but unjust burdens and/or unequal opportunities when carrying out an important practice. Suppose this position is coherent and persuasive, a commonly voiced and potentially fatal objection remains: exemption proliferation.

The proliferation objection is essentially a slippery slope objection. It says that if we grant some exemptions, then to be consistent we will have to grant so many exemptions that cumulatively they undermine, for example, social cohesion, the purpose and effectiveness of the law, legal obligation, and political authority. So even if we assume that exemptions are indeed necessary for some to avoid unjust burdens, the proliferation objection says this eventually comes at too high a price. It is difficult to postulate a threshold for when exemptions cause such issues. Nevertheless, exemption proliferation at least poses a significant theoretical challenge for proponents of exemptions.

Exemption proliferation is partly driven by immigration as new religious, cultural, and ethnic groups try to maintain practices that may be in tension with existing laws, rules, or norms (Patten 2017, 204). Fragmentation of existing groups can also be a driver for exemption proliferation. For example, the fragmentation of religious denominations in the United States since the 1960s 'is liable to be a source of considerably more varied claims for religious exemptions than was the case when the mainline churches enjoyed more ascendancy' (Schwarzchild 2016, 193). And in multicultural societies which seek to respect value pluralism, we should

81

not expect exemption claims to 'become any less common' (Maclure and Taylor 2011, 63). In sum, we ought to be increasingly conscious of exemption proliferation.

An easy way to overcome exemption proliferation would be to reject the idea of exemptions as a whole (Barry 2001; Leiter 2012; Dworkin 2013). After all, if we prohibit all exemptions – or almost all[1] – then there is nothing to proliferate. I do not take this path. Rather than mount yet another justification of exemptions, I assume that a regime of limited exemptions is justified on the basis of protecting the integrity of individuals (Bou-Habib 2006; Maclure and Taylor 2011; Vallier 2015; Laborde 2017; Seglow 2017).[2] Not only are integrity-based theories dominant in contemporary political philosophy, they are especially susceptible to the proliferation objection. This is because they typically take a subjective approach to integrity, which affords individuals a significant say in determining if they should follow a law or rule. Though proponents of integrity-based theories have been alive to the proliferation objection, there has not yet been a systematic discussion of the issue.

This chapter aims to address this gap. In section 1, I clarify the structure and target of the proliferation objection. In section 2, I outline the features of integrity-based theories and evaluate how each feature helps or hinders proliferation. I show that integrity-based theories are indeed vulnerable to the proliferation objection primarily due to their individualized, subjective approach to integrity. In sections 3 and 4, I discuss the sincerity test and the balancing test, respectively. The tests have been justified independently of their effect on proliferation, but here I argue that they can also be a means for limiting proliferation in ways consistent with the core features of integrity-based theories. However, I conclude that integrity-based theories are somewhat hostages to fortune since it is difficult to predict the contingencies that partly determine the effectiveness of the tests.

1. THE PROLIFERATION OBJECTION

The first conceptual distinction to be made is between the proliferation of exemptions that are *claimed* and the proliferation of exemptions that are *granted*. If legislatures or courts are inundated with exemption claims but rarely, if ever, grant those claims, then the objection is limited to concerns about clogging up the court system or the balkanisation of society (Schwarzchild 2016, 194–98). Whereas, if legislatures or courts actually grant numerous exemptions, then concerns about the erosion of legal obligation and political authority are crystallized. That said, the proliferation of claims is still significant since if fewer people have a legitimate claim to be heard in the first place, then fewer exemptions are likely to be granted. This fact anticipates two stages for stemming exemption proliferation: (a) whether someone has a claim or not, and (b) whether that claim should be granted. For example, we will see in section 3 that the sincerity test concerns stage (a), while in section 4, the balancing test concerns stage (b).

Next, we can measure the proliferation of exemptions in two different ways. First, it can be measured by the range of exemptions. Here the worry is that once exemptions are granted in some areas of life, exemptions will inevitably be sought in other areas of life. The recent history of exemptions granted by legislatures and courts suggests this worry is not unwarranted as they have extended to a wide range of areas, including but not limited to: animal slaughter, uniforms, identification, education, unemployment benefit, employment, business hours, healthcare, tax, property and land development, drugs, military service, and imprisonment.[3] When proliferation is measured in this first way, the objection lends itself more to abstract worries about legal obligation and political authority since individuals get to opt out of numerous laws or rules that others must follow.

The second measure of proliferation is the number of exemption holders. This is distinct from the first measure as we can imagine a large number of people being permitted an exemption in only one of the above areas, or a small number of exemption holders across a wide range of areas. When proliferation is measured in this second way, the objection lends itself to concrete policy concerns. For example, one might be concerned that an exemption for the religious use of a controlled substance could open the door to widespread drug use. Indeed, in *Employment Division of Oregon v. Smith* 494 U.S. 872 (1990) one of the reasons given for denying the exemption was that it would open the door to widespread and dangerous drug use (Nussbaum 2008, 152). Since the purpose of drug legislation is to protect people from such drug use, granting exemptions apparently would undermine that legitimate purpose.

The second measure of proliferation raises abstract concerns too. Suppose, for instance, that the state grants exemptions only in the area of education. Specifically, it allows parents that object to sections of the standard curriculum on religious grounds to home-school their children. Now suppose that hundreds of thousands of religious parents exercise the exemption and withdraw their children from public education to home-school them according to a curriculum that is consistent with their religious beliefs. As a result of this one type of exemption – albeit in a fundamental area of life – concerns about social cohesion and autonomy arise.

The perfect storm for dissenters of exemptions is, of course, that the range of exemptions *and* exemption holders proliferate. After all, if there were numerous kinds of exemption but only a handful of exemption holders, there would not be any serious cause for concern. Nevertheless, this conceptual discussion allows us to anticipate the fact that some measures for addressing the proliferation objection may centre on reducing exemption holders and/or the range of exemptions.

The final conceptual distinction to consider in this section is between volitional and nonvolitional exemptions. This distinction is pivotal to understanding that the exemption-proliferation objection is almost always directed at only one particular category of exemptions, namely, volitional exemptions. A volitional exemption is granted when a law or rule wrongly conflicts with an individual's wishes or beliefs. Exemptions granted on the basis of religious convictions, moral conscience, or cultural traditions fall under the category of volitional exemptions. In contrast, a nonvolitional exemption is granted when a law or rule wrongly conflicts with an individual's physical or mental needs. Exemptions granted on the basis of disabilities fall under the category of nonvolitional exemptions.

Nonvolitional exemptions are widely accepted, while volitional exemptions are a source of deep political and moral controversy (Maclure and Taylor 2011, 66–69; May 2017, 193). Consider a school that prohibits students from bringing dangerous objects to school, such as knives and syringes. Suppose a Sikh student claims an exemption to carry the kirpan, while a diabetic student claims an exemption to carry a medical syringe. No reasonable person would consider rejecting the diabetic's claim, whereas the Sikh's claim would be hotly contested. Or consider the fact that exemptions for service dogs in public places are widely accepted, whereas exemptions for pets are not.

An underlying reason for the difference in the controversy generated by volitional and nonvolitional exemptions is the idea that, as a matter of justice, individuals are morally responsible for their beliefs in a way that they are not for their physical or mental hardships. This means we 'are not afflicted by our beliefs as alien impositions; rather we identify with them'. As rational epistemic and practical agents, 'we revise, reform, and even reject our beliefs; but even where we do not, we regard our beliefs as ours and, as agents, hold ourselves (and each other) accountable for them' (Seglow 2017, 179). In short, there is a principle of individual moral responsibility.

An upshot of this principle is that individuals are expected to internalize at least some of the costs that result from their beliefs (Seglow 2017, 180; Jones 1994). That is to say, if you find manifesting your beliefs costly despite just background conditions and legitimate laws and rules, then you should bear those costs. It would be unjust to expect third parties to do so. If you are not willing to bear the costs, then it is up to you to modify or jettison your costly beliefs. Supporters of exemptions need not entirely reject the idea of individual responsibility. Instead, they can – and do – disagree with opponents to exemptions on what kind of costs are morally permissible, what counts as just background conditions, and what makes laws and rules legitimate. Nevertheless, it is plain how the idea of individual responsibility can be marshalled to provide a justice-based objection to exemptions in general.

But to fully understand the place of volitional exemptions in the proliferation objection, we must observe how they impinge not just on justice, but on the ideas of legal obligation and political authority. In short, volitional exemptions give extraordinary power to individuals to dictate their own legal obligations. As Simon Căbulea May (2017, 193) explains, volitional exemptions imply 'that an individual should not have to follow a law that other people have to follow precisely because she does not want to follow it. This is peculiar because it is in the nature of the law to impose obligations that members of the public must respect whether they wish to or not'. As noted earlier, a limited number of exemptions and/or claimants may not pose a threat to fundamental ideas of legal obligation and political authority, but May wants to press the theoretical challenge that exemption proliferation poses. He goes on to write, if 'just any sort of volitional conflict warranted an exemption, then the concept of legal obligation would be threatened with incoherence' (May 2017, 193–94). The challenge then is to establish a theory of exemptions that delineates special volitional conflicts from 'just any sort of volitional conflict'. This is precisely what integrity-based theories of exemptions try to do, which brings us to section 2.

2. INTEGRITY

Suppose an employee's favourite colour is red. There is a rule that all employees must wear a uniform, which happens to be blue. The employee seeks an exemption from the rule so that he can wear his favourite colour at work. Now suppose he has a colleague who is Christian and believes she must bear witness to her faith by visibly wearing a crucifix, including at work. However, imagine there is also a rule that all employees must not wear jewellery at work. The Christian employee seeks an exemption in order to wear her crucifix.[4]

Let us suspend the question of whether either employee should actually be granted an exemption, and ask a more fundamental question: are the two employees' claims of equal moral weight in the first place? For integrity-based theories, the answer is no given that exemptions may be warranted only when an individual's moral integrity is at stake.[5] The first employee has a mere preference or whim. Were he prevented from wearing a red uniform, he would be unhappy. Even if it were an intense and longstanding preference he could be very unhappy, but he would not suffer a setback to his moral convictions. Whereas, were the Christian employee prevented from wearing her crucifix at work, she would not merely be unhappy. Instead, her integrity would be harmed, which is to say, she would fail to live up to a conviction that is constitutive of her moral identity. Or in other words, she would not be who she thinks she should be. As such, under integrity-based theories the first employee has no legitimate grounds for an exemption claim; only the second employee does.

It appears, then, integrity-based theories have a response to May's challenge that not 'just any sort of volitional conflict' should warrant an exemption. By differentiating moral convictions from mere preferences, integrity-based theories attempt to isolate a special category of practices that may warrant an exemption (Maclure and Taylor 2011, 76–77; Laborde 2017, 197–217). From the outset, then, an initial hurdle is placed in front of exemption proliferation by ruling out a raft of practices that are not a matter of integrity.[6]

But how do we know whether a practice is a matter of integrity or not? The sturdiness of the hurdle depends on how, if at all, we can answer that question. If we want to permit exemptions but cannot reliably and nonarbitrarily filter out claims that do not relate to integrity, then we run the risk of allowing any and all exemptions. Hence, the difficulty in identifying the line between people's moral convictions and mere preferences is 'at the heart' of the proliferation objection (Maclure and Taylor 2011, 91–92).

If we could refer to a circumscribed list of practices that are objectively related to integrity, then we could reliably push back against the proliferation objection. Any practice put forward that does not relate to integrity – such as preferring to wear the colour red – would be quickly and definitively rejected. While it is easy for me to stipulate in a hypothetical case that one practice is a mere preference while the other is a moral conviction, in reality, an objective list is extremely problematic.

Against the background of reasonable value pluralism and the burdens of judgement, however, integrity has 'an irreducibly subjective dimension' (Maclure and Taylor 2011, 92). When there is reasonable disagreement about morality, an objective view of integrity is conceptually and morally misguided. We cannot and should not stipulate the moral convictions that individuals should live up to. That is for each individual to decide. A subjective view of integrity encapsulates that moral independence. It says that I maintain *my* integrity only when I live up to what *I* consider to be right or wrong, not what *others* consider right or wrong, or what is *truly* right or wrong (Bou-Habib 2006, 117–18; Laborde 2017, 204).

While a subjective view of integrity is appropriate in view of reasonable value pluralism, it clearly exacerbates the chances of proliferation. It does so in terms of potential exemption holders *and* the range of exemptions. With regard to exemption holders, a subjective view facilitates precisely the kind of extraordinary power that concerned May above since it allows each individual to determine when their integrity is at stake. Although, that power is somewhat bounded. Since an exemption entails some people not being subject to a law or laws that others are obliged to follow, it seems reasonable that others are owed a justification.[7] Under integrity-based theories, that justification needs to be grounded in the idea of living up to moral convictions rather than satisfying mere preferences. Thus, in making an exemption claim, an individual must be prepared to cogently articulate how a practice is a matter of integrity for her (Maclure and Taylor 2011, 99; Seglow 2017, 183). For instance, the practice may be part of her inquiry into the 'ultimate questions' in life or realize special relationships or achievements that contribute to her measure of a successful life.

With regard to the proliferation of the range of exemptions, a subjective view also allows each individual to determine where matters of integrity arise in their lives. For example, the manifestation of one's religious beliefs is not objectively circumscribed to the home or places of worship. Rather, an individual may determine that certain religious practices extend to public life, including education and the workplace. Furthermore, a subjective view respects the fact that people treat different areas of life with different degrees of importance. For instance, identification photos might seem morally insignificant to many of us. Yet, for many individuals it is a morally significant that they still be permitted to wear religious headwear in identification photos, and for members of some Amish, Mennonite, and Hutterite communities even the very act of having one's photo taken is morally problematic. The same could be said about uniforms, business hours, and so on.

So, what measures for countering proliferation are available to subjective integrity-based theories of exemptions? One possibility is to grant exemptions only on an individual case-by-case basis. This is a natural step since the family of integrity-based theories of exemptions under discussion concern not just subjective integrity *per se*, but the subjective integrity of *individuals*. In principle, an individual case-by-case basis should at least slow down proliferation compared to granting exemptions *en masse* to, for example, religious or cultural groups. In practice, however, this is not how exemptions function. As Cécile Laborde (2017, 203 fn. 19) explains, exemptions usually provide categorical protection of practices for the sake of 'administrative convenience'. For instance, a blanket exemption for religious symbols in the workplace is made available to any relevant employee rather than have each employee claim their own special exemption.

From a justificatory point of view, it remains the case that blanket exemptions are 'not rights enjoyed by groups as groups: they are enjoyed by individuals whose individual integrity is at stake' (Laborde 2017, 221 fn. 65; also see Kymlicka 1995 and Jones 2010). From a proliferation point of view, however, blanket exemptions facilitate a rapid increase in the number of exemption holders. Though integrity-based theories could say only individuals may bring exemption claims – and indeed it is usually individuals that bring landmark or test cases to courts – once a claim is successful, practicalities necessitate extending the exemption to other similarly placed individuals. This may avoid the problem of clogging up the courts with numerous individual claims, but it comes at the cost of creating potentially countless exemption holders.

So, integrity-based theories need a measure that limits the number of claims that are upheld. At this point it is important to reiterate that integrity-based theories attempt to isolate a special category of practices that *may* warrant an exemption. Integrity-based theories do not say that simply because an individual's integrity-related practice is burdened by a law or rule, she should therefore be granted an exemption. Rather, her integrity is one interest among many. As such, she has a *pro tanto* claim to an exemption that must be weighed against other interests, such as the rights of others, the costs to others and the functional purposes of a law or rule (Maclure and Taylor 2011, 100–101; Laborde 2017, 202; Patten 2017; c.f. Jones 2017). In many cases, these interests will outweigh *pro tanto* claims, thereby mitigating proliferation. I will discuss this balancing test in more detail in section 4.

Prior to the balancing test, are there measures available to integrity-based theories for limiting the range of *pro tanto* exemption claims? For instance, could integrity-based theories restrict claims to only religious practices? Some proexemption theorists do in fact single out religious practices for special protection (Laycock 1996; McConnell 2000; Koppelman 2006). However, integrity-based theories – particularly of the subjective kind – reject the notion that religion is special and thus only religious practices may warrant exemptions. The practice in question need not be religious in nature, aim, nor grounding. It can be purely secular so long as the practice is a matter of moral conviction rather than mere preference (Maclure and Taylor 2011, 92–97).

For this reason, subjective integrity-based theories of exemptions overlap and underpin 'liberal egalitarian theories of religious freedom' (Laborde 2017, chap. 2). A defining characteristic of liberal egalitarian theories is that religious freedom is not a distinctive freedom. Instead, religious freedom is derivative of a more general moral value, such as integrity. In other words, religious practices are protected not because they are religious, but because they are an instantiation of the protection-worthy value of integrity. Against a background of secularization and reasonable value pluralism, religion does not have a monopoly over matters of integrity. Thus, exemptions should not be exclusive to religious practices. Naturally, this widens the scope for proliferation, but it is a bullet that liberal egalitarian and subjective integrity theories of exemptions must bite.

Regardless of whether a practice is religious or secular, can we at least exclude practices that are morally abhorrent such as infant sacrifice, honour killings, and genocide? Clearly individuals should not receive an exemption to engage in such practices. But does a subjective view of integrity mean morally abhorrent practices are at least *pro tanto* worthy of exemptions? I think the answer should be yes.

For some, the idea that morally abhorrent practices could be a matter of integrity is fundamentally mistaken (Koppelman 2009). However, this moralized view is incompatible with a subjective view of integrity. A subjective view allows for the fact that individuals may seriously err in their moral judgements, yet wholeheartedly believe they are right. For instance, an individual may consider infant sacrifice to be a sacred duty, which if not performed poses spiritual and existential peril. Clearly this individual would consider infant sacrifice a matter of integrity then. But, all things considered, it is better that he lives without integrity. A subjective integrity theorist is able to say this since integrity is just one value among others, including the basic rights of others such as the right to life (Lenta 2016, 254). Though a moralized view of integrity helps limit *pro tanto* claims in the first place, I believe this comes at the cost of theoretical consistency. A subjective view more accurately captures the moral convictions of all individuals but exemptions for morally abhorrent practices can still be denied under the balancing test.

To conclude this section, let us consider one more class of practices that perhaps should be denied *pro tanto* status, specifically, silly or trivial practices. By 'silly' or 'trivial' I mean practices that appear to most people to be so comical or inconsequential that they could not possibly be a matter of integrity. The concern about silly or trivial practices is a common manifestation of the worry about exemption proliferation. Proexemption theorists have grappled with chicken suits (Nussbaum 2008, 169), baseball caps (Maclure and Taylor 2011, 77), and clown hats (Laborde 2017, 199–200). The issue is not merely theoretical either. Pastafarians – members of the parodic Church of the Flying Spaghetti Monster who believe that must wear colanders on their heads in identification photos – have in fact received exemptions in various jurisdictions. And Laborde – who defends a subjective integrity-based theory of exemptions – concedes that it may not be possible to exclude Pastafarians (Laborde 2017, 207 fn. 37).

This discussion also returns us to the hypothetical example that opened this section. What if the employee insists that wearing a red uniform is a matter of integrity for him? Must we accept this and assume he has a *pro tanto* claim to an exemption? Under a balancing test, his claim might be denied on the grounds that the costs to the employer of providing bespoke uniforms is unfairly high, but the concern about silly or trivial practices here is that they should not have *pro tanto* status in the first place.

Given that I have claimed subjective integrity-based theories should not deny morally abhorrent practices *pro tanto* status, it would be absurd of me to now say that silly or trivial practices should be denied *pro tanto* status. The individuality that underpins a subjective view of integrity means that we must allow for others being committed to practices that we find silly or trivial. After all, many of us find religious practices silly or trivial, but no proexemption theorist would deny them *pro tanto* status.

It remains the case that a claimant must still be able to articulate how a practice is a matter of integrity for him. Yet, if this only amounts to a mere assertion – however well-articulated – from the claimant, it is a relatively easy test to meet, even for practices that are allegedly silly or trivial. For example, imagine that the employee says wearing red at all times is deeply important since it is an act of remembrance and reverence for generations of his family that served and died in an army that wore red uniforms. The idea is a familiar one even if the importance of wearing red is not, since many individuals wear or carry mementos of lost loved ones.

In any case, the mere assertion that a practice is integrity-related seems insufficient. To justify being exempt from a rule or law that others must follow, it seems reasonable to ask if a claimant *really* believes a practice is integrity-related. This question is relevant to all exemption claims, but particularly so when a practice appears to be silly or trivial (Adams and Barmore 2014, 64). What is required, then, is a test of the claimant's sincerity. This brings us to section 3.

3. SINCERITY

Recall that integrity entails living up to one's moral convictions. When a practice is a matter of moral conviction, we would expect a sincere claimant to make a serious effort to perform that practice. By contrast, an insincere claimant would make no, little, or erratic effort to perform a practice she professes is a matter of moral conviction. The lack of serious effort strongly suggests that the practice does not have the kind of pull on her conscience that an integrity-related practice should. In the context of integrity, then, sincerity is defined as the 'coherence between what is said and what is done by the claimant' (Laborde 2017, 207). Where there is sufficient coherence, the claimant does have a *pro tanto* claim to an exemption and *vice versa*. As such, the existence of a *pro tanto* claim is not solely dependent on the mere assertions of the claimant – her deeds must match her words also.

Whether there is coherence is a question of fact. It is something that can be studied objectively via evidence of the claimant's actions. An objective basis is essential for any sincerity test to be principled and reliable. After all, if mere assertions from a claimant are insufficient to grant an exemption, then 'mere disbelief of a claimant' is insufficient to deny an exemption (Greenawalt 2000, 205). The objectivity of the sincerity test takes on special significance in the context of proliferation and integrity-based theories. We saw that the subjective dimension of integrity-based theories was the principal source for the proliferation objection. It allowed individuals extraordinary power to determine their obligations. A sincerity test based on objective factors should allow us to rein in subjectivity, and thus exemption proliferation too.

Crucially, the objectivity of the sincerity test need not undermine a subjective view of integrity. The test asks whether there is coherence between the claimant's actions and *her* moral convictions as she *perceives* them. For this reason, the sincerity test should not be used as an underhanded way to test the truth of a claimant's beliefs, particularly in the case of religious beliefs (Greenawalt 2000, 200–201; Loewentheil and Platt 2018, 270–72). For example, a court should not consider a claimant to be insincere simply because her interpretation of a religious practice diverges from the mainstream. To do so would be imposing orthodoxy, which is flatly incompatible with the individualized, subjective view of integrity that underpins liberal egalitarian theories of religious freedom (Maclure and Taylor 2011, 82–83). To reiterate, courts should be testing the internal consistency between the claimant's beliefs and actions, not the consistency between the claimant's beliefs and external sources such as the majority's beliefs or traditional texts.

So what kind of evidence is appropriate for demonstrating sincerity? A major source is documentation and witness testimony concerning patterns of behaviour consistent with the object of the exemption. For instance, in *Watson v. Green* 569 F.3d 115 (2009), a claimant seeking an exemption from military service as a conscientious objector submitted a series of letters that attested to his antiwar beliefs and participation in antiwar marches. Or in *Howard v. United States* 864 F. Supp. 1019 (D. Colo. 1994), witnesses testified that the claimant had regularly attended religious services and study groups. Equally, documentation and witness testimony concerning inconsistent behaviour or a failure to bear costs can be used as evidence of insincerity. For example, in *Reed v. Faulkner* 842 F.2d 960, 963 (1988), the claimant was observed by prison staff violating the religious diet and grooming practices for which he sought an exemption.

Of course, no individual is perfect and so claimants should not be expected to demonstrate a flawless history of consistent behaviour (Adams and Barmore 2014, 63; Loewentheil and Platt 2018, 254). Indeed, there may be good reasons for the claimant's inconsistent behaviour, particularly where it would be costly for the claimant to be consistent. Evidence that one has borne the costs of exercising one's beliefs is a strong indicator that a practice is matter of integrity – it shows that one is willing to take a stand and make sacrifices. Yet, in some cases the costs may be unreasonably high, especially when other moral convictions are at play. For instance, an employee may sincerely want an exemption in order to attend religious services but has thus far acquiesced in her employer's demands because providing for her family was more important than losing her job in order to attend religious services. Though that was her choice, whether that was a *fair* choice is precisely under debate in the exemption case. Justice may require she receive an exemption so she can attend religious services *and* provide for her family under her existing employment. Thus, although documentation and witness testimony provide some objective basis, there is interpretive work still to be done. Judges and other officials will have to carefully evaluate the body of evidence and consider alternative explanations for inconsistent behaviour.

Despite these complications, the sincerity test can still function as a measure against the proliferation of *pro tanto* exemption claims. It is often claimed that courts are loathe to question the sincerity of claimants. Indeed, in the recent *Burwell v. Hobby Lobby* 573 U.S. (2014) case, Justice Ginsburg proclaimed that the court 'must accept as true' any assertions of a sincere belief. Yet, legal scholars have shown there is in fact a rich history of the courts denying exemptions on the basis of insincerity using documentation and witness testimony of inconsistent behaviour (Greenawalt 2006, chap. 7; Adams and Barmore 2014; Loewentheil and Platt 2018). In fact, had the sincerity test been applied in the *Hobby Lobby* case then there was substantial evidence that the claimants were insincere and thus should not have had a *pro tanto* claim to an exemption (Loewentheil and Platt 2018, 274–76).

And what about silly or trivial practices? Consider again Pastafarians. Had a sincerity test been applied in those cases, I believe there was sufficient evidence to deny them a *pro tanto* claim to an exemption. This is because Pastafarians rarely, if ever, wear colanders on their heads except when an identification photo is being taken. Furthermore, Pastafarians have not demonstrated a willingness to bear the costs of their beliefs, such as forgoing a driving license – and thus the liberty to drive – when they were told they could not wear colanders in their identification photos.

The sincerity test has a role in not just countering the proliferation of *pro tanto* claims, but also in countering the proliferation of exemption holders once a blanket exemption has been granted. Suppose one sincere claimant is successful in a test or landmark case. Indeed, this particular claimant may be a 'new convert' to a practice and thus it would be unfair to expect them to produce a record of consistent behaviour (Loewentheil and Platt 2018, 277). In any case, as noted in section 2, it is common practice for a blanket exemption to be granted following the first successful claim. The sincerity test can still be deployed where evidence comes to light that an individual using a blanket exemption is doing so insincerely. For instance, an employee may take advantage of a blanket exemption for time off to attend religious services, but there is evidence that the employee consistently violates his purported religious beliefs outside of working hours.

However, we must conclude this section with an important caveat about the robustness of the sincerity test. Since the test is based on the simple coherence between the claimant's words and deeds, it could be undermined by a determined claimant that does not really believe his practice is matter of moral conviction. Instead, the claimant simply wants material gains such as a tax exemption. Knowing that a sincerity test would be applied, the determined but insincere claimant could build a record of consistent behaviour under false pretences. Such cases are another bullet that integrity-based theories of exemptions will have to bite. As Laborde (2017, 207) states, 'judges cannot and should not pry on individual consciences'.

That said, since the claimant is seeking an exemption for a practice that is currently burdened by a law or rule, building a record of consistent behaviour is not costless and, in many cases, the costs will be significant, such as forgoing a driving licence. Thus, the sincerity test offers some meaningful deterrent. Then again, if we assume that most claimants have genuinely felt convictions, then the sincerity test cannot do all the work in countering proliferation. As such, we require an additional test to counter the number of exemptions that are actually granted. This brings us to the balancing test in the next section.

4. BALANCING

Recall that an assumption of the balancing test is that integrity is one value among many. Though an exemption helps protect the integrity of exemption holders, the exemption will invariably have consequences for countervailing interests, such as the rights of others, the cost to others, and the functional purposes of a law or rule. Where the countervailing interests outweigh the interest of the claimant in maintaining his integrity, the state has a 'compelling interest' to deny the exemption and enforce the universal application of a law or rule.[8]

We have previously encountered a straightforward case for the balancing test. Recall that where a morally abhorrent practice would harm the basic rights of others such as the right to life, the state clearly has a compelling interest to deny an exemption. However, the majority of cases are not as clear-cut. First, take the claimant's side of the scales. It can be difficult to properly appreciate the weight of a practice for a claimant, particularly when it seems trivial to the majority, such as having a reflective triangle on the back of one's vehicle (Patten 2017, 214). Congruent with the subjective view of integrity, judges and other officials should be as understanding as possible of the claimant's point of view, but this is obviously not easy in practice (Nussbaum 2008, 139).

The claimant's side of the equation is further complicated if we believe that not all integrity-related claims have equal weight. Paul Billingham (2017, 5–9) argues we should adopt this view using the 'centrality' and 'obligatoriness' of practices to determine their weight. If a practice is deemed obligatory – such as Sikh men wearing a turban at all times – then the claim is weightier than if the practice was not obligatory – such as Christians wearing a crucifix. However, in keeping with the subjective view of integrity and avoidance of religious orthodoxy, a practice need not be obligatory to be a matter of integrity and it is left to the individual to determine how central a practice is to their religion. As such, Christians that seek an exemption to wear a crucifix at work, for example, can have a *pro tanto* claim to an exemption, but, that claim is less weighty than Sikhs that seek an exemption to wear a turban at work. Naturally, claims that are less weighty are more likely to be outweighed and so the balancing test is at least helpful for limiting proliferation in cases of non-obligatory practices.

Now consider the countervailing interests on the other side of the scales. Different countervailing interests will arise in different cases, each case will likely have numerous countervailing interests, each of which will not always be easily quantified. Take, for example, exemptions from uniform rules. One countervailing interest is the cost to the employer if the exemption entails the provision of bespoke uniforms. But how do we decide if the cost is too great? It needs to be decided according to a wider theory of distributive justice, over which there is of course considerable disagreement. And should we take into account the employer's desire to have a consistent image for their organization? If so, how do we measure and then compare it to the integrity of employees?

As Martha Nussbaum (2008, 153–54) points out, we should also have a healthy scepticism when the functional purposes of the law are cited as a reason for denying an exemption. Recall that in *Employment Division v. Smith*, the denigration of the paternalistic purposes of drug regulations was cited as a reason for denying an exemption for Native Americans to use peyote in their religious ceremonies. Slippery slope arguments of this kind depend on the veracity of their empirical predictions, and in *Employment Division v. Smith* and similar cases, the evidence suggests that worries about the spill-over effects in drug use are unfounded. Thus, under the balancing approach it appears that the state does not have a compelling interest in the absolute application of drug regulations. Similarly, we ought to have common sense about how many people are interested in making use of blanket exemptions since peyote use has not accelerated following the *Religious Freedom Restoration Act* (Nussbaum 2008, 163–64).

The above empirical doubts create a complicated picture for the proliferation objection. On the one hand, it suggests that the balancing test may be wrongly deployed in some cases, and thereby more exemptions should have been granted. Yet, on the other hand, it suggests that we should not be very concerned about a proliferation of individuals exercising a blanket exemption or taking advantage of an exemption for ulterior motives. As such, the force of the proliferation objection is weakened in the first place.

As a result of all the above complexities, it is difficult to say how effective a balancing test will be at countering proliferation. For this reason, Peter Jones (2017, 173) writes that 'legal exemptions, both religious and nonreligious, are better conceived as exercises in adhockery' and Jonathan Seglow (2017, 189) insists we ought to accept that the 'accommodation of deeply held religious and other convictions is too complex an issue to be settled by algorithms.' Nonetheless, in tandem with a strong principle of individual moral responsibility, a substantial number of claims have been rejected using a balancing test. Thus, it can be an effective measure for countering proliferation even in the face of numerous *pro tanto* claims (Nussbaum 2008, 146). Furthermore, proliferation itself could be considered a countervailing interest. Where there is sufficient evidence that granting an exemption would open the floodgates, courts ought to consider this under the balancing test.

5. CONCLUSION

To conclude, integrity-based theories of exemptions are vulnerable to the proliferation objection. This is primarily due to their individualized, subjective approach to integrity, which affords individuals significant latitude for challenging the legitimacy of laws and rules. We can turn to the sincerity test for an objective means of limiting the number of *pro tanto* claims without compromising the individualized, subjective view of integrity. And the balancing test offers a means for limiting the number of claims that are then upheld. But integrity-based theories are not entirely out of danger, at least in theoretical terms. This is because it is difficult to predict the contingencies inherent in the sincerity and balancing tests, such as the determination of claimants with ulterior motives, or the costs that should be borne by third parties.

REFERENCES

Adams, Ben, and Cynthia Barmore. 2014. 'Questioning Sincerity: The Role of the Courts After Hobby Lobby'. *Stanford Law Review Online* 67: 59–66.
Barry, Brian. 2001. *Culture and Equality*. Cambridge: Polity Press.
Billingham, Paul. 2017. 'How Should Claims for Religious Exemptions Be Weighed?' *Oxford Journal of Law and Religion* 6 (1): 1–23.
Bou-Habib, Paul. 2006. 'A Theory of Religious Accommodation'. *Journal of Applied Philosophy* 23 (1): 109–26.
Burwell v. Hobby Lobby 573 U.S. (2014).
Dworkin, Ronald. 2013. *Religion Without God*. Cambridge, MA: Harvard University Press.
Employment Division of Oregon v. Smith 494 U.S. 872 (1990).
Eweida v. United Kingdom [2013] ECHR 37.

Greenawalt, Kent. 2000. 'Five Questions about Religion Judges are Afraid to Ask'. In *Obligations of Citizenship and the Demands of Faith*, edited by Nancy L. Rosenblum, 196–244. Princeton, NJ: Princeton University Press.

Greenawalt, Kent. 2006. *Religion and the Constitution, Volume I: Free Exercise and Fairness*. Princeton, NJ: Princeton University Press.

Howard v. United States 864 F. Supp. 1019 (D. Colo. 1994).

Jones, Peter. 1994. 'Bearing the Consequences of Belief'. *Journal of Political Philosophy* 2 (1): 24–43.

———. 2010. 'Cultures, Group Rights, and Group-Differentiated Rights'. In *Multiculturalism and Moral Conflict*, edited by Maria Dimova-Cookson and Peter Stirk, 38–57. London: Routledge.

———. 2017. 'Religious Accommodation and Distributive Justice'. In *Religion in Liberal Political Philosophy*, edited by Aurélia Bardon and Cécile Laborde, 163–76. Oxford: Oxford University Press.

Koppelman, Andrew. 2006. 'Is It Fair to Give Religion Special Treatment?' *University of Illinois Law Review* vol. 2006: 571–604.

———. 2009. 'Conscience, Volitional Necessity, and Religious Exemptions'. *Legal Theory* 15 (3): 215–30.

Kymlicka, Will. 1995. *Multicultural Citizenship*. Oxford: Oxford University Press.

Laborde, Cécile. 2017. *Liberalism's Religion*. Cambridge, MA: Harvard University Press.

Laycock, Douglas. 1990. 'The Remnants of Free Exercise'. *The Supreme Court Review* vol. 1990: 1–68.

———. 1996. 'Religious Liberty as Liberty'. *Journal of Contemporary Legal Issues* 7: 313–56.

Leiter, Brian. 2012. *Why Tolerate Religion?* Princeton, NJ: Princeton University Press.

Lenta, Patrick. 2016. 'Freedom of Conscience and the Value of Personal Integrity'. *Ratio Juris* 29 (2): 246–63.

Loewentheil, Kara, and Elizabeth Reiner Platt. 2018. 'In Defence of the Sincerity Test'. In *Religious Exemptions*, edited by Kevin Vallier and Michael Weber, 247–78. Oxford: Oxford University Press.

Maclure, Jocelyn, and Charles Taylor. 2011. *Secularism and Freedom of Conscience*. Cambridge, MA: Harvard University Press.

May, Simon Căbulea. 2017. 'Exemptions for Conscience'. In *Religion in Liberal Political Philosophy*, edited by Aurélia Bardon and Cécile Laborde, 191–203. Oxford: Oxford University Press.

McConnell, Michael. 2000. 'The Problem of Singling Out Religion'. *DePaul Law Review* 50:9–12.

Nussbaum, Martha. 2008. *Liberty of Conscience*. New York: Basic Books.

Patten, Alan. 2017. 'Religious Exemptions and Fairness'. In *Religion in Liberal Political Philosophy*, edited by Aurélia Bardon and Cécile Laborde, 204–19. Oxford: Oxford University Press.

Reed v. Faulkner 842 F.2d 960, 963 (1988).

Schwarzchild, Maimon. 2016. 'Do Religious Exemptions Save?' *San Diego Law Review* 53 (1): 185–200.

Seglow, Jonathan. 2017. 'Religious Accommodation: Responsibility, Integrity, and Self-Respect'. In *Religion in Liberal Political Philosophy*, edited by Aurélia Bardon and Cécile Laborde, 177–90. Oxford: Oxford University Press.

Sherbert v. Verner 374 U.S. 398 (1963).

Vallier, Kevin. 2015. 'The Moral Basis of Religious Exemptions'. *Law and Philosophy* 35 (1): 1–28.

Vallier, Kevin. 2018. 'Public Justification'. Last modified 1 March 2018. https://plato.stanford.edu/entries/justification-public/.

Watson v. Green 569 F.3d 115 (2009).

NOTES

1. Barry (2001, 49), Leiter (2012, 101), and Dworkin (2013, 136) all make exceptions for when exemptions should be granted.

2. As a result, this chapter focuses on exemptions for individuals rather than groups or institutions.

3. See Greenawalt (2006) for a survey of the various exemption granted in the United States by both by legislatures and courts.

4. This is inspired by the real case of *Eweida v. United Kingdom* [2013] ECHR 37, in which a British Airways employee sought an exemption to wear a crucifix over her work uniform.

5. Maclure and Taylor (2011, 76–77) and Laborde (2017, 199–200) use similar comparisons to reach this conclusion.

6. May (2017, 200–202) is sceptical that integrity-based theories can explain why 'non-moral projects' should not also receive exemptions. However, I doubt the counterexamples he raises really are as a nonmoral as he assumes, and so I do not think the proliferation he envisages is plausible.

7. Whether one must provide a justification based on shareable rather than merely accessible reasons may also be a way of limiting exemptions. This depends on the background theory of public reason, which I do not have the space to discuss here. However, on first impressions, it seems accessible reasons are more conducive to a subjective view of integrity than shareable reasons. On shareable v. accessible reasons, see Vallier (2018).

8. In the philosophical literature, this approach is commonly known as 'reasonable accommodation' (e.g., Maclure and Taylor 2011). In legal practice it is associated with the 'Sherbert test' from *Sherbert v. Verner* 374 U.S. 398 (1963) and judgements of the European Court of Human Rights (see Billingham 2017, 1–2).

SIX

Religion and the Claims of Citizenship

The Dangers of Institutional Accommodation

Andrea Baumeister

Many of the most contentious claims for religious accommodations, such as exemptions from antidiscrimination legislation dealing with gender and sexual orientation, reflect demands by organized religion to a right to corporate self-governance. Such claims typically seek to strengthen the autonomy of religious institutions by granting them the power to control the status and entitlements of community members and to regulate their relationship with nonmembers.[1] The grounds for and legitimate scope of such religious institutional autonomy remain strongly contested in contemporary debates regarding freedom of religion in a liberal polity.

For religious institutionalists, a robust defence of institutional religious autonomy constitutes a vital component of any plausible account of freedom of religion in a liberal polity.[2] Indeed, on this account, organized religion occupies a unique position within the liberal constitutional state: grounded in the independent, transcendental nature of religious authority, the jurisdictional independence of organized religion plays an essential role in a liberal constitution as both a check on the powers of secular government and a prerequisite for the religious liberty and civic equality of religious citizens.

In the face of such attempts to depict institutional religious autonomy as integral to the constitutional principles of a liberal polity, this chapter argues that, far from being vital to the success of a liberal polity, the notion of organized religion as a distinct, exogenous jurisdictional sphere poses a profound challenge to the foundational principles of a modern, liberal, democratic, constitutional state committed to individual liberty, civic equality, popular sovereignty, and democratic self-limitation. As liberal egalitarians[3] rightly note, in a liberal polity claims to self-govern-ance by religious institutions are neither basic nor absolute, but are best viewed as an aspect of a wider liberal commitment to associational autonomy grounded in the dignitary and conscience-based rights of their members. Claims to corporate religious self-governance must, therefore, be balanced against other rights and important state interests. Conse-quently, the legitimate scope of religious institutional self-governance is a matter of public policy and subject to regulation by legitimately consti-tuted political authority.

While there is much to commend liberal egalitarian analyses of the relationship between state and organized religion and the potential im-pact of claims to corporate religious self-governance upon the rights and liberties of individuals, the liberal egalitarian preoccupation with indi-vidual liberty and the coherence interests of voluntary associations obscures important considerations regarding the integrity of the public political sphere as a prerequisite for the effective exercise of political autonomy and democratic self-limitation. Moreover, liberal egalitarian attempts to recast religious organizations as just one of a variety of forms of civil society association lose sight of the distinctive challenges inherent in claims to religious self-governance. In the light of these concerns, this chapter argues that in a liberal polity, claims to corporate religious self-governance are not only delimited by liberal egalitarian worries regard-ing individual integrity and personal autonomy, but must also respect civic republican concerns for the integrity of the public political sphere and the background conditions that facilitate political autonomy.

1. INSTITUTIONAL ACCOMMODATION AND THE SOVEREIGNTY OF ORGANIZED RELIGION

For religious institutionalists, freedom of religion first and foremost re-fers to the allocation and separation of political and religious domains of authority (McConnell 1985). On this account, the separation between state and organized religion is best seen as a structural feature of a liberal constitution akin to the separation of powers between legislature and executive and federal and state government and marks the distinction between two independent realms of jurisdiction: the political and the religious (Smith 2016; Garnett 2016). This 'separation' does not place re-ligion under a special disability in public life, but safeguards the integrity and autonomy of the religious realm by limiting government control and regulation of religion (McConnell 1985). Moreover, the jurisdictional in-dependence of the church does not constitute a concession by the state, but stems from the transcendental nature of religious authority invested by God in the church. Organized religion thus occupies a special position within a liberal polity: its right to exist and to engage in corporate action is neither derived from nor dependent upon the state (Muñiz-Fraticelli 2014). Indeed, since a 'liberal state . . . cannot reject in principle that religion may be true', it cannot claim that 'its authority is in all matters supreme', as this would be tantamount to denying 'the possibility that transcendental authority could exist' (McConnell 1985, 15). Given the commitment to state neutrality, this deference must be extended to churches in general, thus safeguarding religious pluralism. The freedom of the church therefore sets exogenous limits to the authority of the state (Muñiz-Fraticelli 2014). Conceived in such jurisdictional terms, the institutional sovereignty of organized religion is basic and absolute. The freedom of the church is, therefore, neither grounded in the religious freedom rights of the individual members of religious organizations, nor can it be balanced against other rights or important state interests (Garnett 2016). Given its sovereign status, the state should therefore accord organized religion the same respect and dignity it extends to other sovereign entities (Smith 2016). Thus, just as fellow nation-states respect one another's jurisdictional autonomy, the state must acknowledge the limits on its own jurisdiction and must recognize the church as an 'organized society with its own laws and jurisdiction' (Garnett 2016, 50).

Indeed, the jurisdictional independence of organized religion is vital to the success of a liberal constitution as both a 'check on the potentially expansive and oppressive powers of the state'(Smith 2016, 33) and a prerequisite for the religious liberty and civic equality of religious citizens. As an institution outside and meaningfully independent of the state, organized religion 'enhances freedom by limiting government' (Garnett 2016, 56). Not only does organized religion provide an institutional buffer between individuals and the state which enhances the capacity of citizens to resist state encroachment, religious institutions can also generate, inculcate, and propose competing norms and alternative visions of social life that can benefit society at large (Garnett 2007). Indeed, organized religion plays a unique role in the transmission, communication, and enforcement of morality and justice and thus helps to instil in citizens the values and virtues essential for civic responsibility (McConnell 1985).

Moreover, although not grounded in the religious freedom rights of individual members, institutional religious sovereignty constitutes a vital prerequisite for individual religious liberty and the civic equality of religious believers. Religious faith and experience have a communal and institutional dimension, which gives meaning to and provides the setting for religious activity. For proponents of the freedom of the church, this communal and institutional dimension marks out religion from individual moral thought and underlines the distinctive place that religious organizations occupy within a liberal polity (McConnell 1985; Garnett 2016).

Not only is freedom of religion 'lived and experienced though institutions, it is also protected, nourished and facilitated by them' (Garnett 2016, 46). From this perspective, the autonomy and sovereignty of organized religion provides the infrastructure essential for the effective exercise of individual religious liberty, guarantees a social space for a truly meaningful pluralism, and constitutes a vital prerequisite for individual faith (Garnett 2016, 2007; McConnell 1991). In addition, institutional accommodations designed to protect religious self-governance play a vital role in safeguarding the equal standing of religious citizens and can help to make religious citizens 'feel at home' within a liberal polity (McConnell 2000, 103). Religious citizens are not only members of the commonwealth, but also have allegiance to a higher transcendental authority. By minimizing the potential for a conflict of jurisdiction between spiritual and temporal authorities, corporate religious self-governance minimizes the risk of religious citizens being confronted with conflicting demands and obligations and thus enables 'people of all religious persuasions to be citizens of the commonwealth with the least possible violence to their religious convictions' (McConnell 2000, 103).

While for religious institutionalists a robust defence of the institutional sovereignty of organized religion constitutes an essential component of any plausible account of freedom of religion, key claims advanced by religious institutionalists in favour of this position are ultimately not persuasive. Far from being essential to the success of a liberal constitution, the notion of organized religion as a unique, sovereign realm outside the jurisdiction of the state cannot be reconciled with the foundational principles of a modern liberal democratic polity.

Whereas religious institutionalists seek to portray the jurisdictional independence of organized religion as a vital prerequisite for the religious liberty and civic equality of religious citizens, attempts to equate institutional religious sovereignty with the protection of the interests of members of religious communities fail to account for the impact of established power relations and conflicting interests within religious communities upon the rights and liberties of their members, including their right to freedom of religion. The question of what constitutes 'true faith' and how established doctrines, beliefs, and practices should be interpreted is often contested within religious communities. What is more, these debates frequently reflect conflicting interests and established power relations. For example, recent feminist discourses not only point to the detrimental effects of many established religious practices upon women, but have also highlighted the difficulties women members of religious communities face in their attempts to secure greater freedom and equality within a religious setting.[4] For instance, within the context of contemporary debates regarding the origin, nature, and interpretation of Jewish and Muslim personal and family law, women members of these communities have challenged inequitable practices that enable men to exercise power over women such as Jewish and Muslim divorce laws, which permit husbands to refuse to consent to the dissolution of a marriage in accordance with Jewish and Muslim family law even if the relationship has been formally terminated by the state (Shachar 2001; Loenen 2002). Men can thus deny women the opportunity to remarry within their faith and to have children from subsequent relationships recognized as 'legitimate'; a threat that can be deployed as a strategic bargaining chip in divorce proceedings.

As these debates and contestations illustrate, claims by religious authorities cannot simply be taken to be synonymous with the interests of individual members of the wider religious community. In the face of such concerns, to argue – as McConnell (1991, 725) does – that it is 'for the believers and their religious communities to decide, without government help' 'whether members are "subjugated" or brainwashed by early-childhood propaganda' not only fails to acknowledge the impact of power relations within hierarchical religious communities, but also suggests that organized religion falls outside the jurisdiction of the state. In effect it denies that the state has a legitimate interest to regulate the self-regulation of religious communities so as to secure the rights and interests of vulnerable and marginalized group members, including their right to freedom of religion. Such a stance is difficult to reconcile with the foundational commitment of a liberal polity to safeguard the equal rights and civil standing of all citizens and cannot be readily defended by an appeal to the right of vulnerable or marginalized group members to exit the community. Not only is this a right that children will inevitably struggle to exercise, institutional accommodations can significantly raise the costs of exit for adult members. For example, the opt out from Social Security provisions negotiated by the Amish community makes it extremely costly for members to leave the religious community late in life (Barry 2001). Moreover, as campaigns by women members to reform Jewish and Muslim family law illustrate, marginalized members of religious communities typically do not reject their religious heritage, but seek greater freedom and equality within a religious context.

It undoubtedly is in principle possible to ground corporate rights in an appeal to the joint interests of members of the group (Seglow 2015). However, to justify institutional accommodations designed to strengthen corporate governance over communal affairs via an appeal to the interests of community members in religious liberty and civic equality requires not merely meaningful exit rights, but also internal decision-making procedures designed to guarantee an effective voice for potentially vulnerable group members that are in stark contrast to the hierarchical power relations characteristic of many religious communities.[5]

These worries are particularly troubling given the all-encompassing character of claims to religious authority. Religious organizations not only 'can and do assert competence and authority over every aspect of individual church members' lives', their central mission of 'saving souls' undermines any clear distinction between members and nonmembers (Schragger and Schwartzman 2013, 945). Indeed, as the support of religious institutionalists for the extension of freedom of religion claims to for-profit commercial corporations[6] illustrates, religious institutionalist claims to jurisdictional independence 'seem to countenance very few limits on church immunity' (Schragger and Schwartzman 2013, 946).

While citizens' sincerely held religious commitments may well on occasions be at odds with secular law, it is not clear that such conflicts necessarily provide strong grounds for corporate religious self-governance rather than legal exemptions designed to protect the freedom of conscience of the individual. Moreover, although religious institutions may well foster civic responsibility and may at times provide an effective check against injustice and the abuse of political power, organized religion is not unique in this regard. While independent civil society associations undoubtedly play an important role in providing the infrastructure and collective resources that can help individuals to become responsible citizens able to resist the abuse of political power and to hold the state to account, such considerations speak in favour of a robust defence of a general right to freedom of association rather than the institutional sovereignty of organized religion.

The claim that the institutional sovereignty of organized religion is vital to the success of a liberal constitution is, therefore, difficult to sustain. In fact, to insist on the independence of a sovereign religious jurisdiction challenges the foundational principles of a modern liberal democratic constitutional state committed to individual liberty, civic equality, popular sovereignty, and democratic self-limitation.

While religious institutionalists may well be right to insist that a due regard for freedom of religion implies that there should be 'a space within a church that government should presumptively treat as the church's business not the governments' (Smith 2016, 26), their account misconstrues important aspects of the nature and purpose of 'separation' in a modern liberal democratic state. In a modern liberal polity, the principle of 'separation' not only safeguards religious pluralism and the integrity of the religious realm, but also protects the political sphere from the sectarian claims of religion. Indeed, the very emergence of the modern liberal democratic state is marked by the separation of the amalgamation of religion and politics. The legitimacy of the modern constitutional state is not grounded in an appeal to the sacred, religious or transcendental, but the 'democratic opinion- and will-formation of citizens within civil society' (Habermas 2011, 21). It thus reflects the principle of popular sovereignty and democratic self-limitation and 'must be immanent, reflexive, fallible and contestable by those subject to it' (Cohen 2015b, 118). The purposes of the modern constitutional polity are 'free-standing' and strictly 'innerworldly'. The pursuit of redemption or the ultimate meaning of life therefore do not constitute a legitimate political end. The character of the modern constitutional state is egalitarian, and its fundamental constitutional principles should not promote particular social identities that are 'less inclusive than the citizenry as a whole' (Cohen 2013, 514). Hence, justifications of its public law and policy must be accessible to those subject to it and cannot be based on an appeal to absolute, transcendental authority.

The authority of religious institutions, in contrast, rests on an appeal to 'external', 'otherworldly' sources and is underpinned by a concern not with collective self-determination, but with salvation and redemption. While democratic legitimacy claims are fallible and contested, religious authority is grounded in absolute truth and unquestionable authority. And whereas the modern constitutional polity emphasizes inclusivity, the beliefs and values which inform the practices of religious institutions rest on revealed truth only fully accessible to those who belong to a particular religious tradition (Habermas 2011). Indeed, if brought to bear within the political realm, religious authority claims potentially pose a distinctive threat to the integrity and independence of the modern constitutional state. While the legitimacy of the modern constitutional state is firmly grounded in immanent sources, political theology seeks to ground the authority of the state in God's authority and aims to connect law and political power with religious belief and practice.[7]

In the face of such potential challenges, 'separation' protects the inclusive and egalitarian character of the modern liberal polity. The modern liberal polity belongs to all citizens regardless of their particular worldviews and marks the sphere where citizens come together on an equal footing to collectively shape the polity and to decide upon the pursuit of public purposes. The foundational values of liberty and equality not only protect a space for individual freedom of conscience, but are also the foundation of the civic republican political values distinctive of a liberal democratic political community. Viewed from this perspective, 'separation' is vital to safeguard a democratic space for public purposes[8] and to protect 'the civic equality, civil identity . . . autonomy and inclusiveness of the political community' (Cohen 2013, 514).

This idea of citizenship as a 'common project' in pursuit of public purposes that citizens 'collectively will' on terms that are 'consistent with the status of all persons as free and equal' (Hartley 2016, 318) is notably absent from religious institutionalist accounts of the modern liberal polity. Indeed, the notion of religious organizations as sovereign bodies outside the jurisdiction of the state constitutes a profound challenge to the principles of popular sovereignty and democratic self-limitation that ground the legitimacy of the modern liberal democratic constitutional state. In a constitutional liberal democracy, it is the people who are the ultimate source of 'all publically legitimate exercises of coercive power' and, while liberal constitutional democracy requires a separation of powers, it places 'all state organs under civil law', denies 'sovereignty to any one of them', and makes all accountable to the people as 'the sole source of the (in principle revisable) constitutional order' (Cohen 2015a, 201). This is why the justification of public law must be immanent and access-ible to and can be challenged by the people. Although in a liberal consti-tutional democracy, associational plurality and fundamental rights and liberties, including the right to freedom of religion, are not concessions by the state, these do not constitute exogenous limits to the authority of the state. In a liberal polity, personal and political autonomy are equiprimor-dial (Habermas 1996). Just as the idea of popular sovereignty implies the protection of basic rights and liberties so as to ensure that citizens are sufficiently independent, the effective protection of personal autonomy can only be achieved if all citizen participate in the formulation and inter-pretation of the rights and norms that govern the polity. The notion of organized religion as an autonomous jurisdiction immune to regulation and constitutional oversight is not compatible with the principles of pop-ular sovereignty and democratic self-limitation that ground the legitima-cy of the modern, liberal, democratic, constitutional state. Moreover, the commitment of the modern constitutional state to neutrality is not merely procedural, but reflects a substantive commitment to the nonneutral val-ues of liberty and equality that define the distinctive civic republican ethos of a liberal democratic political community. This commitment to liberty and equality as political values is definitive of the freestanding claims of citizenship; claims that are not merely independent of religious beliefs, but also limit the role that religious convictions can play in the justification of public law.[9] Indeed, the notion of organized religion as an exogenous jurisdictional sphere cannot be reconciled with the founda-tional principles of the modern, liberal democratic, constitutional state.

2. INSTITUTIONAL ACCOMMODATION AND FREEDOM OF ASSOCIATION

Recent liberal egalitarian reconceptualizations of freedom of religion as one element of a fair scheme of individual liberties offer a potentially more promising framework for analysing claims to self-governance by religious organizations. For liberal egalitarians, the separation between state and organized religion does not mark the boundary between two distinct domains of authority, but constitutes a secondary principle grounded in the foundational liberal commitment to individual liberty and equality (Eisgruber and Sager 2007; Laborde 2017). While religious institutionalists seek to ground institutional accommodations in the dis-tinctive constitutional status of organized religion, liberal egalitarians in-sist that religion is neither special nor unique, but constitutes one of a variety of conceptions of the good central to individuals' sense of identity and integrity (Laborde 2017). On this reading, the separation of state and organized religion is good in as far as it protects individual liberty by 'preventing the public realm from establishing a religious doctrine that denigrates or marginalizes some group of citizens' (Nussbaum 2008, 11). Therefore, the primary purpose of the principle of separation is to guard against religious discrimination.

From this perspective, the desire of religious organizations 'to live by their own standards, purposes and commitments' is not an expression of the special place that religious organizations occupy in a liberal polity, but is best seen as an aspect of a wider liberal commitment to association-al autonomy grounded in respect for the interests individuals have 'to pursue a conception of the good that is central to their identity and integ-rity' (Laborde 2017, 174, 175).[10] On this analysis, religious organizations are just one of a wide variety of voluntary associations and their interest to live by and interpret their own standards, purposes, and commitments reflects the interest in associational integrity of voluntary associations in general (Laborde 2017). Therefore, in as far as religious organizations qualify for institutional accommodations, they do so not because they are religious, but because they enable members to 'integrate core aspects of their beliefs and commitments with associational goals and values' (La-borde 2017, 182). This interest in associational integrity not only implies that organizations must be free to refuse or rescind membership, but may also provide good grounds for more far reaching accommodations, such as exemptions from antidiscrimination legalisation dealing with race, gender, and sexual orientation, provided the association's 'professed doc-trine . . . demands such differential treatment' and there is a close fit between 'the association's main purpose and the specific activity or func-tion for which it claims an exemption' (Laborde 2017, 179, 185). The Cath-olic Church, for example, can legitimately demand an exemption from antidiscrimination legislation in relation to the appointment of priests, because this constitutes a core religious activity and the professed doc-trine of the Catholic Church stipulates an all-male clergy. Moreover, vol-untary associations may on occasions be able to claim special expertise to interpret their own standards, purposes, and commitments. Given churches' special theological expertise, the state should not take positions on theological issues, such as the rationale for religious employment deci-sions (Laborde 2017).

For liberal egalitarians, religious institutions are, therefore, not a pre-requisite for religious liberty, but the product of the freedom of associa-tion of religious citizens. Hence, claims to self-governance are grounded not in the sovereignty of organized religion, but in 'the fact that individu-als' dignitary and conscience-based rights can only be vindicated because they are exercised through institutions' (Schragger and Schwartzman 2013, 966). Although members of religious communities may not see their religious commitments as a personal choice, from the perspective of the liberal state, participation in religious communities is voluntary (Schragger and Schwartzman 2013). Therefore, to justify institutional accommodations designed to strengthen corporate self-governance, religious authorities must show that they have the consent of members and that the standards, purposes, and commitments the accommodation seeks to protect can 'credibly claim to represent the group on whose behalf they act' (Shorten 2015, 254). While religious groups need not be internally democratic, this implies at a minimum that 'members must be free to leave the group at no excessive cost' (Laborde 2017, 174). Moreover, to carry weight, religious authorities must show that their interpretation of the group's standards, purposes, and commitments does not unreasonably exclude the views and interests of some members (Shorten 2015).

Since religious organizations' right to self-governance is grounded in the dignitary and conscience-based rights of their members, for liberal egalitarians, claims to religious corporate self-governance are neither basic nor absolute and can be balanced against other rights and important state interests. Indeed, while fundamental liberal rights linked to freedom of association are not concessions by the state, liberal egalitarians insist that the final authority to determine the legitimate scope of associational self-governance rests with the state as the legitimately constituted public authority representative of and accountable to all citizens (Laborde 2017). From this perspective, the proper boundary between state and organized religion and the legitimate scope of institutional religious autonomy are matters of public policy.

There is much to commend liberal egalitarian accounts of religious institutional self-governance.[11] Not only is the foundational liberal constitutional principle of state sovereignty pivotal to this approach, liberal egalitarian principles are also well placed to address concerns regarding consent to religious authority and the position of vulnerable and marginalized members of religious communities. While liberal egalitarians have not always paid sufficient attention to the standing of marginalized members of religious communities, consistently applied, the focus on personal integrity and the equality and liberty of individuals extends the principle of equal protection to those within religious communities.[12] This not only implies that the state should take 'special care of those whose consent is suspect (such as children)' (Schragger and Schwartzman 2013, 962), but also suggests that on a liberal egalitarian account, institutional accommodations designed to perpetuate discriminatory or in-egalitarian practices that are likely to have a detrimental impact on members' interests, would be difficult to justify (Seglow 2015).[13]

Moreover, the liberal egalitarian focus on modes of association offers a valuable framework to address concerns regarding the limits of religious self-governance and the potential impact of the claims of religious associations on nonmembers. To qualify for institutional accommodations, associations must be identificatory, that is to say there must be a clear alignment between their purposes, structure, and membership (Shorten 2015; Laborde 2017). While on these grounds churches and other religious organizations can make a strong claim for associational discretion, the same cannot be said for demands by commercial for-profit organizations, such as the claims by the owners of Hobby Lobby for an exemption on religious grounds from the contraception mandate under the US 2010 Affordable Care Act (Laborde 2017). While in core religious organizations, the mode of association is clearly identificatory, this not the case for employees of commercial organizations. Indeed, even religious organizations cannot expect to be exempt from employment legislation in relation to employees not engaged in religious work. The further removed an employee's role is from the core religious purposes of the association, the less grounds there are for exemptions on religious grounds from general employment legislation (Schragger and Schwartzman 2013).

As these examples illustrate, the liberal egalitarian emphasis on individuals' integrity and conscience-based rights offers effective protection for citizens' personal autonomy. However, claims to religious self-governance not only have a bearing on questions of individual integrity and identity, but are also liable to impact on the integrity of the public political sphere as a prerequisite for the effective exercise of political autonomy and democratic self-limitation. The liberal egalitarian preoccupation with individual liberty and the coherence interests of voluntary associations obscures important considerations in this regard. Moreover, liberal egalitarian attempts to recast religious organizations as just one of a variety of forms of civil society association lose sight of the distinctive challenges inherent in claims to religious self-governance.

Many religious organizations are engaged not only in the pursuit of direct religious purposes central to core religious practices, but also perform a wide variety of public welfare functions within wider civil society, such as education, healthcare provisions, adoption services, or care for the elderly. While a due regard for the liberal principles of state neutrality and equal treatment suggests that religious organizations – just like other civil society organizations – should, in principle, be free to play a full role in civil society, attempts by religious organizations to invoke the idea of freedom of religion to gain exemptions from generally applicable laws that govern the provision of such services raise a range of concerns regarding the integrity of the public political sphere, not all of which can be readily addressed in terms of individual liberty and the associational integrity of civil society associations.

The difficulties in this regard can be illustrated by reference to the controversies in the UK surrounding the campaign by the Catholic Church for Catholic Adoption Agencies to be exempt from the requirement under the Equality Act (Sexual Orientation) Regulations 2007 to offer adoption services to gay and lesbian couples.[14] On the analysis advanced by liberal egalitarians such as Eisgruber and Sager (2007), demands for Catholic Adoption Agencies to be exempt from the 2007 Regulations constitute primarily a question of 'free exercise' and the protection of religious conscience. After all, the requirement to provide adoption services for gays and lesbians cannot be readily reconciled with the mainstream teaching of the Catholic Church endorsed by large sections of the Catholic community. Given a commitment to freedom of association and state neutrality, this suggests that the demand for an exemption for Catholic Adoption Agencies should be granted, provided the services denied to same-sex couples could be readily offered by other organizations, thus safeguarding the legal rights of gays and lesbians to access adoption services. In fact, Catholic Adoption Agencies should be free to bid for state funding on the same terms as other service providers. This line of reasoning was pivotal to the case presented by Catholic Care Leeds in its appeal to the Upper Tribunal ([2012] UKUT 395 (TCC)).

However, for fellow liberal egalitarians like Cohen (2013), Laborde (2017), and Lever (2017), this analysis fails to take account of the 'public facing' character of the services provided by Catholic Adoption Agencies. These agencies do not merely cater for members of their religious community, but aim to provide a service to the 'public at large'. For Cohen, Laborde (2017, 185), and Lever this implies that Catholic Adoption Agencies cannot claim to be '"religious" in the sense that matters to standing in exemptions from discrimination claims'. That is to say Catholic Adoption Agencies cannot claim to constitute identificatory associations that exhibit a clear 'alignment among their purposes, structure, membership and public' (Laborde 2017, 186). Catholic Adoption Agencies, therefore, fail to qualify for an exemption from the 2007 Regulations because, as organizations serving the 'public at large', they lack a 'relevant coherence interest that would allow them to refuse to serve all members regardless of race, gender or sexuality' (Laborde 2017, 185). As Lever (2017, 236–37) acknowledges, this line of reasoning implies that if Catholic Adoption Agencies were to cease to benefit from public funding and changed their remit to explicitly cater only to the faithful, the state could not object to such agencies refusing 'to place children with homosexual couples', provided 'there are suitable alternatives available for everyone else'.

While this focus on the 'public facing' character of Catholic Adoption Agencies highlights important considerations absent from Eisgruber and Sager's analysis, it still obscures key issues at stake in this case. Within modern liberal democracies it is widely acknowledged that government is responsible for public welfare and the provision of a wide range of public services. Indeed, adoption agencies constitute not merely a 'public facing' service, but a public service, that is to say a service that citizens have charged the state to provide for all members of the polity. Access to such public services is typically a marker of membership of the polity and signifies a citizens' status and standing. In fact, not only does the provision of public services such as welfare and healthcare play a role in facilitating the participation of potentially vulnerable citizens in public life, what public services are provided, how, and for whom shapes the ethos of civil society and is indicative of the civil identity of a political community. This character and ethos provides the setting for the processes of democratic opinion- and will-formation that ground the legitimacy of the modern constitutional state and constitute the context within which citizens collectively shape the polity and decide upon the pursuit of public purposes. While voluntary sector organizations may support the state in the provision of public services, a due regard for the civil identity and ethos of a political community implies that the state has a legitimate interest in the operation of such agencies and their impact on wider civil society.

In the UK, public policy in relation to the provision of public services is informed by a strong commitment to nondiscrimination and equal public recognition of gays and lesbians, 'where "recognition" means accepting their identity as normal, legitimate and unexceptional' (Jones 2015, 554). Such recognition is vital to safeguard the capacity of traditionally marginalized groups to make 'full use of the rights and opportunities inherent in the status of citizen' (Galeotti 2002, 96). Indeed, to exempt organizations engaged in the provision of public services from antidiscrimination legislation on the grounds of sexual orientation could be construed as state support for the continuation of discriminatory practices that threaten the equal public standing and dignity of a vulnerable minority and would undermine the general ethos and wider objectives inherent in public policy.[15] These considerations were pivotal to the ruling by the Upper Tribunal against Catholic Care Leeds. While the availability of other adoption services may well have lessened the immediate impact on homosexual couples, the Tribunal concluded that this did not mitigate the harm caused by the 'feeling that discrimination on grounds of sexual orientation was practiced at some point in the adoption system nor would it remove the harm to the general social value of promotion of equal treatment for heterosexuals and homosexuals' ([2012] UKUT 395(TCC) at para 66).

The liberal egalitarian focus on the coherence interests of voluntary associations engaged in the provision of public services cannot readily capture the concerns regarding the character and ethos of public service provision expressed by the Upper Tribunal in its ruling against Catholic Care Leeds. Exemptions from antidiscrimination legislation for organizations engaged in the provision of public services are problematic not only in as far as such organizations are 'public facing' or reliant on public funds, but also because they undermine the egalitarian and inclusive character and ethos of public service provision. Since public service provision is indicative of the civil identity of a political community and serves as a marker of membership of the polity, access to such services must reflect the inclusive and egalitarian character of the liberal political community. To fail to do so is to undermine the integrity of the public political sphere as a democratic space in which citizens come together on an equal footing to collectively shape the polity. As the reference by the Upper Tribunal to the 'adoption system' indicates, this not only implies that religious organizations that support the state in the provision of public services to 'the public at large' have no legitimate claim to be exempt from antidiscrimination legislation, but also suggests that religious organizations should not be permitted to subvert the egalitarian character of public service provision by selectively restricting their intended 'customer' base.[16] Given that public services are by definition services for the public, members of the polity should not be denied access to some aspects of adoption provisions on the grounds of race, gender, or sexuality.

Not only do liberal egalitarian arguments obscure important considerations regarding the integrity of the public political sphere, liberal egalitarian attempts to recast religious organizations as just one of a variety of forms of civil society association also lose sight of the distinctive challenges inherent in claims to religious self-governance. Although liberal egalitarians like Laborde (2017) are undoubtedly right to stress that religious organizations are not unique in claiming a special expertise to interpret and apply the standards, purposes, and commitments that define their associations, her attempt to compare appeals to 'otherworldly' standards by religious organizations to the judgements of secular professional organizations obscures the distinctive character of religious claims to self-governance. While 'courts may well "routinely defer to employers' judgements about subjective professional judgements in highly specialized fields"' (Laborde 2017, 194), because judges lack the specific knowledge and expertise to evaluate such claims, judgements regarding secular professional qualifications are open to critical rational evaluations in a manner that religious authority claims regarding the 'gifts and graces' essential to be a good minister are not. Whereas in the former case the lack of judicial competence is the product of technical specialization, in the latter it stems from the fact that the justifications in question are inaccessible to the standards of public reason. Although this feature may well not be unique to the claims of religious authorities, it nonetheless illustrates the distinctive challenge inherent in claims to institutional religious self-governance. Indeed, the appeal to 'otherworldly' justifications in the judgements of religious authorities makes it particularly likely that claims to self-governance by religious organizations will prove challenging within a liberal polity committed to immanent and generally accessible justifications of public law and policy.

3. INSTITUTIONAL ACCOMMODATION AND THE INTEGRITY OF THE PUBLIC POLITICAL SPHERE

In a liberal polity, claims to self-governance by religious institutions are neither basic nor absolute, but are grounded in the dignitary and conscience-based rights of their members and must be balanced against other rights and important state interests. The legitimate scope of religious institutional self-governance is, therefore, a matter of public policy and subject to regulation by legitimately constituted political authority. Indeed, given the potential impact of claims to institutional religious sovereignty upon the integrity, ethos, and civil identity of a liberal democratic political community, demands by religious institutionalists for a robust defence of the independent jurisdiction of the church free from state regulation are tantamount to trying to bring to bear the principles of political theology in the public political realm. That is not to suggest that fundamental liberal rights linked to freedom of association constitute concessions by the state. A due regard for the associational integrity of religious organizations may at times provide good grounds for exemptions from generally applicable laws for religious organizations with a direct religious purpose and engaged in core religious practices, whose professed doctrine is at odds with generally applicable laws such as antidiscrimination legislation.

Although there is much to commend the liberal egalitarian focus on the effective protection of citizen's personal integrity and autonomy, in a liberal polity the separation of state and organized religion also safeguards the integrity of the public political sphere committed to inclusivity, civic equality, popular sovereignty, and democratic self-limitation. The liberal egalitarian preoccupation with individual liberty and the coherence interests of voluntary associations obscures important considerations in this regard. These worries point to the need for an account of the limits of institutional accommodation that is cognisant not only of liberal egalitarian concerns for individual liberty, but also civic republican worries regarding the background conditions that facilitate the effective exercise of political autonomy. Liberal egalitarians generally recognize that self-governance claims by voluntary associations are impermissible if they impact on their members' political citizenship (Schragger and Schwartzman 2013). Indeed, for Cohen (2013), demands for a segmental legal pluralism that enables religious organizations to exercise jurisdiction over coreligionists pose a challenge not merely to individual liberty, but also to the integrity of the public political realm and the legitimate scope of political authority. However, even Cohen's (2013, 2015 a and b) insightful critiques of both religious institutionalists and fellow liberal egalitarians such as Eisgruber and Sager have been too focused on US-specific debates regarding constitutional law and state funding to explore the wider implication of civic republican concerns.[17] Given the intricate link between public service provision and the character and ethos of the public political sphere, these concerns are particularly pressing in relation to the participation of religious organizations in the provision of public services. A commitment to the principle of state neutrality implies that religious organizations should be free to fully participate in civil society. However, if the state is to effectively safeguard the inclusive and egalitarian character of a liberal democratic political community, it can legitimately insist that religious organizations respect the civic ethos of public service provision. This not only suggests that religious organizations that support the state in the provision of public services such as education, healthcare, and adoption must provide these services to 'the public at large' in a manner consistent with the civic identity of a liberal democratic political community, but also implies that such organizations, regardless of their sources of funding, should not be permitted to subvert the inclusive and egalitarian character of public service provision by selectively restricting their intended customer base in an attempt to meet the 'coherence test'.

While religious organizations should be free to select the type of public services they provide and can legitimately seek to cash out the general ethos of public service provision in a manner that is particularly appealing to members of their religious community, the services they provide must meet the general criteria of public service provision. Thus, religious organizations opposed to abortion may choose not to participate in the provision of reproductive healthcare, while schools run by religious organizations may cash out the values and principles of public education in a manner that is particularly appealing to coreligionists. However, while religious organizations may tailor their contribution to public services to the needs of particular segments of the population, such 'specialization' must be compatible with the inclusive and egalitarian character of a liberal polity and its emphasis on nondiscrimination and nondomination. Thus, regardless of intended customer base or sources of funding, religious organizations may not discriminate in the provision of public services on the grounds of race, sex, or sexuality. Indeed, unless there are good countervailing public reasons,[18] the default position in public service provision should be one of 'equal access for all'.

Taken together, a due regard for both individual and public political integrity and autonomy place significant limits on legitimate claims to self-governance by religious institutions. Indeed, although not unique, the appeal to 'otherworldly' justifications in the judgements of religious authorities makes it particularly likely that claims to self-governance by religious organizations will prove problematic within a liberal polity committed to immanent and generally accessible justifications of public law and policy.

REFERENCES

Barry, Brian. 2001. *Culture and Equality*. Cambridge: Polity

Cohen, Jean L. 2013. 'Political Religion vs Non-Establishment: Reflections on 21st-Century Political Theology: Part 1'. *Philosophy & Social Criticism* 39 (4–5): 443–69; Part 2, *Philosophy & Social Criticism* 39 (6): 507–21.

———. 2015a. 'Freedom of Religion Inc.: Whose Sovereignty?'. *Netherlands Journal of Legal Philosophy* 44(3): 169–210.

———. 2015b. 'Rethinking Political Secularism and the American Model of Constitutional Dualism'. In *Religion, Secularism and Constitutional Democracy*, edited by Cecile Laborde and Jean Cohen, 113–56. New York: Columbia University Press.

Deveaux, Monique. 2006. *Gender and Justice in Multicultural Liberal States*. Oxford: Oxford University Press.

Eisgruber, Christopher L., and Lawrence G. Sager. 2007. *Religious Freedom and the Constitution*. Cambridge, MA: Harvard University Press.

Galeotti, Anna Elisabetta. 2002. *Toleration as Recognition*. Cambridge: Cambridge University Press.

Garnett, Richard. 2007. 'The Freedom of the Church'. *Journal of Catholic Social Thought* 4 (1): 59–86.

———. 2016. 'The Freedom of the Church (Toward) An Exposition, Translation and Defence'. In *The Rise of Corporate Religious Liberty*, edited by Micha Schwartzman, Chad Flanders and Zoë Robinson, 39–62. Oxford: Oxford University Press.

Habermas, Jürgen. 1996. *Between Facts and Norms*. Cambridge, MA: MIT Press.

———. 2011. '"The Political": The Rational Meaning of a Questionable Inheritance of Political Theology'. In *The Power of Religion in the Public Sphere*, edited by Eduardo Mendieta and Jonathan VanAntwerpen, 15–33. New York: Columbia University Press.

Hartley, Christine. 2016. 'Vallier, Kevin, Liberal Politics and Public Faith: Beyond Separation'. Book Review, *Ethics* 127 (1): 315–19.

Jones, Peter. 2015. 'Toleration, Religion and Accommodation'. *European Journal of Philosophy* 23 (3): 542–63.

Laborde, Cecile. 2017. *Liberalism's Religion*. Cambridge, MA: Harvard University Press.

Lever, Annabelle. 2017. 'Equality and Conscience: Ethics and the Provision of Public Services'. In *Religion in Liberal Political Philosophy*, edited by Cecile Laborde and Aurelia Bardon, 233–46. Oxford: Oxford University Press.

Loenen, Titia. 2002. 'Family Law Issues in a Multicultural Setting: Abolishing or Affirming Sex as a Legally Relevant Category? A Human Rights Approach'. *Netherlands Quarterly of Human Rights* 20 (4): 423–43.

McConnell, Michael W. 1985. 'Accommodation of Religion'. *The Supreme Court Review* 1–59.

———. 1991. 'Accommodation of Religion: An Update and a Response to Critics'. *George Washington Law Review* 60: 685–742.

———. 2000. 'Believers as Equal Citizen'. In *Obligations of Citizenship and Demands of Faith. Religious Accommodation in Pluralist Democracies*, edited by Nancy L. Rosenblum, 335–402. Princeton, NJ: Princeton University Press.

Muñiz-Fraticelli, Victor. 2014. *The Structure of Pluralism: On the Authority of Associations*. Oxford: Oxford University Press.

Nussbaum, Martha. 2008. *Liberty of Conscience. In Defence of America's Tradition of Religious Equality*. New York: Basic Books.

Phillips, Anne. 2007. *Multiculturalism without Culture*. Princeton, NJ: Princeton University Press.

Schragger, Richard, and Micah Schwartzman. 2013. 'Against Religious Institutionalism', *Virginia Law Review* 99 (5): 917–85.

Seglow, Jonathan. 2015. 'Religious Sovereignty and Group Exemptions A Response to Jean Cohen'. *Netherlands Journal of Legal Philosophy* 44 (3): 231–39.

Shachar, Ayelet. 2001. *Multicultural Jurisdictions*. Cambridge: Cambridge University Press.

Shorten, Andrew. 2015. 'Are There Rights to Institutional Exemptions?' *Journal of Social Philosophy* 46 (2): 242–63.

Smith, Steven D. 2016. 'The Jurisdictional Conception of Church Autonomy'. In *The Rise of Corporate Religious Liberty*, edited by Micah Schwartzman, Chad Flanders, and Zoë Robinson, 19–37. Oxford: Oxford University Press.

Wolterstorff, Nicholas. 2012. *The Mighty and the Almighty*. Cambridge: Cambridge University Press.

NOTES

1. See Shorten's (2015) analysis of institutional exemptions.

2. For example, McConnell (1985, 1991, 2000), Smith (2016), Garnett (2007, 2016), Muñiz-Fraticelli (2014).

3. For example, Laborde (2017).

4. For example, Deveaux (2006), Phillips (2007).

5. While Seglow (2015) suggests that meaningful exit rights may mitigate the case for internal democracy, the debates surrounding campaigns by women members to reform Jewish and Muslim family law indicate that attempts to offset 'exit' and 'voice' are liable to leave marginalized group members with difficult and at times unsustainable choices between their religious faith and their rights.

6. For a critical analysis of religious institutionalist claims, see Cohen's (2015a) discussion of *Burwell v. Hobby Lobby Stores, Inc.*

7. For example, traditional Christian theology maintains that God authorizes and enjoins the authority of the state to protect rights and curb injustice (Wolterstorff 2012).

8. That is to say the pursuit of policies, laws, or governmental actions that benefit the political community in general.

9. While among mainstream political liberals it is widely accepted that this limitation implies that politicians and officials in public institutions must justify legal coercion exclusively in terms of public reasons – that is to say reasons shared, accessible, or acceptable to all – the extent to which these constraints apply to the political statements of 'ordinary' citizens in the informal public political realm remains contested.

10. While the desire to pursue a conception of the good central to one's identity and integrity can give rise to demands for associational autonomy that is not necessarily the case. As Martin rightly notes in chapter 5 of this volume, the subjective and individualized approach of integrity-based theories grants individuals considerable scope to determine highly personal moral obligations.

11. Liberal egalitarians place significantly more restrictions on the legitimate scope of corporate religious self-governance than proponents of more minimal strands of liberalism, such as Billingham in this volume.

12. While Eisgruber and Sager (2007) are keen to ensure nondiscrimination between religious and nonreligious groups, 'they fail to apply these principles to vulnerable *individuals* and minorities within religious groups' (Cohen 2015b, 137).

13. As Seglow (2015, 238) notes, on a liberal egalitarian account religious authorities not only need to show that a particular piece of legislation or rule significantly burdens their beliefs, but also have to demonstrate that ordinary members consent (or at least acquiesce) to their control and that the 'proposed exemption that the leadership seeks would not set back the interests of ordinary members'.

14. In response, some Catholic adoption agencies ceased operation, while others cut their formal ties with the Church in order to comply with the rules.

15. What is at issue here is not necessarily the question of endorsement as such, but the impact of public perceptions on wider policy objectives.

16. Selective restrictions of the intended customer base was an issue in UK debates regarding adoption services. For example, *St Margaret's Children and Family Care Society v. Office of the Scottish Charity Regulator* (Case ref: APP 02/13).

17. The United States also lacks comprehensive national nondiscrimination legislation akin to the UK Equality Act 2010 (Nussbaum 2008).

18. For example, a school run by a religious organization may prioritize coreligionists in their admission policy, if a failure to do so would disproportionally restrict the ability of this group of parents to have their educational preferences met.

SEVEN

(Not) Shaking Hands with People of the Opposite Sex

Civility, National Identity, and Accommodation

Christoph Baumgartner

In November 2015, two Muslim schoolboys in the Swiss municipality of Therwil decided to stop shaking hands with their female teachers for religious reasons. While the school initially found a provisional solution that tolerated their behaviour, the case received wide media coverage after it was mentioned on Swiss television in April 2016. Subsequently, educational-political authorities of the canton Basel-Country, where Therwil is located, decided that the two schoolboys were obliged to shake hands with all their teachers, male as well as female teachers. If they refused to comply, they could be fined, or even expelled from school. This case is only one among several instances where the refusal of religious people to shake hands with people of the opposite sex[1] triggered heated debates, and sometimes even resulted in multiple lawsuits. In 2004, for instance, Imam Ahmad Salam refused a handshake with the then sitting Dutch Minister of Integration Rita Verdonk, and she criticized his behaviour harshly. In 2006, a female Muslim teacher at a public high school in Utrecht in the Netherlands was suspended after she had informed her colleagues via e-mail that she would no longer shake hands with men because of religious objections.[2] Also in 2016, an Algerian women who is married to a French man was denied French citizenship because she refused to shake the hand of a male official in the citizenship ceremony for religious reasons (Breeden 2018).

In Europe, only a very small number of people refuse, for religious reasons, to shake hands with someone of the opposite sex. Moreover, unlike typical cases of religious accommodation such as so-called ritual slaughter, or the consumption of psychoactive substances like peyote and ayahuasca in religious rituals, the handshake-issue is not about exemptions from general laws; there is no general legal obligation to shake hands with both men and women. It does, however, involve a specific and context-bound exemption of sorts from a general social norm, and the normative structure of the handshake-issue is analogous to typical cases of religious accommodation. Furthermore, the fact that people were suspended and lost their jobs because their religion prevented them from shaking hands with people of the opposite sex indicates that something significant is at stake for all the people and institutions involved, and that we need to think about the normative criteria that can help us to determine how one can aptly respond to the demand of some people not to shake hands with someone of the opposite sex. In this chapter, I explore the nature of the conflicts and controversies in European societies (which is the focus of this chapter) regarding the refusal of some Muslims to shake hands with people of the opposite sex.[3] I will first examine motives from Islamic legal discourse, which are at the basis of the refusal to shake hands. After that, I reconstruct two arguments that support a general requirement to shake hands with both men and women, especially in the context of public institutions. Subsequently, I explore anthropological findings, which concern ways in which some Muslims in Belgium and the Netherlands deal with their religious commitments not to shake hands with people of the opposite sex, and with the challenges and problems they have to face as a result. Finally, turning to normative analysis, I tentatively respond to the question of how one should deal with the demands of some people who, because of their religion, refuse to shake hands with people of the opposite sex in the context of public institutions such as schools, and whether a general requirement to shake hands with both men and women is legitimate.

1. THE HANDSHAKE IN ISLAMIC LEGAL DISCOURSE

What are the reasons that in their view compel some practicing Muslims to refrain from shaking the hand of someone of the opposite sex even if this person extends her or his hand?

According to Islamic law, sexual relations are only allowed within the context of a marriage, and legal schools argue that social interactions between men and women who are unrelated by immediate kin ties are potential sources of social disorder and discord (*fitna*) (see Mahmood 2005, 106–13; Bucar 2012, 54–58). To protect proper relationships between men and women, and through this the social order, Islamic law includes a complex set of regulations concerning privacy and modesty. Islamic legal discourse is strongly gendered in that matter, and the female body is often understood as having significant power to ignite men's sexual desire (see, e.g., Mahmood 2005, 106; Spectorsky 2010, 190). Both men and women are required to abide by modesty regulations, but, as Saba Mahmood points out:

> it is women who bear the primary responsibility for maintaining the sanctity of relations between the sexes. This is because the juristic Islamic tradition assumes that women are the objects of sexual desire and men the desiring subjects, an assumption that has come to justify the injunction that women should 'hide their charms' when in public so as not to excite the libidinal energies of men who are not their immediate kin. (Mahmood 2005, 110)[4]

Most of the female body, usually with the exception of face, hands, and feet, is regarded as private parts (*'awra*), and hence to be covered in public, while men's *'awra* is limited to the area between the navel and the knees (Lange 2013, 44; Mahmood 2005, 107; Spectorsky 2010, 190). Next to such provisions relating to people's – and especially women's – appearance in public, Islamic modesty regulations also include norms that are related to direct social interactions. Women should, for instance, lower their gaze in their interactions with men; a man and a woman must avoid being alone together in seclusion, that is, out of sight and hearing of others; and – most importantly for this chapter – people of the opposite sex must not have immediate skin-to-skin contact, and hence must refrain from shaking hands (see Katz 2017, Krawietz 2013, and Schlatmann 2016, 170). Importantly, these modesty regulations do not apply in the context of immediate family members (*mahram*),[5] and also not in interactions with people of the same sex and children. Here, it is assumed that no illicit sexual relations and interactions will be provoked, for instance, by exposure of a woman's *'awra*, or by touching the hand of somebody of the opposite sex. Touching people of the opposite sex, however, who are not one's immediate kin, 'and with whom therefore sexual relations are possible', is forbidden (Batum 2016, 969.) This relational aspect is important for an adequate understanding of the refusal to shake hands; the reason why some Muslims refrain from shaking hands with someone of the opposite sex is not that they would consider those people somehow inferior, impure, or not worthy of a handshake, and is in no way related to the religion of the person whose hands is rejected—the modesty regulations apply to social interactions between Muslims as well. Rather, the practice of not shaking hands is part of a larger set of modesty regulations that is based on the belief that extramarital sexual relations are morally wrong and pose a threat to social order, and on the assumption that shaking hands with a person of the opposite gender outside the family is a potential source of such illicit sexual relations.

2. THE MEANING AND MORAL SIGNIFICANCE OF THE HANDSHAKE IN CURRENT EUROPEAN SOCIETIES

Handshaking is a very common quotidian greeting practice in many contemporary societies, especially in Western cultures (Katsumi et al. 2017, 346). Until the nineteenth century, however, the handshake had a different meaning; before that time, everyday greeting and parting gestures in Europe included noncontact practices such as bowing, curtsying, or taking off one's hat – practices by which upper classes of society distinguished themselves from others. The handshake served to formally settle disputes, and as formal seal of reconciliation (Roodenburg 1991, 173–74). In the course of the nineteenth century, the handshake became an increasingly popular and rather egalitarian greeting gesture that has been regarded 'as a sign of friendliness, hospitality, formality, and trust' (Katsumi et al. 2017, 346). Although class, gender, and (sub)cultural differences are significant when it comes to, for instance, frequency and firmness regarding the handshake – think of varieties such as the homie handshake, high five, or the fist bump – shaking hands has developed into a relatively egalitarian and very common greeting and parting gesture since the nineteenth century in Western cultures.

In legal procedures and even more so in public controversies about refusals to shake hands with people of the opposite sex, two arguments are especially influential. The argument that is brought forward most frequently to support a general requirement to shake hands with both men and women claims that the handshake is a token of equal respect, and that refusing to shake hands with a person of the opposite sex expresses disrespect or an unfair discrimination on the basis of gender, and possibly even both. Call this the argument from equal respect. A second argument adds to this a further assertion, namely that shaking hands with men and women is an essential part of the 'national culture' of societies such as Germany, Switzerland, or the Netherlands. Since public institutions, such as schools, are prominent places of manifestation and transmission of national culture, the argument says, shaking hands should be compulsory within such institutions. Call this the argument from national culture. Let me examine both arguments further.

The argument from equal respect construes the handshake as a practice of civility that displays a genuinely moral commitment namely equal respect, which is denied if somebody refuses a handshake. Rita Verdonk, for instance, confronted Ahmad Salam with the question of whether he would not consider her as equal and accused him of disrespecting women. In a similar vein, the legal opinion that was produced to prepare the Therwil decision emphasizes the common role of the handshake as an expression of civility and respect (see BKSD 2016, 5), as do several other legal decisions (for the Netherlands see, e.g., Alidadi 2017, 213–23, and Orgad 2015, 73). This aspect of the handshake and the refusal to shake hands respectively can be reconstructed in terms of philosophical theories of civility and manners. Authors such as Sarah Buss (1999), Cheshire Calhoun (2000), Anna Elisabetta Galeotti (2017), and Karin Stohr (2006; 2012), for instance, argue that civility, and practices that are part of it like the handshake, are communicative forms of conduct that involve the – often nonverbal – display of respect or other moral attitudes. A nonverbal display of respect, for instance through a handshake, consists of acts, Calhoun argues, 'that the addressee of civility might reasonably interpret as making it clear that I recognize some morally considerable fact about her as worth treating with respect' (Calhoun 2000, 259.) Similarly, Buss characterizes good manners as 'essential to acknowledging the direct value of anyone who deserves to be treated with respect' (Buss 1999, 803). If an act of good manners or civility is conducted in public so that other people witness it, those bystanders also need to be familiar with the meaning of the act, since otherwise the important communicative function of civility – to display and communicate a moral attitude – cannot be fulfilled, or only to a limited extent.[6]

The morally considerable fact to which Calhoun refers in the quote above, and the recognition of which is displayed through an act of civility, can be different in different acts of civility – that somebody recognizes a person as a queen, for instance, can be communicated through bowing or curtseying. Giving the queen a high five, however, will probably not be understood as communicating respect, but count as inappropriate or even disrespectful, no matter what the person attempting to give the queen a high five intends to communicate. Unlike in the case of, for instance, bowing before a queen, the handshake does not display the recognition of a person's special status as dignitary, but the recognition of the other person as morally equal. This could be achieved by different gestures as well, so the form of the handshake is in important respects arbitrary, which is demonstrated by the fact that people in different cultures use different forms and gestures to recognize others as morally equal. But despite this arbitrariness with regard to the form, acts of civility cannot be easily dispensed with or transformed by individuals or small groups, because existing practices and gestures are connected with and embedded into stable expectations that are widely shared in a society. They can only function as communicative acts because virtually all members of a society are familiar with their meaning, and act accordingly. In the particular case of a refusal to shake hands, the situation is complicated even more, since in European societies the act of not shaking the hand of another person who extends her or his hand not only fails to communicate the recognition of the other person as equal; rather, in European societies the refusal to shake hands is generally understood as genuine expression of disrespect or moral disapproval.[7] People can and actually do use the refusal to shake hands to communicate to the person who offers a handshake and to possible witnesses of this act that they disapprove of something the other person did, or what the person stands for – a specific 'morally considerable fact', to use Calhoun's phrase.[8] In the context of my analysis, the morally considerably fact that is highlighted by the refusal to shake hands with a person of the opposite sex is exactly that: the fact that the respective person is somebody of the opposite sex. And since a refusal to shake hands appears as, and counts as an expression of moral disapproval and disrespect, the refusal to shake hands with a person of the opposite sex *communicates* a rejection of gender equality – quite independently of the actual motives and intentions of the person who refuses to shake hands.

The second argument for a requirement to shake hands with both men and women, the argument from national culture, adds to the argument from equal respect a further dimension by construing the handshake, including shaking hands between people of the opposite sex, as an important component of a national culture or *Leitkultur* of the respective country.[9] Since this national culture is understood as being normatively significant for all members of society, the handshake is more directly invested with value than it is according to the argument from equal respect. Whereas for the latter, the handshake functions as common practice that displays respect, the argument from national culture construes the handshake as a practice that is constitutive for membership in society, and as an important sign of good citizenship. Against this background, the refusal to shake hands with people of the opposite sex is understood as both signaling lack of respect and, importantly, as indicating that the person who refuses to shake hands does not really partake in what characterizes a country, namely its national culture, and hence does not really belong to it. Such a framing of people who do not want to shake hands with someone of the opposite sex as cultural and societal outsiders was powerfully present in recent public political debates and election campaigns in Germany and the Netherlands. In the 2017 federal election campaign, Germany, both the then-sitting Federal Minister of the Interior Thomas de Maizière and the conservative political party Christian Social Union, explicitly included handshaking into a *Leitkultur* with which, they said, all people in Germany should comply. In the same year, Dutch Prime Minister Mark Rutte emphasized during the election campaign that shaking hands is one of the practices that are 'normal' in the Netherlands, and that any member of Dutch society should be expected to shake hands with both men and women. Such contributions that define handshaking as an important component of a normatively charged national culture or *Leitkultur* (leading or dominant culture of a society to which foreigners should assimilate; see Manz 2004; Pautz 2005; Ohlert 2015) often go hand in hand with antiimmigration rhetoric, and are part of a broader process, the culturalization of citizenship. For the Netherlands, this has been described as 'a process in which norms, and values and symbols and traditions (including religion) have come to play a pivotal role in defining what can be expected of a Dutch citizen' (Slootman and Duyvendak 2015, 151.) The culturalization of citizenship adds informal and emotional aspects to the legal dimensions of citizenship, and to be fully recognized as belonging to the Netherlands, people – and especially immigrants – are also expected to 'adjust to Dutch culture, to Dutch norms and values, in order to avert the impending danger of insufficient social cohesion' (Slootman and Duyvendak 2015, 152). In this context, the notion of 'Dutch culture' is understood as a largely homogeneous system of norms, values, practices, traditions, and so forth, that is carried and shared by virtually all people who 'belong to the Netherlands'. More-over, this Dutch culture is perceived by proponents of a culturalization of citizenship as in need of protection against 'foreign' influences. Accord-ingly, Dutch national culture and identity 'must "cannibalize" other iden-tities in order to turn immigrants into reliable citizens' (Geschiere 2009, 166). People who resist this process, and want to maintain minority prac-tices and traditions, are construed as 'cultural others' (see, e.g., Balken-hol, Mepschen, and Duyvendak 2016 and Uitermark, Mepschen, and Duyvendak 2013), and somebody's refusal to shake hands with people of the opposite sex in particular is understood as an indication that this person is not adapted to the national culture, and does not really belong in the Netherlands. Or, to put it differently, the argument from national culture claims that to develop full membership of a society such as the Netherlands, and to demonstrate and perform it, all people in society are supposed to shake hands with both men and women. People who are not willing to do this, although they know about the significance of the hand-shake in the particular society, indicate by their refusal that they do not really and wholeheartedly belong to this country. For people working at public institutions like public schools, this is considered especially prob-lematic, because, as already stated above, such institutions should repre-sent national culture, and contribute to transmitting it to future genera-tions.

3. THE HANDSHAKE IN EVERYDAY LIFE OF MUSLIMS IN BELGIUM AND THE NETHERLANDS

How do Muslims deal with the tensions I've described between the Is-lamic requirement not to have immediate skin-to-skin contact with peo-ple of the opposite sex who are not *mahram* on the one hand, and the often very strong expectation in Western European societies to shake hands with both men and women on the other hand? In such contexts, being a practicing Muslim who wants to fully comply with Islamic mod-esty regulations is a contested identity. Anthropologist Annemeik Schlat-mann even reports from her fieldwork in the Netherlands that 'the west-ern custom of handshaking when greeting each other is by far the one that disturbs the peace of mind of the Shi'i Muslims I interviewed most. Shaking hands is a daily recurring, inevitable personal confrontation between Islamic norms and western social practices' (Schlatmann 2016, 169–70). Consequently, only very few Muslims refuse to shake hands with people of the opposite sex strictly and without exception. Many others try to negotiate between their religious commitments and the social requirement of the handshake – they shake hands when necessary, but avoid it if possible, and make sure that this process of negotiation does not negatively affect their religious commitments and sensibilities. Anthropological research in this field (especially with regard to the situation in Belgium and the Netherlands) identifies several motives that prompt such negotiation processes; I want to mention two, here.

Social and economic opportunities. In her research about how Turkish-Dutch Muslim students dealt with the handshake issue, Deniz Batum shows that the practice of not-handshaking can have positive symbolic value, within (parts of) an Islamic community, and that it can be important in the ethical formation of some Muslims (see Batum 2016). This is different, however, in social interactions with non-Muslims; here, shaking hands with both men and women has a positive communicative function and symbolic value. Batum's interlocutors experienced shaking hands with both men and women as 'a social obligation, refusing to do so is rude rather than an ethical choice of self-making' (Batum 2016, 977). Moreover, they described the willingness to shake hands with both men and women as crucial for full social participation, and as key to the competitive Dutch job market and to upward mobility (Batum 2016, 976–77). Because of this, they developed a flexible approach: although they continued to consider handshaking as wrongful practice and as a transgression of their religion, they recognized the significant social meaning of the handshake in the Netherlands, and in some social contexts – usually related to employment – they did shake hands, at least to start with in getting to know someone, for instance to qualify for a job in the eyes of their non-Muslim fellow citizens. Deniz Batum describes this approach for one of her interlocutors as follows:

> As she considers the handshake as a practice embedded in Dutch social life, she argues for being flexible and accommodating rather than strictly keeping with modesty. A certain bargaining takes place in her thinking between strict observation of piety and economic emancipation, in which the latter is found to be more important in the long run. (Batum 2016, 976)

Similar practices have been identified in research by Nadia Fadil (2009; concerning Belgian Maghrebi Muslim women) and Annemeik Schlatmann (2016; concerning the Shi'i Muslim youth in the Netherlands). Both authors point out that such processes of accommodation can be reconsidered later. Some interlocutors reported that they decided to shake hands in situations such as job interviews, and at the start of a new job. At a later stage, when people knew each other better, they addressed the handshake issue in conversations with colleagues and superiors, and often employers respected their request not to shake hands with people of the opposite sex, and introduced alternative greeting gestures (Fadil 2009, 444; Schlatmann 2016, 175).

Representation of Islam, and social peace. A second important motive that prompts processes of negotiation between religious demands on the one hand, and social norms on the other hand, relates to existing negative stereotypes of Muslims and Islam as cultural 'other' and alien to liberal democracy and 'Western' modernity, being prone to misogyny and religious violence. Annnemeik Schlatmann's research demonstrates how such stereotypes can motivate, and sometimes force, Muslims to be flexible with regard to the handshake in order 'to counter the representation of Islam as a hostile religion' (Schlatmann 2016, 178. For Muslims' efforts to counter public images of Islam as a violent religion, see Es 2018.) To represent Islam as a peaceful and tolerant religion, and to avoid harming the public image of the Muslim community, some of Schlatmann's interlocutors decided to stop refusing to shake hands with people of the opposite sex, although they considered this as sinful (Schlatmann 2016, 173–74; see also Batum 2016, 97). This situation constitutes a social-religious predicament in which practising Muslims have to decide whether they should be 'good Muslims' – in a religious sense – and comply with Islamic modesty regulations even if this makes them suspicious in the eyes of non-Muslim citizens and harms the image of Islam, or whether they should be 'good Muslims' – in a social sense – and adapt to the customs of the non-Muslim majority in society even if this demands that they transgress their religious codes or rules (see Schlatmann 2016, 174). Fadil describes a similar case that is less explicitly related to the public image of Islam and more focused on the avoidance of social unrest in general. One of Fadil's female interlocutors decided to shake hands with men in situations where a refusal would cause 'some sort of *fitna*', as she phrases it. 'And my prime objective is to serve, not to disserve. But I just make sure not to make a habit out it' (Fadil 2009, 445). Interestingly, the woman uses the Arabic term *fitna* to explain why she decides not to comply with one of the Islamic modesty regulations – the very same term that provides the rationale of the provision not to shake hands with people of the opposite sex who do not belong to one's *mahram* (see above). 'While a diligent application and adherence to Islamic rules generally figures as a way to avoid *fitna*,' Fadil points out, 'an interesting inversion appears here, where not abiding by particular religious conducts becomes a way to achieve this same Islamic virtue' (Fadil 2009, 446.).

Summing up the different claims that are involved in the handshake-issue in societies such as Belgium, Germany, the Netherlands, or Switzerland, one can say the following. The Islamic provision not to shake hands with people of the opposite sex who are not immediate kin is rooted in regulations of modesty and privacy that are meant to prevent illicit sexual relations, which are considered morally wrong and a threat to social order. In European societies, on the other hand, proposals for a general requirement to shake hands with both men and women are informed by the claim that the handshake is a common gesture displaying equal respect (and the refusal to shake hands a token of disrespect). A further argument claims that the handshake is invested with a specific normativity, because it is part of the national culture of countries such as Germany or the Netherlands. Finally, if practising Muslims for whom shaking hands with people of the opposite sex is wrong and sinful are confronted with the demand to shake hands, they sometimes develop strategies to mediate between the requirements of their religion and the social requirement to shake hands. However, even if they succeed in doing this, they often continue considering handshaking with people of the opposite sex who are not their immediate kin wrong and sinful. It is against this background that I now analyse the issue in normative terms, and attempt to provide some tentative considerations regarding the question how we should respond to people who, for religious reasons, refuse to shake hands with someone of the opposite sex.

4. HOW TO RESPOND TO REFUSALS TO SHAKE HANDS WITH PEOPLE OF THE OPPOSITE SEX?

Since the scope of my analysis is limited to liberal democratic and pluralistic societies such as the Netherlands, I take for granted a number of normative principles such as gender equality and the right to freedom of religion. Liberal democratic societies aspire to build a polity that is based on such principles, and hence the question I am interested in is not whether we should accept, for instance, gender equality and freedom of religion, but what these principles imply for the handshake-issue. With regard to freedom of religion, I further assume that it is, in principle, possible and legitimate that measures of accommodation are granted if this is necessary to allow people to practice their religion while at the same time being able to participate on a par with others in social and economic interactions. Such accommodations usually consist of exemptions for designated minorities from general laws, if these laws severely burden the practising of religion, or bar people from fair opportunities in society because of their religion (see, e.g., Bou-Habib 2006, Nussbaum 2008; Patten 2017; Seglow 2017). Since the handshake-issue primarily concerns a social convention rather than formal social institutions or constitutional matters, I use Jonathan Seglow's broad understanding of religious accommodation as a practice that 'involves shaping laws, rules, or codes in such a way that they carve out a space for those with deep conscientious convictions, usually religious ones' (Seglow 2017, 177). People who want to refrain from shaking hands with people of the opposite sex perceive refraining from the handshake as part of their religion. Accordingly, not shaking hands with people of the opposite sex is a prima facie candidate for a practice that should be accommodated. Or, to put it differently, the question at issue is whether public institutions such as public schools should be permitted, or perhaps even encouraged, to make shaking hands with both men and women compulsory. Do the two arguments sketched out above provide sufficiently strong reasons for such a general requirement to shake hands with both men and women in the context of public institutions such as public schools? Let me examine the two arguments one by one.

The decisive claim of the argument from equal respect is that people who refuse to shake hands with people of the opposite sex fail to display equal respect that everybody deserves, independent of, for instance, somebody's gender. This problem results from the different meaning that the handshake has for most people in European societies on the one hand, and Muslims who interpret the handshake on the basis of Islamic modesty regulations on the other hand. If this is the point of the matter, then the two normative principles that are at stake are the principle of equal respect on the one side, and the right to practice one's religion without damage to one's social, political, and economic status on the other side. A practical solution of this potential conflict could consist in allowing people who, based on their religion, don't want to shake hands, to use alternative greeting and parting gestures that can be unambiguously recognized as tokens of respect, so as to guarantee the nonviolation of the principle of equal respect. A little bow while putting one's hand on one's chest, for instance, could be a functional equivalent of the handshake. This gesture could allow practising Muslims to abide by Islamic modesty regulations, while at the same time ensuring the display of equal respect in social interactions with both men and women. To even strengthen the unambiguousness of such an alternative gesture, people who don't want to shake hands with people of the opposite sex could be encouraged to generally refrain from handshaking in public-professional settings, and use an alternative gesture in interactions with both men and women. Actually this was the essence of the internal agreement between the Swiss school in Therwil and the two Muslim boys before the broader public and educational-political authorities drew attention to it: the two pupils were allowed to refrain from shaking hands, but they had to stop shaking hands with male as well as female teachers—to avoid the impression of unfair discrimination on the basis of gender—and they still were expected to greet in an equally polite manner, but without physical contact (see Bleisch 2016, 103).

Such an accommodation doesn't constitute a violation of the principle of equal respect, I suggest, because the rationale behind the modesty regulations in general and the prohibition of skin-to-skin contact with people of the opposite sex doesn't imply that women are morally inferior to men.[10] Allowing of alternative greeting gestures as functional equivalents of the handshake instead of making the handshake with both men and women compulsory at public institutions resembles the swearing-in or affirmation ceremony in the House of Representatives in the Netherlands and other institutions of the state. New Members of Parliament or public officials can choose whether they swear ('I swear . . . So help me, almighty God!') or affirm ('This I declare and affirm!') that they will faithfully perform the duties of the office (see Tweede Kamer der Staaten General). From the perspective of the state, these two versions are fully equivalent, and statistics aside, neither can be considered the standard. This is different in the case of the proposed accommodation with regard to the handshake, where shaking hands remains the standard and traditional Western custom, and is replaced by an alternative gesture only for those people who, because of their religion, refuse to have skin-to-skin contact with people of the opposite sex.

Things are more complicated with regard to the argument from national culture, for at least two reasons. First, this argument is based on very controversial assumptions about the concept of a 'national culture' and its normative status. And secondly, the argument allows of at least two different interpretations. As for the concept of national culture, a number of authors have pointed out that the idea of a more or less stable and homogeneous 'national culture' that is shared by virtually all members of society rests on essentialist and oversimplified assumptions regarding culture, and can hardly be sustained. '[A] national character (identity, culture, creed, etc.)', Liav Orgad points out, 'is an elusive concept' (Orgad 2015, 234; see also Baumann 1999 and Scheffler 2007). And even authors who argue that a national culture is of constitutive value for a nation and has important political functions, for instance helping to build trust in society and stabilize democracy, define the scope of national culture relatively moderately (see Miller 1995; Miller 2008; Orgad 2015). They locate, for instance, the 'culture' – the protection of which, as they suggest, can legitimately be expected by the majority – for the most part on the level of one or more shared languages, general traditions, and common values. So how should one interpret, or further develop the argument from national culture against this background? Two strategies are possible, but neither, I suggest, succeeds in justifying a general requirement to shake hands with both men and women in public institutions. The first strategy understands the handshake as a communicative sign that shows that somebody endorses a particular (national) culture, and belongs to the respective society. Here, shaking hands would be significant because of its specific communicative function as representing and indicating somebody's belonging to a particular national culture. But still, what is invested with normativity, here, is national culture, and not the handshake, which is significant only as a means to 'say something'. This makes this strategy vulnerable to the same criticism that is voiced against the argument of equal respect: other gestures could be used as functional equivalents and could indicate one's belonging to a national culture equally well. A second strategy could avoid this problem by construing the handshake as a constitutive and essential part of a national culture, thus elevating it onto the level of a shared language or values like gender equality. This would integrate handshaking into the core of a national culture that deserves, according to proponents of, for instance, cultural majority rights, to be preserved and protected against influences from people who do not, or not yet, partake in the national culture. One can interpret the claims regarding *Leitkultur* and Dutch culture that some politicians voiced in election campaigns (see above) as being in line with such a strategy, but to my knowledge none of them has ever provided reasons why the handshake should have such as status. Rather the opposite, practices like handshaking and other social standards and rules of civility are constantly submitted to contestation and revision, which is demonstrated by the relatively recent history of the handshake as egalitarian greeting gesture (see above), and numerous emancipatory struggles in the course of which similar practices have been reinterpreted, and sometimes modified, like opening doors to women, to which I will return below.

6. CONCLUSION

Up to this point, the normative analysis of the handshake-issue suggests that people who, because of their religion, refuse to shake hands with someone of the opposite sex can be accommodated. Accordingly, a general requirement to shake hands with both men and women at public institutions is morally problematic. Reasons for this are that the refusal to shake hands is based on a religious commitment to comply with Islamic modesty regulations. The two arguments for a general requirement to shake hands fail to rebut a claim for accommodation: The argument from equal respect allows of alternative contactless greeting gestures so that practicing Muslims can unambiguously communicate equal respect to both men and women, while at the same time fully complying with Islamic modesty regulations. The argument from national culture, on the other hand, is based on controversial assumptions regarding culture in general and national culture in particular, and the source of normativity with which the handshake is said to be invested.

One could object to my argumentation that the anthropological findings, which I described above, suggest that similar things could be said with regard to the religious commitment not to shake hands with people of the opposite sex. It is true that the practising Muslims whose responses are documented in studies by Batum, Fadil, and Schlatmann decided to give in to social expectations they experienced as burdening, and as hampering their efforts to adhere to Islamic modesty regulations. My proposal to accommodate nonhandshaking by agreeing on alternative practices for people who for religious reasons object to shaking hands with someone of the opposite sex does not reach out to these aspects of the issue. The space that is carved out by accommodation measures concerning the handshake-issue is a space where religious people are protected against coercive measures that would prevent them from practising their religion. It is not merely kind and benevolent if an employer tolerates their refusal to shake hands with people of the opposite sex. Rather it is unjust if people are expelled from school, or suspended from their jobs as teacher, because they refuse to shake hands with someone of the opposite sex. I have not argued, however, that justice requires the space that is carved out through accommodation to be a space in which religious practices and ideas are not burdensome, or cannot be questioned by others. In European societies, people who for religious reasons don't shake hands with someone of the opposite sex will still have to face and endure the presence of customs and expectations they perceive not only as wrong or sinful, but as constraints and burdens on practising their belief. Also relevant here is the critique of assumptions regarding female bodies, male sexuality, and the assigning of responsibility for preventing illicit sexual relations primarily to women (see above, footnote 4). The transformation of the practice of opening doors to women that I mentioned earlier demonstrates how ideas about gender equality can lead to reinterpretations and modifications of rules of civility: opening doors to women had been considered a conventional way to display men's consideration and respect for women, but is now often understood as patronizing and 'rooted in demeaning assumptions about women's weakness and need for male protection' (Calhoun 2000, 262–63; see also Galeotti 2017, 543). The fact mentioned above that Muslim feminists criticize traditional Islamic gender roles indicates that Islamic modesty regulations can also be in the center of such transformative struggles, and justice does not require anybody to refrain from contributing to debates about such processes. Since the accommodation that I suggest keeps existing rules of civility and corresponding expectations in place, such accommodation doesn't prevent negotiation processes such as those described above being catalysed by existing customs and expectations. Subjects and authors of such negotiation and transformation processes, however, are religious people themselves, in their religious communities.

ACKNOWLEDGEMENTS

An earlier draft of this chapter was presented at a conference on Public Life and Religious Diversity at Harris Manchester College, Oxford University, and the research colloquium Religious Studies at Utrecht University. I would like to thank participants for their feedback. Particular thanks to Christian Lange, Birgit Meyer, Andrew Shorten, and Jonathan Seglow for very helpful comments.

REFERENCES

Alidadi, Katayoun. 2017. *Religion, Equality and Employment in Europe*. Oxford and Portland, Oregon: Hart Publishing.

Balkenhol, Markus, Paul Mepschen, and Jan Willem Duyvendak. 2016. 'The Nativist Triangle: Sexuality, Race and Religion in the Netherlands'. In *The Culturalization of Citizenship. Belonging and Polarization in a Globalizing World*, edited by Jan Willem Duyvendak, Peter Geschiere, and Evelien Tonkens, 97–112. London: Palgrave Macmillan.

Batum, Deniz. 2016. 'Handshaking in the Secular: Understanding Agency of Veiled Turkish-Dutch Muslim Students'. *GÉNEROS—Multidisciplinary Journal of Gender Studies* 5 (1): 962–85.

Baumann, Gerd. 1999. *The Multicultural Riddle. Rethinking National, Ethnic, and Religious Identities*. New York: Routledge.

BKSD Bildungs-, Kultur- und Sportdirektion Kanton Basel-Landschaft. 2016. Rechtsabklärung vom 14. April. Schüler verweigern Lehrerinnen den Handschlag. https://www.baselland.ch/politik-und-behorden/direktionen/bildungs-kultur-und-sportdirektion/medienmitteilungen/verweigerter-handedruck-an-schule-therwil/downloads/haendedruck_rechtsabklaerung.pdf.

Bleisch, Petra. 2016. 'Der "Fall Therwil"—(Nicht-)Händeschütteln in der Schule als Frage berufsethischen Handelns'. *Zeitschrift für Religionskunde* 3: 102–07.

Bou-Habib, Paul. 2016. 'A Theory of Religious Accommodation'. *Journal of Applied Philosophy* 23 (1): 109–216.

Breeden, Aurelia. 2018. 'No Handshake, No Citizenship'. *New York Times*, 21 April. https://www.nytimes.com/2018/04/21/world/europe/handshake-citizenship-france.html.

Bucar, Elizabeth. 2012. *The Islamic Veil*. Oxford: Oneworld Publications.

Buss, Sarah. 1999. 'Appearing Respectful: The Moral Significance of Manners'. *Ethics* 109 (4): 795–826.

Calhoun, Cheshire. 2000. 'The Virtue of Civility'. *Philosophy and Public Affairs* 29 (3): 251–75.

Es, Margreet, van. 2018. 'Muslims Denouncing Violent Extremism'. *Journal of Muslims in Europe* 7 (2): 146–66.

Fadil, Nadia. 2009. 'Managing Affects and Sensibilities: The Case of Not-Handshaking and Not-Fasting'. *Social Anthropology* 17 (4): 439–54.

Galeotti, Anna Elisabetta. 2017. 'Cultural Conflicts: A Deflationary Approach.' *Critical Review of International Social and Political Philosophy* 20 (5): 537–55.

Geschiere, Peter. 2009. *Perils of Belonging. Autochthony, Citizenship, and Exclusion in Africa and Europe*. Chicago: University of Chicago Press.

Katsumi, Yuta, Suhkyung Kin, Keen Sung, Florin Dolcos, and Sanda Dolcos. 2017. 'When Nonverbal Greetings "Make It or Break It": The Role of Ethnicity and Gender in the Effect of Handshake on Social Appraisals'. *Journal of Nonverbal Behavior* 41: 345–65.

Katz, Marion H. 2017. 'Gender and Law'. In *Encyclopedia of Islam, THREE*, edited by Gudrun Krämer, Denis Matringe, John Nawas, and Everett Rowson. Brill Online. http://dx.doi.org.proxy.library.uu.nl/10.1163/1573-3912_ei3_COM_27397.

Krawietz, Birgit. 2013. 'Body, in Law'. In *Encyclopedia of Islam, THREE*, edited by Gudrun Krämer, Denis Matringe, John Nawas, and Everett Rowson. Brill Online. http://dx.doi.org.proxy.library.uu.nl/10.1163/1573-3912_ei3_COM_23722.

Lange, Christian. 2013. 'Vom Recht sich zu verhüllen. Dimensionen der Privatsphäre im muslimischen fiqh'. In *Jahrbuch für Verfassung, Recht und Staat im islamischen Kontext* , edited by Peter Scholz, Christine Langenfeld, Jens Scheiner and Naseef Naeem, 35–52. Baden-Baden: Nomos.

Mahmood, Saba. 2005. *Politics of Piety: The Islamic Revival and the Feminist Subject.* Princeton, NJ: Princeton University Press.

———. 2016. *Religious Difference in a Secular Age: A Minority Report.* Princeton, NJ: Princeton University Press.

Manz, Stefan. 2004. 'Constructing a Normative National Identity: The *Leitkultur* Debate in Germany, 2000/2001'. *Journal of Multilingual and Multicultural Development* 25 (5–6): 481–96.

Miller, David. 1995. *On Nationality*. Oxford: Oxford University Press.

———. 2008. 'Immigrants, Nations, and Citizenship'. *The Journal of Political Philosophy* 16 (4): 371–90.

Nussbaum, Martha. 2008. *Liberty of Conscience: In Defense of America's Tradition of Religious Equality*. New York: Basic Books.

Ohlert, Martin. 2015. *Zwischen 'Multikulturalismus' und 'Leitkultur'. Integrationsleitbild und –politik der im 17. Deutschen Bundestag vertretenen Parteien*. Wiesbaden: Springer VS.

Orgad, Liav. 2015. *The Cultural Defense of Nations*. Oxford: Oxford University Press.

Patten. Alan. 2017. 'The Normative Logic of Religious Liberty'. *The Journal of Political Philosophy* 25 (2): 129–54.

Pautz, Hartwig. 2005. 'The Politics of Identity in Germany: The Leitkultur Debate'. *Race & Class* 46 (4): 39–52.

Roodenburg, Herman. 1991. 'The "Hand of Friendship": Shaking Hands and Other Gestures in the Dutch Republic'. In *A Cultural History of Gesture: From Antiquity to the Present Day*, edited by Jan Bremmer and Herman Roodenburg, 152–89. Cambridge: Polity Press.

Scheffler, Samuel. 2007. 'Immigration and the Significance of Culture'. *Philosophy and Public Affairs* 35 (2): 93–125.

Schlatmann, Annemeik. 2016. 'Shi'i Muslim youth in the Netherlands: Negotiating Shi'i Fatwas and Rituals in the Dutch Context'. PhD diss., Utrecht University.

Seglow, Jonathan. 2017. 'Religious Accommodation: Responsibility, Integrity, and Self-Respect'. In *Religion in Liberal Political Philosophy*, edited by Cécile Laborde and Aurelia Bardon, 177–90. Oxford: Oxford University Press.

Slootman, Marieke, and Jan Willem Duyvendak. 2015. 'Feeling Dutch: The Culturalization and Emotionalization of Citizenship and Second-Generation Belonging to the Netherlands'. In *Fear, Anxiety, and National Identity. Immigration and Belonging in North America and Western Europe*, edited by Nancy Foner and Patrik Simon, 147–68. New York: The Russell Sage Foundation.

Spectorsky, Susan A. 2010. *Women in Classical Islam: A Survey of the Sources*. Leiden and Boston: Brill.

Stohr, Karin. 2006. 'Manners, Morals, and Practical Wisdom'. In *Values and Virtues. Aristotelianism in Contemporary Ethics*, edited by Timothy Chappell, 189–211. Oxford: Clarendon Press.

———. 2012. *On Manners*. New York: Routledge.

Tweede Kamer der Staaten General. n.d. 'New Members of the House of Representatives'. www.houseofrepresentatives.nl/new-members-house-representatives.

Uitermark, Justus, Paul Mepschen, and Jan Willem Duyvendak. 2013. 'Populism, Sexual Politics, and the Exclusion of Muslims in the Netherlands'. In *European States and Their Muslim Citizens: The Impact of Institutions on Perceptions and Boundaries,* edited by John Bowen, Christophe Bertossi, Jan Willem Duyvendak, and Mona Lena Krook, 25–255. Cambridge: Cambridge University Press.

NOTES

1. In my use of the term 'opposite sex' (instead of 'gender') I follow the dominant terminology in the literature about such cases.

2. See Alidadi (2017, 213–23).

3. In Orthodox Judaism, there are similar regulations that restrict physical interactions with people of the opposite sex. In this chapter, I focus on controversies about Muslims who refused to shake hands with people of the opposite sex, but I expect that some of the considerations and arguments apply to cases involving orthodox Jews as well.

4. Elizabeth Bucar points out that discussions on *'awra* and *fitna* in classical Islamic law focused mainly on the prevention of illicit sexual encounters. They linked *fitna* to modesty practices of women 'by marking women's bodies as dangerous and disorderly' (Bucar 2012, 58). It is important, however, to notice that Bucar and Mahmood describe traditional Islamic legal discourse, here. Mahmood emphasizes that Muslim feminist scholars have criticized the differential gender roles that are included in such legal reasoning, and points out that in various contexts – she mentions Iran – Muslim activists argue that equality of men and women in the eyes of God also means that men and women 'equally share the burden of guarding against illicit sexual desire and conduct' (Mahmood 2005, 112).

5. The Arabic term *mahram* refers to the immediate family; members of this group cannot marry, and hence cannot have licit sexual relations. A women's male *mahram* include her father, father-in-law, sons, stepsons, brothers, and nephews (cf. Spectorsky 2010, 190).

6. The reference to people other than the target of civility is from Stohr (2006, 193). Other people who witness an act of civility are important, since civil or uncivil behavior can strengthen or damage the social standing of the recipient.

7. See BKSD (2016, section 2.3.3). 'Even if Islam seems to understand a refusal of the handshake as expression of respect for women, it is still to be evaluated according to the meaning it has in our local value system. Here the refusal is understood as resulting from a patriarchal attitude according to which women are not equal to men' (my translation).

8. An illustrative example of this is an event in 1966 when the then sitting President of the Federal Republic of Germany Heinrich Lübke visited the Togolese Republic; Lübke did not want to shake hands with the President of Togo Gnassingbé Eyadéma because Eyadéma was said to have contracted a killer to eliminate his predecessor Sylvanus Olympio, who was a friend of Lübke. He knew, however, that an open refusal to shake hands with President Eyadéma would have been understood as straightforward insult, so he encased his right arm with a plaster cast, which allowed him to avoid the symbolic gesture of the handshake with Eyadéma without causing a diplomatic scandal.

9. In the following I provide a rather charitable reconstruction of the argument from national culture. In actual debates, more Islamophobic and nationalistic versions of this argument have also been voiced.

10. See the description of Islamic modesty regulations above. Of course one can criticize these regulations and a number of the underlying assumptions, such as the view that the prime responsibility for (the prevention of) illicit sexual relationships is on the side of women and their bodies (see above, footnote 4). This is not the same, however, as denying women equal moral status and equal respect.

Part III

The New Challenges of Religious Diversity

EIGHT

Compromise and Religious Accommodation

Élise Rouméas

Religious accommodation is pervaded by negotiated deals and *ad hoc* arrangements. Major reforms, such as compulsory state education, could not have passed without concessions made on each side. Public institutions, such as hospitals, prisons, and schools, have had to respond to increasing demands from religious individuals requesting special accommodations. Urban spaces have been the scenes of tailored adjustments ensuring that minority religious communities could have access to places of worship. Some of these formal or informal agreements may be described using the label of 'compromise'. As this chapter argues, there is a space for compromise in a politics of religious accommodation.

There has been much discussion on religious accommodation, on the one hand, and a growing interest in the ethics of compromise, on the other, but little dialogue has taken place between the two bodies of literature. Political theorists have debated the justifiability of exemptions to generally applicable laws (Barry 2001, Jones 2016, Laborde 2017, Laborde and Bardon 2017, Maclure and Taylor 2011, Quong 2006, Seglow 2011). Many have argued that there are reasons of justice to exempt some individuals from the burden of particular rules on grounds of convictions, religious or otherwise. Such legal exemptions include, paradigmatically, conscientious objection to military service or the exemption for religious slaughter. In addition to legal exemptions, cases have been made for special accommodations in school or in the workplace to allow religious individuals to combine their occupational requirements with their conscientious commitments.

The idea of compromise often appears in the background of discussion around religious accommodation. Being accommodating requires a degree of flexibility, a willingness to concede and to work out mutually satisfactory arrangements. Compromise as such has been a topic of discussion among political philosophers and theorists (Bellamy 1999, Benjamin 1990, Fumurescu 2013, Gutmann and Thompson 2014, Jones and O'Flynn 2013, Margalit 2010, May 2005, Pennock and Chapman 1979, Rostbøll and Scavenius 2018, Weinstock 2013, Wendt 2018). Authors have discussed, among other things, the reasons to concede in face of moral or political disagreement, the morality of compromise, and its relationship with fairness.

This chapter argues that compromise is a desirable feature of religious accommodation. I am primarily concerned with compromise *as a way of making decision*, rather than compromise *as a decision*. The process of compromise – the exercise of exchanging concessions – can lead to a variety of outcomes. I am not arguing that these outcomes are qualitatively better than the outcomes of, say, deliberation or voting. Instead, I claim that compromise, as a decision-making procedure, has a key role to play in dealing with the practicalities of accommodation on grounds of religion or belief.

The chapter begins with an account of compromise. Compromise is defined as a decision-making procedure based on reciprocal concessions. I distinguish compromise from bargaining on the one hand, and from deliberation, on the other, and I present a view of compromise centred around the norm of reciprocity. The next section identifies different instances of religious accommodation in which compromise has a role to play, including when accommodations are not required by justice, when they stir conflicting claims, and when they generate new unfairness. The final section argues that compromise should be an essential component of religious accommodation, at least in some cases. Compromise expresses an ethos of mutual concern and achieves innovative arrangements that distribute the burdens among the parties involved. Several examples illustrate the argument.

1. COMPROMISE AS A DECISION-MAKING PROCEDURE

I define compromise as a decision-making procedure based on reciprocal concessions. In a situation of conflict between two or more parties holding incompatible claims, compromise is way of reaching an agreement: each party discounts its initial aspiration until the collective finds a mutually satisfactory arrangement.

The term 'compromise' has been used to refer to both a process and an outcome (Golding 1979, 7). As a process, compromise is a method to make collective decisions based on reciprocal concessions. As an outcome, it is a proposal that works as a second-best for parties involved in a conflict. Each party has an aspiration point, what they hope to achieve, and a conflict point, the threshold at which they refuse an agreement and remain in conflict. The compromise falls somewhere in between.

It is rather common in the literature to distinguish compromise from bargaining (Benditt 1979, Leydet 2006). The crucial difference lies in the attitude of the parties. To bargain is to further one's interest as much as possible through a process of give-and-take. Participants to a bargain are primarily utility-maximisers and they do not share a joint strategy. To compromise involves taking into consideration other parties' interests through a process of exchanging concessions. Compromisers are conciliatory and willing to make some sacrifices to reach a mutually satisfactory solution. In that respect, compromise can be construed as a thinly moralized version of bargaining, which is more cooperative.

In practice, it is difficult, often impossible, to neatly distinguish between a bargain and a compromise. Actors' motivations are mixed, opaque, and preparedness to compromise can emerge in the midst of fierce bargains. Negotiations are messy and proposals to 'split the difference' are not always equitable. Many processes fail. The politics of compromise remains an ongoing process of trial and error.

Compromise has also been contrasted with deliberation (May 2005, Elster 2000, Leydet 2006, Weinstock 2017). Compromise differs from deliberation insofar as concession differs from revision of beliefs. An agent making a concession is yielding something to another agent in the context of a dispute. A concession is a necessary, but not a sufficient condition to reach a compromise. If the concession is unilateral – the other agent does not reciprocate – the outcome can be interpreted as a painful defeat or as a generous and noble act, but it fails to be a compromise. A compromise is defined by a reciprocal exchange of concessions.

Revision, by contrast, is not about yielding something to someone, but rather about endorsing an updated or alternative view, more publicly justifiable than the initial one. Unlike concession, revision does not entail a loss. Agents share public reasons in the hope of reaching a common ground, and they are willing to update their own view in the process. The exchange of reasons sheds light on each position, allows for mutual understanding and critical scrutiny, and ideally leads to the formation of a consensus.

Compromise works differently. It requires no such a thing as a revision of belief. Participants typically hold the exact same view before and after a compromise: they remain steadfast about the core of the matter under dispute. There is no need to formulate arguments on behalf of a specific position to work out a compromise. Instead, parties negotiate concessions by offering to concede in return, and by convincing others that it is worth discounting one's aspirations for the sake of securing an agreement. Both deliberation and compromise involve rational persuasion, but their aim is different. Participants in deliberation aim to critical-ly assess each other's reasons. Compromisers aim to convince others to make certain concessions in return for others. In the messiness of political life, these practices may be hard to disentangle, but the theoretical distinction remains relevant and compelling.

Some authors have conceptualized the distinction between reasons for revision and reasons for concession by speaking of 'first-order' and 'second-order reasons' (May 2005, Weinstock 2013). First-order reasons for revision concern the respective merits of conflicting positions. They support and justify political convictions. In the abortion controversy, prolife or prochoice arguments are first-order reasons. My conviction on, say, the right of fetuses to life, gives me a first-order reason to hold a certain position on whether a right to abortion is justified. Second-order reasons for compromise concern the attitude one should have in face of a disagreement. How firmly should I hold on to my position? They include principled reasons, such as mutual respect, as well as pragmatic considerations, such as preserving a harmonious relationship with a political opponent. For example, my firm belief in freedom of conscience can lead me to concede that abortion should not be publicly funded, even if it should be made widely accessible.

The distinction between consensus and compromise stems from this distinction. Participants to a consensus converge on a proposal that is perceived as correct, or superior to the other options on the basis of first-order reasons. Compromisers reluctantly accept an arrangement (on the basis of second-order reasons) that they perceive as inferior to their initial aspirations (on the basis of first-order reasons). Compromisers only secure a second-best option, whereas a consensus solution is perceived as a first-best by those endorsing it.

So far so good. Now that I have highlighted the distinctiveness of compromise with respect to bargaining and deliberation, I must account for what makes compromise procedurally effective and (potentially) fair.

Some might resist the claim that compromise should be called a procedure. When compared to voting, compromise seems quite an informal way of making decisions. We compromise all the time in interpersonal relationships. Compromise occurs almost unexpectedly and fails to be reached when parties actively seek it. In a collective discussion, practices of bargaining, compromise, and deliberation may be hard to disentangle. The exchange of persuasive arguments may coexist with the use of promise and threat (Elster 2000). Compromise is not a very formal and neat process for making decisions.

Yet, compromise indicates an effective procedural path to overcome conflicts. This path can be described in three steps.

The first step is the readiness to let go of one's initial aspirations, at least in part. Compromise relies on a risky gamble, the gamble of conceding in the hope of securing an agreement. Various second-order reasons to concede have been highlighted in the literature, some pragmatic, such as peace, and others principled, such as respect for the opponent or a communitarian ethos (Gutmann and Thompson 2014; May 2005; Weinstock 2017). Choosing compromise implies being open to a cooperative solution that will take into consideration the interests of all parties involved. To be sure, compromisers are not disinterested. They do hope to further their interests in the process. But unlike strategic bargainers, they are also cooperatively minded. They are willing to adjust their strategy to reach a mutually beneficial outcome.

Such a cooperative attitude is valuable for instrumental reasons. Cooperation is useful to achieve a collective outcome, as parties coordinate their strategies and share information. Furthermore, cooperation is susceptible to produce better outcomes than noncooperative ways of allocating preferences. Each party is ideally situated to provide factual knowledge about her specific situation and to articulate her interest. Cooperatively minded parties can work out arrangements that are both well-informed and mutually beneficial.

I will not provide evidence for the instrumental value of cooperation. Instead, I want to argue that this value does not lie exclusively in the outcome it generates. Cooperation is also valuable because it expresses certain values, such as collective autonomy and equal respect. For instance, it matters that employees in a firm can cooperate to design the rules that bind them. The cooperative setting creates a situation of rough equality when it comes to solving the problem at hand. The input of all parties is equally needed for a collective outcome to be found. The cooperative dimension of compromise can allow for such an equal participation. But these values are not specific to compromise and are conveyed by other procedures as well. In particular, majority rule expresses collective autonomy and equal respect for each participant's voice.

What is perhaps specific to compromise is the ethos of mutual concern that underlies the logic of concessions giving. No decision can be taken without granting part of the opponent's demands and thus discounting one's aspirations. The act of conceding expresses an acknowledgement of the opponent's perspective and a readiness to adopt at least some of their claims. There is no need to adopt such a standpoint in a voting process. Although an ethos of mutual respect is present in deliberation, it merely demands to take seriously the opponents' views by critically engaging with them, not by granting anything to them. There is something specific, and intrinsically valuable, in the readiness to cooperate by conceding.

The second step is the reciprocal move. One concession should respond to the other party's concession until an agreement is found. The norm of reciprocity governs the logic of loss-loss: concessions should be appropriate and proportionate (Becker 1986; Gould 1988; Gouldner 1960). A collective exercise takes place to achieve a rough equivalency between concessions. Each party is responsible for evaluating its sacrifice in light of the other's sacrifice. This can be a tedious process, and it can fail at any time. The concession of the other side may be deemed insignificant, while it appears painfully costly in the eyes of the one who concedes.

The last step follows from this collective evaluation: it is the act of mutual consent. When parties reckon that the dynamics of concession has led to an acceptable outcome, they agree with the arrangement. The possibility of mutual consent is a check which helps to prevent asymmetrical deals that poorly reflect the norm of reciprocity.

In my account, reciprocity (associated with consent) is the key norm that makes compromise procedurally fair. The relationship between compromise and fairness is complex and multifold (Jones and O'Flynn 2013; Wendt forthcoming). This complexity arises in part from the different facets of compromise itself. As I said, compromise can refer to both a process and an outcome. Similarly, the fairness of compromise can refer to both procedural fairness and the substantive fairness of the outcome. The relationship between the two also demands clarification: is the fairness of the outcome a mere product of procedural fairness?

A full account of the relationship between compromise and fairness is beyond the scope of this chapter. What matters for my purpose is that compromise is based on a rule of proportionality – the norm of reciprocity – which guides the allocation of burdens and benefits, or more precisely, the adjustment of losses. Parties are responsible for internally evaluating the equivalency of concessions. Their consenting to the final arrangement indicates that an equilibrium between concessions has been reached.

In practice, compromise remains an imperfect instrument of fairness. Many external considerations weigh upon the procedural fairness of actual compromises. For example, how to account for unfairness in the initial allocation? How do power disparities affect the fairness of compromise?[1] If strict reciprocity occurs in a situation of unfair asymmetry, the existing bias will only be reproduced. Not all conflicts ought to be resolved by compromise. In the next section, I argue that compromise is desirable at least in some instances of religious accommodation.

2. THE SPACE FOR COMPROMISE IN RELIGIOUS ACCOMMODATION

There is a space for compromise in religious accommodation. Accommodation refers to adjustments made on behalf of individuals or groups holding various commitments, especially religious ones, because they clash with existing rules or arrangements. Adjustments can take various forms, including exemptions from general laws or specific regulations, or special arrangements, such as tailoring work schedules or providing for dietary requirements on religious grounds.

Some religious accommodations are aptly construed as *concessions*. Suffice it to look at the list of examples given by the Bouchard and Taylor report on 'reasonable accommodations' and 'informal agreements' (Bouchard and Taylor 2008). Most of them seem to involve a small concession on the part of the institution accommodating religious claims. To cite but a few examples: In 2002, the hospital Sainte-Justine authorized some Jews to install a special fridge for kosher food in the patients waiting room. In 2006, the Antoine-Brossard secondary school in Montreal authorized three Muslim students to take the swimming exam with female supervisors only and with closed windows (Bouchard and Taylor 2008, 54). In these examples, the cost incurred by the institution seems rather small. In other examples, the adjustment is more susceptible to raise discontent. For instance: In 2001, the administration renamed the Christmas tree near the Montreal town hall 'the tree of life'. And it was temporarily removed in November 2002 (Bouchard and Taylor 2008, 69). In November 2006, the hospital CLSC Sainte-Rose in Laval allowed a Jewish patient to skip the queue to be treated on time to be discharged for the beginning of Shabbat (Bouchard and Taylor 2008, 55).

Other arrangements stem from processes of give-and-take and distribute the costs between the parties involved. For instance, Denis Maillard (2017, 210–11) describes the case of a small French business where four employees out of seven requested a scheduling arrangement during the time of Ramadan. They wanted to start work early and leave early. The first year, their manager denied them the accommodation without any discussion. The following year, she adopted a different approach and initiated a collective discussion on how to best organize the working schedule during Ramadan. Non-Muslim workers complained that the scheduling arrangement requested by their coworkers would have a detrimental impact on their own workload. It was indeed at the end of the workday that much of the activity was happening. The Muslim workers gave up on their initial request, but they were able to take some days off during the following Ramadan. This worked as a satisfactory compromise between them, their coworkers, and the manager.

To be clear, the concept of compromise should not be used to interpret each and every case of accommodation. Some legal exemptions are rather one-sided – the state carving an exception into a law to unburden some citizens holding minority religious beliefs – while others arise from negotiated processes. But my main claim is normative, not empirical: some instances of accommodation *should* be addressed with compromise.

Which specific instances of accommodation call for compromise? Three situations are compelling candidates. The first one is when an accommodation is not required by justice, but still desirable. The second one is when an accommodation occurs at the intersection of conflicting rationales of justice and a balancing exercise is necessary. The last one is when an exemption generates new unfairness that demands some form of compensation.

The first instance is quite straightforward: the spirit of compromise motivates accommodations beyond the demands of justice. Not all accommodations are required by justice. In fact, many are best conceived of as *ad hoc* arrangements arising from the mere willingness to be accommodating. Peter Jones thus argues that legal exemptions need not be 'grounded in justice' (Jones 2017). Instead, they are better construed as '"defensible" or "reasonable" arrangement in all of the relevant circumstances' (Jones 2017). The example cited above of the special kosher fridge in the hospital Sainte-Justine is a good example of a generous gesture towards the Hassidic Jewish community which seems supererogatory – more than what is necessary for the hospital to fulfill its duties. As a self-inflicted sacrifice, the act of concession has an altruistic dimension to it.[2] Concession, or the willingness to compromise, finds a space beyond what justice requires.

Even if some religious accommodations are not required by justice, they need to be handled fairly in order to avoid injustices. Accommodations often happen at the intersection of competing claims that need to be taken into consideration. This is the second instance I have in mind. Consider the example cited above of the Jewish patient allowed to skip the queue to honor the beginning of Shabbat. Surely, healthcare professionals at the hospital CLSC Sainte-Rose in Laval must have balanced several considerations before reaching that decision: How urgent were the cases of other patients that day? How central for the Jewish patient faith was the ritual of Shabbat? Were there healthcare professionals available to treat him on time without excessive costs?

Similar scenarios are frequent in the workplace environment, as the example of the Muslim workers in the French business illustrates. Many competing considerations can influence whether a specific scheduling arrangement should be granted to a religious worker. The worker has an interest in combining her professional activity with the obligations of her faith. This can be justified by invoking the protection of individual integrity and the interest in coherence between one's normative commitments and one's actions (Laborde 2017; Seglow 2017). The firm has an interest in economic profitability. Accommodating some religious claims may end up being costly and detrimental to the business productivity. And workers have an interest in equitable treatment. Some nonreligious workers may have weighty reasons to request scheduling flexibility as well. The balancing exercise between different interests is complex and highly contextual. For example, the size of the business matters, as well as the nature of the activity. A shortage of staff is more consequential in a fire department than in a clothing store. Compromise can usefully arbitrate between different claims by directly involving the parties involved in a conflict. They are best situated to express their demands and articulate their interests.

The last instance stems from the previous one: there are cases of conflicting claims in which a degree of reciprocity matters, especially when a law or a regulation is associated with an ideal of fair cooperation, that is, when it matters for reasons of fairness that the burdens of cooperation are distributed rather equally among participants. As I argued earlier, a central element of the normative framework of compromise is reciprocity. In practice, accommodations often look like *one-sided concessions*. Many of the examples cited above do not involve any concession on the part of the beneficiary of an exemption. In some cases, reciprocity is not to be expected. For instance, when an exemption aims at rectifying a situation in which a religious minority is unfairly disadvantaged – in a majority bias scenario (Laborde 2017) – it makes little sense to expect a reciprocal concession from the beneficiary of an exemption.

However, many scenarios do not fit the majority bias case. A paradigmatic example is the exemption from military service. The debate around conscientious objection to military service occurred in France in the early 1960s. The dispute was portrayed as a dilemma between the equality of all before the law and freedom of conscience. At the time, conscientious objectors were mostly Jehovah's Witnesses refusing to bear arms for religious reasons, as well as some members of mainstream religions, Protestants and Catholics, and some anarchists and secular pacifists. A very contentious negotiation eventually gave rise to a legal status for conscientious objectors. The status was a compromise between the defenders of the status quo and those advocating a full-fledged exemption. It fell somewhere in between, giving the option of a two-year civilian service under restrictive conditions.

It mattered for the justification of the conscription that all young men were treated equally, irrespective of their social background. Men were equal before the law and before the obligation to participate in the collective effort and risk of defending the nation. As a result, legal exemptions were not costless for objectors. They had to complete a lengthy civilian service instead of the standard military service. The civilian service was the cost that the beneficiary of an exemption had to bear in exchange of the benefit of being exempting from military service. An element of reciprocity appeared in this exemption to respond to a concern of fairness: it was unfair that some would risk their young lives while others would be exempted from any burden. The civilian service mitigated the asymmetry by compensating for the unfairness generated by the exemption.

When several parties with conflicting interests are involved and reciprocity matters, compromise is a useful way of making collective decisions and resolving conflicts. Military service is not the only instance of accommodation where fairness demands some measure of reciprocity. In some cases, it might be appropriate to ask workers benefiting from scheduling arrangements on religious grounds to compensate for the benefits they receive. Here, the idea of reciprocal concessions, at the core of compromise, can help to work out a fair arrangement in allocating costs and benefits.

3. WHAT COMPROMISE EXPRESSES AND ACHIEVES

There are two reasons why compromise, understood as a series of negotiated reciprocal concessions, should be a key component of a politics of religious accommodation. The first reason relates to what compromise *expresses*, what I call an ethos of mutual concern. The second reason relates to what compromise *achieves*, namely innovative arrangements based on reciprocity. These reasons are not exhaustive and they do not apply exclusively to religious accommodation. Compromise is needed in many other domains. Yet, the context of religious accommodation is a fertile ground for compromise, as it involves situations of conflicting claims that call for *ad hoc* resolutions.

The first reason why compromise is desirable in religious accommodation lies in what it expresses. The cooperative attitude at the core of compromise expresses an ethos of mutual concern. Recall the first step in the process of compromise: the compromiser accepts a self-inflicted loss for the sake of finding a cooperative solution. No one can ensure that such sacrifice will be reciprocated. It is both a risky gamble and a generous gesture towards the other side.

Compromise has been associated with the values accommodation and inclusiveness. Yet, not everyone agrees that they give us principled reasons to compromise. Simon Căbulea May argues that accommodation does not require compromise, but inclusive procedures (May 2005). A democratic government is under no obligation to work out a compromise with an opponent's position. Policies need not represent the diversity of views among political parties and citizens. Yet, there are other ways to ensure the inclusiveness of procedures without having to resort to compromise. Specifically, policy deliberations can seek to improve their openness to political pluralism and the participation of ordinary citizens. A process of law-making can be inclusive without generating a compromise policy.

Daniel Weinstock replies to May's objection by stressing the limits of democratic procedures, which are not always fair nor inclusive (Weinstock 2013). Power asymmetries or educational differentials create deliberative distortions. Some groups struggle to have their voice heard, while others dominate the debate and control the agenda. Given such biases, partially integrating the input of political opponents can work as a corrective mechanism. Compromise is a way to make up for failures of democratic inclusion in practice. An accommodating society is preferable to a 'winner-take-all society'.

The contentious question in this discussion is whether the values of accommodation and inclusiveness give us principled reasons to compromise at the policy level. My claim is related: I argue that compromise expresses mutual concern.

A good way of illustrating this expressive value is to contrast compromise with another way of making collective decisions. The French firm PAPREC, a recycling undertaking located in the Northern Parisian suburb, designed a Charter of *laïcité* proscribing any religious signs (Maillard 2017, 70). The four thousand employees of the firm, a diverse group composed of fifty-six nationalities, adopted the Charter by 'referendum'. In this example, majority rule is used to ratify a set of rules governing the exercise of religious freedom in the firm. Whether the process was fair remains to be seen, but I leave this question aside. The use of majority rule fosters the participation of those affected and is an exercise in collective autonomy. It also gives equal weight to the voice of each participant. But it does not require the same cooperative attitude as the one involved in a compromise. An analogous decision taken through a process of compromise would demand an active engagement with those who disagree with the Charter as well as an effort to meet at least some of their demands. Choosing compromise over majority rule would signal a much deeper concern for others' perspectives, including minority views. It would require concessions to be made on both sides, a reciprocal sacrifice.

In the French military service example mentioned above, a concern for minority views is expressed in the midst of fierce debates in Parliament. Member of Parliament René Capitant declared: 'Jehovah's Witnesses, however few they are, have their belief. Would they be only one of these witnesses, his belief would no less warrant our respect.' In a similar vein, MP Eugène Claudius-Petit claimed: 'I am not a conscientious objector; I do not have to approve conscientious objectors; I have to try to understand them and I also have to strive to apply the law of democracy to the very end, for democracy is truly perfect only when the smallest minorities feel protected.' The concern for a religious minority, the Jehovah's Witnesses, was presented as a compelling reason to choose compromise.

In addition to its expressive value, compromise is desirable because of what it achieves. Compromise is a useful procedure to make decisions and resolve conflicts. Compromise can handle conflicting preferences in three different ways: division, integration, and substitution. These different scenarios can all be present in the three instances of compromise mentioned in the previous section. While the former distinction refers to the circumstances of compromise, this one distinguishes different types of compromise by examining how they treat preferences.

The first scenario consists in dividing and allocating a disputed re-source. Compromisers find an intermediary point C between positions A and B hold by agents in conflict. Consider a case where two religious communities dispute a piece of land on which to build a place of worship. One way of allocating the contested resource is to divide the territory among the parties. Another option is to let one party use the land, in exchange of a side payment given to the other party. Or, if feasible, a common place of worship can be built and shared among the parties, as it is sometimes the case with multifaith spaces. Compromise by allocation need not be strictly about splitting the disputed good, but can use compensative mechanisms or share the time of use.

For instance, the city of Roubaix (France) and its Muslim community struck a compromise on the question of the place of worship.[3] The Da'Wa mosque did not meet the criteria of safety required to host eight hundred attendants on Friday evenings. The city authorized the Muslim community to use the public gymnasium *Buffon*, in exchange for the small sum of ninety euros an hour. A side payment compensated for the concession granted by the city. The elected authorities were described as 'conciliatory' by the local newspaper *La Voix du Nord.* They declared: 'We couldn't leave them without a solution'.[4] Some concessions were made on various sides, given that the public gymnasium was usually used by the local school. But it was finally agreed that 'the gym mats will be replaced a few hours on Friday by the prayer mats'.[5] The arrangement worked until 2016, when the renovated mosque eventually reopened.

The second compromise scenario consists in integrating elements from antagonistic camps in a collective decision. No one's view is fully endorsed, but aspects of opposing views are reflected in the outcome. What makes it a compromise is the fact that the decision is perceived as a second-best by the parties who adopt it. Many legislative bills combine inputs from several political groups. A law on abortion can decriminalize the voluntary interruption of pregnancy while not allowing public funding for abortion. A law enforcing compulsory state education can nevertheless include the possibility of homeschooling under certain conditions. Such compromise laws are very common. They do not take the side of one rationale of justice over another, but exhibit instead a normative patchwork. Although they can be accused of lacking coherence and integrity, they can play a key role in incrementally changing the status quo on polarized matters.

An interesting example of 'compromise by integration' was achieved in 2011, in the Montreal Correction Services Department. Following the case of prison guard Sondos Abdelatif winning a case after being fired for wearing a hijab at work, an innovative arrangement was found for accommodating Muslim correctional agents: they could now be equipped with hijabs with Velco strips that meet the safety requirements of the correctional facility. In this example, the integration between the requirement of safety and the obligation of faith found a tangible conciliation in an innovative device (St-Onge 2015, 19–20).

The last compromise scenario consists in substituting an alternative option to the parties' conflicting demands. In the face of incompatible claims, a 'third way' is adopted that works as a second-best for compromisers. Substitution involves finding an original alternative to overcome a conflictual deadlock. Consider the hypothetical case where religious leaders from different sects are invited to lead a public ceremony of collective mourning after a tragedy. The leaders disagree with one another's approach to religious ritual and fail to reconcile their different practices. They finally agree to substitute prayers and hymns with low-key ecumenical speeches. None of the parties is fully satisfied with the outcome, but a way out of the impasse has been found.

The politics of religious accommodation includes attempts to find 'ecumenical' substitutes to sectarian symbols. On 10 October 2000, the city of Outremont, Canada, adopted a resolution to substitute the traditional prayer with a 'secular invocation' (Bouchard and Taylor 2008, 50). This decision was made following a complaint of the *Mouvement laïque québecois* (MLC), an association promoting secularism. The details of the negotiation are not publicized, but the outcome indicates a 'compromise by substitution': it does not fully abandon the practice of the prayer nor maintain the status quo, but adopts a third option, the secular invocation, namely the public reading of a text about prudent government. In January 2017, the secular invocation was again replaced by a minute of silence.[6] Whether these substitutes really are ecumenical remains to be seen, but they aim to transcend sectarianism with an alternative option.

All three compromise scenarios can succeed in resolving conflicts. Compromise crucially leads to a reconfiguration of the conflict options. Each scenario adds options to the discussion table, whether it be an allocation plan, a hybrid law proposal, or an *ad hoc* alternative to incompatible claims. When there are compelling reasons on each side of a controversy, the addition of new options can reshuffle the ranking of preferences. A new option may work as a second-best, and be endorsed by the parties, eager to avoid both the repellent third-best option and the threat of conflict. Compromisers do not have full knowledge of potential outcomes prior to negotiating. Information regarding others' preferences and future decisions is imperfect. The process of exchanging concessions broadens the range of alternatives and is favourable to cooperatively working out an acceptable arrangement.

I have argued that compromise is a useful way of making decisions and resolving conflicts: but does it resolve them fairly? To what extent is the process of compromise a sufficient safeguard for fairness?

In light of the account of compromise given in this chapter, I situate the intersection between compromise and fairness in the norm of reciprocity. Reciprocity is the guiding principle for a fair resolution of a conflict through compromise. Recall that reciprocity demands an appropriate and a proportionate response to a concession made. This need not be a strict equivalency between the losses, but at least a proportioned response (White 2003, 49–59). The parties themselves are qualified to evaluate the concessions made and express their approval or disapproval by giving or denying their consent to an agreement. Because of the rule of reciprocity and the necessity of mutual consent, the outcome is likely to reflect a distribution of burdens which is perceived as fair by the parties involved.

To be sure, reciprocity is not a sufficient condition for a substantively fair outcome. Unfair background conditions will not be corrected by a reciprocal exchange of concessions. Compromise is not adequate when it comes to rectifying an unjust state of affairs. Unequal bargaining power can perpetuate or even worsen the situation of the disadvantaged party. Compromise is not advisable in contexts of significant power disparities or when justice demands an uncompromising stance. Consider the example of a compromise with a highly controversial outcome: the 'Seattle compromise' on female genital mutilation in the late 1990s (Coleman 1998). Faced with a local community of Somali immigrants requesting excision for their daughters, the Harborview Medical Center in Seattle came up with an unexpected proposal. A committee of health professionals suggested a way to meet the religious and cultural demands of Somali families while protecting their daughters from the irreversible damages of traditional excision. The idea was to perform, under medical supervision, a painless and innocuous cut on Somali girls' genitals. Proponents of the compromise plan argued that it would dissuade parents from seeking the traditional rite to be performed with its horrendous medical consequences. What was presented as a benign gesture towards a minority group raised fierce oppositions in the wider public, especially from feminist figures and survivors of female genital mutilation. They claimed that a symbolic cut would legitimize an intolerable practice and that an educational approach was preferable to a misplaced cultural sensitivity. The proposal was ultimately abandoned because it was deemed too controversial.

Here the proposal aimed at taking seriously a minority religious and cultural practice while minimizing the harm inflicted on a vulnerable population. It failed because it was perceived as not serving the best interest of a vulnerable minority within the minority – the Somali girls. Compromise can fail to be inclusive enough or can generate morally unjustifiable outcomes. It is an imperfect procedure, more akin to an ongoing experimentation than to a neat allocation mechanism.

Yet, as I hope to have shown, compromise expresses mutual concern and achieves innovative solutions, under the normative guidance of reciprocity. Many cases of religious accommodation involve the creation of potential unfairness: why exempt young men from bearing arms when others may sacrifice their life for protecting their nation? Why let some workers have more flexibility in their scheduling arrangements on grounds of religion while others also have good reasons to demand flexibility, although they have little to do with conscience? In such cases, a balancing exercise is needed to fairly allocate the burdens and the benefits. Compromise is desirable precisely because it allows the parties involved to adjust the concessions that they are making in a reciprocal manner so as to reach a fair distribution of burdens.

4. CONCLUSION

This chapter has argued that compromise has a key role to play in a politics of religious accommodation. This view is based on an account of compromise as a decision-making procedure based on reciprocal concessions. Compromise can be distinguished from mere bargaining on the one hand, and from deliberation on the other. Unlike bargaining, compromise is imbued with a cooperative spirit. Unlike deliberation, compromise does not aim at revising beliefs or reaching consensus. Compromise achieves agreement through collective and proportionate sacrifices.

I have described the procedure of compromise as consisting of three steps: the act of conceding, the reciprocal move, and the act of mutual consent. The norm of reciprocity lies at the core of compromise. Parties seek to adjust their concessions in a proportionate manner with the concessions of the others so as to avoid blatant asymmetries. In practice, this exercise in mutual adjustment is highly experimental and imperfect. Some external factors can jeopardize the fairness of an actual compromise, such as the existence of power disparities between the parties. Yet, compromise remains desirable, at least in some cases of religious accommodation.

I have highlighted three different instances of religious accommodation in which compromise finds a space. The first is when an accommodation is not required by justice, but advisable on other grounds. The willingness to be accommodating, beyond the call of duty, can give a good reason to compromise. The second instance is when a conflict arises between different claims for which there is no obvious resolution. Compromise can help resolve the conflict by directly involving the parties in the allocation of burdens and benefits. The last instance is when an accommodation is at risk of creating new unfairness by exempting some individuals from a collective burden. The rule of reciprocity at work in compromise can help find an arrangement that fairly distribute the costs.

Finally, I have argued that the added value of compromise in religious accommodation stems from two dimensions. On the one hand, compromise *expresses* an ethos of mutual concern that fits the context of religious accommodation. On the other hand, compromise *achieves* innovative solutions to conflictual deadlocks. It is an effective collective decision-making tool, as well as a normative guide for working out a distribution of burdens that meets the demand of reciprocity.

REFERENCES

Barry, Brian. 2001. *Culture and Equality: An Egalitarian Critique of Multiculturalism.* Cambridge: Polity Press.

Becker, Lawrence C. 1986. *Reciprocity.* London: Routledge & Kegan Paul.

Bellamy, Richard. 1999. *Liberalism and Pluralism: Towards a Politics of Compromise.* London: Routledge.

Benditt, Theodore. 1979. 'Compromising Interests and Principles'. In *Compromise in Ethics, Law, and Politics,* edited by J. Roland Pennock and John W. Chapman, 26–37. New York: New York University Press.

Benjamin, Martin. 1990. *Splitting the Difference: Compromise and Integrity in Ethics and Politics.* Lawrence: University Press of Kansas.

Bouchard, Gérard, and Charles Taylor. 2008. Fonder l'avenir. Le temps de la conciliation. Commission de consultation sur les pratiques d'accommodement reliées aux différences culturelles.

Coleman, Doriane Lambelet. 1998. 'The Seattle Compromise: Multicultural Sensitivity and Americanization'. 47 (4): 717–83.

Elster, Jon. 2000. 'Arguing and Bargaining in Two Constituent Assemblies'. University *of Pennsylvania Journal of Constitutional Law* 345 (2).

Fumurescu, Alin. 2013. *Compromise: A Political and Philosophical History.* Cambridge: Cambridge University Press.

Golding, Martin. 1979. 'The Nature of Compromise: A Preliminary Inquiry'. In *Compromise in Ethics, Law, and Politics,* edited by J. Roland Pennock and John W. Chapman, 3–25. New York: New York University Press.

Gould, Carol C. 1988. *Rethinking Democracy: Freedom and Social Cooperation in Politics, Economy, and Society.* Cambridge: Cambridge University Press.

Gouldner, Alvin W. 1960. 'The Norm of Reciprocity: A Preliminary Statement'. *American Sociological Review* 25 (2).

Guesnet, François, Cécile Laborde, and Lois Lee. 2017. *Negotiating Religion: Cross-Disciplinary Perspectives.* London: Routledge.

Gutmann, Amy, and Dennis F. Thompson. 2014. *The Spirit of Compromise: Why Governing Demands It and Campaigning Undermines It.* Princeton, NJ: Princeton University Press.

Jones, Peter. 2016. 'Accommodating Religion and Shifting Burdens'. *Criminal Law and Philosophy* 10 (3): 515–36.

———. 2017. 'Religious Exemption and Distributive Justice'. In *Religion in Liberal Political Philosophy,* edited by Cécile Laborde and Aurélia Bardon, 163–76. Oxford: Oxford University Press.

Jones, Peter, and Ian O'Flynn. 2013. 'Can a Compromise Be Fair?' *Politics, Philosophy & Economics* 12 (2): 115–35. doi: 10.1177/1470594x12447773.

Laborde, Cécile. 2017. *Liberalism's Religion.* Cambridge, MA: Harvard University Press.

Laborde, Cécile, and Aurélia Bardon. 2017. *Religion in Liberal Political Philosophy.* Oxford: Oxford University Press.

Leydet, Dominique. 2006. 'Pluralisme et compromis'. In *Eloge du compromis: pour une nouvelle pratique démocratique,* edited by Mohammed; Nanteuil Nachi, Matthieu, 81–106. Louvain-la-Neuve: Bruylant-Academia.

Maclure, Jocelyn, and Charles Taylor. 2011. *Secularism and Freedom of Conscience.* Cambridge, MA: Harvard University Press.

Maillard, Denis. 2017. *Quand la religion s'invite dans l'entreprise.* Paris: Fayard.

Margalit, Avishai. 2010. *On Compromise and Rotten Compromises*. Princeton, NJ: Princeton University Press.

May, Simon Căbulea. 2005. 'Principled compromise and the abortion controversy'. *Philosophy and Public Affairs* 33 (4): 317–48.

Pennock, J. Roland, and John W. Chapman. 1979. *Compromise in Ethics, Law, and Politics, Nomos*. New York: New York University Press.

Quong, Jonathan. 2006. 'Cultural Exemptions, Expensive Tastes, and Equal Opportunities'. *Journal of Applied Philosophy* 23 (1): 53–71. doi: 10.1111/j.1468-5930.2006.00320.x.

Rostbøll, Christian F., and Theresa Scavenius. 2018. *Compromise and Disagreement in Contemporary Political Theory: Routledge Innovations in Political Theory*. New York: Routledge.

Seglow, Jonathan. 2011. 'Theories of Religious Exemptions'. In *Diversity in Europe: Dilemmas of Differential Treatment in Theory and Practice*, edited by Gideon Calder and Emanuela Ceva, 52–64. London: Routledge.

———. 2017. 'Religious Accommodation: Responsibility, Integrity, and Self-Respect'. In *Religion in Liberal Political Philosophy*, edited by Cécile Laborde and Aurélia Bardon, 177–90. Oxford: Oxford University Press.

St-Onge, Sylvie. 2015. 'Accommodations in Religious Matters: Quebec and Canadian Perspectives'. In *Managing Religious Diversity in the Workplace: Examples from around the World*, edited by Stefan Gröschl and Regine Bendl, 9–30. Farnham, UK: Gower.

Weinstock, Daniel. 2013. 'On the Possibility of Principled Moral Compromise'. *Critical Review of International Social and Political Philosophy* 16 (4): 537–56.

———. 2017. 'Compromise, Pluralism, and Deliberation'. *Critical Review of International Social and Political Philosophy* 20 (5): 1–20.

Wendt, Fabian. 2018. 'In Defense of Unfair Compromises'. *Philosophical Studies*. Online first. doi.org/10.1007/s11098-018-1154-z.

White, Stuart Gordon. 2003. *The Civic Minimum: On the Rights and Obligations of Economic Citizenship*. Oxford: Oxford University Press.

NOTES

1. One argument against the fairness of actual compromises is the presence of power disparities between the parties. Cécile Laborde expresses scepticism about the use of the term 'negotiation' to characterize the relationship between the state and religious groups (Guesnet, Laborde, and Lee 2017, 67). She argues that this choice of word hides a fundamental power disparity between the sovereign state and social groups. While religious groups can seek to influence the political agenda, they remain legally bound by the final authority of the state. Negotiation gives a false picture of equal standing.

2. This is not in contradiction with the idea of reciprocity. We often expect our acts of kindness towards others to be somehow reciprocated, which does not preclude other-regarding motivations.

3. *La Voix du Nord*, 'Roubaix: les fidèles de la mosquée Da'Wa iront prier le vendredi dans la salle Buffon', 11 December 2014; 'Roubaix : la communauté musulmane va payer 90 € de l'heure pour prier dans une salle municipale', by Bruno Renoul, 20 December 2014; *La Voix du Nord*, 'Roubaix: fermée il y a près d'un an, la mosquée Da'wa a rouvert ses portes', 14 January 2016.

4. *La Voix du Nord*, 'Roubaix: les fidèles de la mosquée Da'Wa iront prier le vendredi dans la salle Buffon', 11 December 2014.

5. *Idem*.

6. *Métro*, 'Une minute de silence en début de Conseil à Outremont', by Frédéric Lacroix-Couture, 22 December 2016.

NINE

Religious Commitments and Equal Opportunities in Public Spaces

Simon Thompson

In a number of European states, laws and regulations of various kinds place limits on individuals' ability to wear certain religious garments or to display certain religious symbols in public space. These limitations apply, for example, to Christian crucifixes, Sikh turbans and Muslim headscarves. The garment which has attracted the most attention, however, has been the Muslim burqa. There have been burqa bans in place in France and Belgium since 2011. In France, loi no. 2010-1192, which came into effect on 11 April of that year, prohibits 'the concealment of the face in public space'. In Belgium, the Act of 1 June 2011 institutes 'a prohibition on wearing clothing that covers the face or a large part of it'. In a number of other European states, similar bans are being introduced, planned, or at least advocated.[1] It is arguable that debates about the justifiability of such bans have often served as proxies for a broader debate about the position of Muslims in non-Muslim societies.

Both political theorists' and legal scholars' analyses of these laws have tended to focus on the proper extent of the right to religion and the limitations which may be placed on that right (e.g., Edwards 2014; Elliot-Williams 2016; Laborde 2012; Lægaard 2015; Yusuf 2014). Thus, critics of burqa bans have argued that, since the right to religion includes the right to manifest one's religious identity in public, these bans are an illegitimate restriction of it. By contrast, defenders of burqa bans have pointed out that the right to religion may legitimately be restricted on various grounds, and they have then argued that at least one of these grounds can be invoked to support them.[2] This focus on rights is completely understandable and entirely appropriate. Rights-talk is the dominant normative language in use today, and there is no doubt that burqa bans can be sensibly and usefully discussed and evaluated in this language. It is very important to know if such bans are compatible with individuals' right to religion or if they are an illegitimate restriction of it.[3]

In this chapter, however, I want to take a somewhat different tack, in order to focus instead on how burqa bans fare when assessed against a principle of equality of opportunity. Even if bans on wearing burqas in public places are not a violation of the right to religion, could it be argued that such bans are still wrong since they undermine the opportunities of some individuals more than others? If it is accepted that all individuals should have roughly equal chances to live the lives of their choosing, does it follow that burqa bans are unjust? More broadly, could it be argued that an equal opportunities approach to this issue has certain advantages over a rights approach? Might it, for instance, enable a more nuanced analysis by making it possible to balance the rival sets of interests which may be at stake?

In order to address these various questions, my argument in this chapter is based on David Miller's analysis of the relationship between equal opportunities and cultural commitments, although my version of his analysis restructures it in several ways, and places more emphasis on some of its elements than on others. First I lay out the main elements of Miller's approach: its principle of equality of opportunity, its analysis of the conflict between general laws and cultural commitments, and its proposed use of democratic dialogue as a means to try to resolve this conflict, and, failing this, as a way of informing decisions about how costs should be fairly distributed between the affected parties. Then I apply Miller's analysis to the specific case of burqa bans: how such laws are justified, how significant a loss of opportunities some individuals experience, what a dialogue between the various parties involved might look like, and how the costs of such laws could be shared between them. In my concluding remarks, I summarize my case for arguing that, judged against an appropriate principle of equality of opportunity, burqa bans place an unjustifiable burden on women who have a commitment to veil in public places.

1. MILLER'S ANALYSIS

In his essay on 'Liberalism, Equal Opportunities and Cultural Commitments' (2013), Miller declares that: 'A liberal society must, among other things, be one that gives each of its members an equal chance to get what they want out of life' (2013, 93).[4] Applying this principle to a multicultural society, he suggests that the diversity of individuals' cultures, and the diversity of commitments that follow from them, need to be taken into account. Hence 'it is a matter of justice that the legal and policy regime should as far as possible provide people with differing cultural commitments with equivalent opportunity sets' (2013, 111). Here the notion of an opportunity set is used to capture the idea that it is not necessary to ensure that everyone has exactly the same opportunities, but only that the range of opportunities which each person has should be roughly equal (2013, 113).

With this principle of equality of opportunity in mind, I can now describe the general problem with which I am concerned. In a multicultural society, different groups endorse different sets of cultural norms, and therefore generally applicable laws may affect each group differently. To be specific, a particular law may reduce one group's opportunity set but not those of others, or reduce one group's set more than it reduces those of others. As Miller puts it: 'The problem arises when cultural norms intersect with the legal or other norms of the wider society in such a way that the group faces constraints over and above those inherent in the culture itself' (2013, 100–101).

To illustrate this problem, Miller considers a group whose 'dress code . . . prevents members from being employed in a significant range of jobs' (2013, 101). For instance, if Sikh men wish to wear turbans, they may not be able to get jobs on building sites or as motorcycle couriers. The general laws making the wearing of hard hats and helmets compulsory for certain jobs reduces the range of employment opportunities for Sikhs but not for members of other cultural groups. It would appear, then, that such a law concerning safety at work comes into conflict with the principle of equality of opportunity.[5]

It is important to understand that, for Miller, conflicts of this kind only present a genuine dilemma for someone committed to a principle of equality of opportunity if both the law in question and the opportunities it threatens meet certain conditions. So far as the law is concerned, it must serve an important public purpose, so that it cannot be reformed or abolished without some significant loss. Referring to a case in which a young Sikh cannot attend the school of his choice, Miller says that 'we must assume that the banning of turbans was part and parcel of a school uniform policy that was seen as generally beneficial to all pupils. Without that assumption, the ban would present itself merely as an arbitrary piece of cultural discrimination' (2013, 107–108). If the uniform policy serves no useful purpose, and if it could therefore be abolished without any significant cost to those affected by it, then, from an equal opportunities perspective, there is no question that it should be abolished, and thus the burdens it imposes lifted.

With regard to opportunities, Miller argues that they only fall within the purview of a principle of equal opportunity if they meet two important conditions. First, 'a liberal society will wish to restrict opportunities whose exercise would be damaging to the interests of its members' (2013,

95). Such harm is direct if the action which an opportunity permits would, to put it in Joel Feinberg's language, wrongfully sets back another's interests (Feinberg 1987). According to Miller: 'If I am to have the opportunity to practise my religion, you cannot have the opportunity to prevent me from practising a religion of which you disapprove.' Such harm is indirect, if, for instance, taking up an opportunity involves 'activities that damage the natural environment' (2013, 95). The idea here seems to be that the natural environment does not in itself have interests which can be set back, but that, as a consequence of damage to that environment, it is the interests of those who live in it which are set back. It is only if the opportunity in question is to perform an activity that does not directly or indirectly harm others that we need worry that some people enjoy this opportunity while others do not.

Second, and, I shall argue, more controversially, Miller also contends that it is not necessary to equalize opportunities where unequal opportunities are necessary to create and maintain social stability: 'Liberals need to be concerned about the conditions under which a liberal society can remain stable over time . . . To achieve this, citizens are likely to need to share not only political principles but also some wider cultural values' (2013, 98). It follows that

> liberal societies may justifiably favour those cultural values that in any given place play this supporting role. For instance, it is not wrong to favour the national language or languages when designing education systems or other public institutions, even if this limits the opportunities of those whose native tongues are different. (2013, 98)

Although speakers of a minority language may have fewer opportunities to have their children educated in that language than do speakers of the majority language in theirs, such an inequality of opportunity may be justified if social stability requires all citizens to be competent in the same language.

If, however, the law does serve an important purpose, if the opportunities are sought not to perform harmful actions, and if the inequality of such opportunities is not necessary for social stability, then the conflict between the law and the principle of equality of opportunity should concern anyone committed to that principle. Miller contends that in these circumstances what is needed is 'a dialogue between representatives of the minority and representatives of the social majority' (2013, 110). In this dialogue, he argues, some questions should be directed at what he calls the 'social majority' which benefits from the existing rule. First, is the rule 'needed at all' or it is 'merely a convention that might have suited people at some earlier time but no longer had any particular rationale' (2013, 110)? If it is useful, then 'could it be modified so that the problems facing the cultural minority were eased' (2013, 110)? Other questions should be asked of the group which Miller refers to as the 'cultural minority'. How important is that 'cultural norm' to the group's collective identity, and what is the evidence for this? Could it relax its interpretation of what compliance with the relevant norm requires (2013, 110)? By conducting such a dialogue, either the majority might agree that the law should be modified or rescinded, or the cultural minority might agree that the relevant norm should be reinterpreted or abandoned. In this case, it may be possible to solve the problem before it becomes necessary to determine how to distribute costs.

If democratic dialogue cannot solve the problem, then there will be costs which must be borne. In this case, by drawing on information gathered in this dialogue, the task becomes one of deciding how to fairly distribute these costs between the majority who benefit from the rule in question and the minority community who are disadvantaged by it (Miller 2013, 109). Broadly speaking, there are three options. First, if a law creating unequal opportunities remains unchanged, and no other action is taken, then all of the costs will be borne by the group whose opportunities are reduced. For example, if the rule that hard hats must be worn on building sites is retained for reasons of workers' safety, then it will impose a burden on Sikh men who, if they wish to wear a turban, will be unable to work on building sites.[6] Second, if the law in question is repealed, in order to equalize all groups' opportunities, then the costs will be borne by all of those for whom the law served some useful purpose. Consider, for example, a school-uniform policy which does not permit the wearing of religious clothing in order to foster a sense of collective identity. If this policy is liberalized, so that such clothing can now be worn, then the cost will be borne by those (the whole school community?) who benefitted from that sense of identity. Third, there are various options in which costs are shared between the parties concerned. For example, consider a case in which a police force's insistence on weekend working means that Orthodox Jews cannot become police officers (Quong 2006). If a change of policy is introduced which enables all police officers to enjoy a similar degree of flexible working, then the burden of that revised policy would be shared between all of them.

2. A CASE TO ANSWER

Having presented my restructured version of Miller's approach to equality of opportunity in multicultural societies, I now want to consider how this approach might be applied to a burqa ban. In order to see that there is at least a case to answer here, let us begin by considering the example of Janice and Jamila, a Protestant and a Muslim, who have similar abilities and ambitions. Both would like to take advantage of the opportunities available to them in the public spaces of their society. However, since a burqa ban is in place, Janice is able to take up the opportunities which untrammelled access to public space affords her, but Jamila can only do so at a significant cost. To generalize, we can see that some Muslim women's commitment to veil in public spaces comes up against the general law banning such veiling, imposing a burden on members of this group which others do not have to bear.[7]

What are we to make of this? Even if there is no right to wear the burqa in public places, is such a ban nevertheless an element of a legal and policy regime which unjustly undermines equality of opportunity? Or, because such a ban serves an important public purpose, should it remain in place despite its adverse effects on such equality? In order to answer these questions, in this section I examine the general law and the opportunity sought to see if the former advances an important purpose, and if the latter is not harmful or if these particular unequal opportunities are not necessary for social stability.

With regard to the ban, it may be recalled that, according to Miller, the law in question must serve some important public purpose. If it does not, then anyone committed to equal opportunities could simply conclude that it should be abolished, and its negative effect on opportunities thus ended.[8] Defenders of burqa bans do claim, of course, that these laws are intended to produce or protect an important social good. To focus on the well-known case of *SAS v. France* (2014), the principal argument for the ban was that it was necessary in the interests of a particular conception of social integration referred to as 'living together'. In the words of the European Court of Human Rights' judgement in this case, the 2010 report of the French parliamentary commission on 'the wearing of the full-face veil on national territory', contended that 'the full-face veil represented a denial of fraternity, constituting the negation of contact with others and a flagrant infringement of the French principle of living together (*le "vivre ensemble"*)' (ECtHR 2014, §16). It therefore concluded that the ban could 'be regarded as proportionate to the aim pursued, namely the preservation of the conditions of "living together" as an element of the "protection of the rights and freedoms of others"' (ECtHR 2014, §157).[9]

In the next section, I shall discuss some of the criticisms which have been made of this argument, and consider how disputes about its plausibility affect the case for burqa bans. For now, my point is that there is at least an argument on the table according to which the reduction of some individuals' opportunities relative to those of others is justified in the name of a significant public good. For this reason, someone committed to a principle of equality of opportunity cannot straightforwardly dismiss burqa bans by arguing that they are what we have seen Miller call 'an arbitrary piece of cultural discrimination' (2013, 107–108).

So far as opportunities are concerned, it may be recalled that, on Miller's account, if individuals seek opportunities to do harm, then they may rightly be denied these opportunities, and any consequent inequality of opportunities is legitimate. An opportunity to do *direct* harm is one in which a person's intended action would wrongly set back another's interests. For example, an individual's opportunity to forcibly remove a crucifix from around another's neck can rightly be denied, without this in any way undermining attempts to achieve equality of opportunity.[10] I can only think of one way in which it could be argued that burqa wearing is directly harmful to others. If individuals have an interest in seeing others' faces when encountering them in public space, and if that interest is of sufficient weight that it should be protected by a right, then burqa wearing may be regarded as an activity that wrongly sets back this interest, and hence violates the corresponding right.

If this argument worked, if it could be demonstrated beyond reasonable doubt that burqa wearing causes direct harm in this way, then defenders of bans would not need to try to refute the charge that such bans wrongly reduce some people's opportunities. But I want to argue that this is not beyond reasonable doubt since there are good reasons to question the existence of a right to see others' faces. One way of making this point is to argue, as do a number of legal scholars, that the existence of the well-established right to privacy suffices to counter the claim that individuals have a right to see others' faces in public space. As Gabrielle Elliot-Williams puts it: 'Since the right to respect for private life is applicable even in public spaces, individuals can hardly have a right of approach or right to attempt to socialize where those advances are unwelcomed' (2016, 346; see also Edwards 2014, 257; Yusuf 2014, 7).

What about the further argument that burqa wearing causes *indirect* harm? According to Miller, such harm occurs when, for instance, taking up an opportunity involves 'activities that damage the natural environment' (2013, 95). In the case of burqa wearing, clearly the *natural* environment is not affected in any way. Might it be argued that the *social* environment is adversely affected? Is it possible that burqa wearing creates or at least contributes to an atmosphere in which others may be indirectly harmed? The possibility that comes most readily to mind is that which I have just considered: namely, that burqa bans are a necessary condition of the possibility of 'living together'. Here, then, the claim is not that a particular burqa-wearing woman directly harms those individuals whom she encounters in public space, but rather that the practice of burqa wearing is indirectly harmful since it creates or plays a part in creating an atmosphere in which goal of 'living together' is undermined. In this way, I would suggest, we are taken back to the claim that burqa bans serve an important political purpose, and thus the remarks I just made about that claim also apply here. To put it in terms of indirect harm, the argument that burqa bans are justified in order to prevent such harm cannot be ruled out of court.

What, finally, of Miller's claim that unequal opportunities may be necessary for social stability? Is he right to argue that in certain circumstances liberals 'should seek to accommodate the minority cultures . . .

but they need not aim for strict equality' (2013, 98)? For Miller's argument to work in the present case, he must be able to show that social solidarity is a necessary condition of social stability. If this were so, then the unequal opportunities created by a burqa ban could be justified in order to create the sense of solidarity necessary to underpin stability. This aspect of Miller's analysis raises a number of highly complex issues concerning the relationship between collective identity, national membership, cultural assimilation, social reproduction, and so on. For the purposes of this chapter, I shall put these complexities aside, and simply say that on this issue I follow the arguments of those of Miller's critics who deny this link between social stability and solidarity. To take just one example, Arash Abizadeh has challenged his claim that the 'social integration, cultural reproduction, and socialization necessary for democratic society can be effected *only if* there exists a shared, national, public culture' (Abizadeh 2002, 499).[11] In this case, since stable societies do not require social solidarity, considerations of stability cannot be used to justify burqa bans.

In light of these remarks, I would conclude that the conflict between bans on burqa wearing and the principle of equality of opportunity cannot be easily dismissed. In this case, I have suggested, it is necessary to move onto the next stage of the process, and to determine if it is possible to resolve this conflict through democratic dialogue.

3. DEMOCRATIC DELIBERATION

In my reworking of Miller's approach to conflicts between general laws and cultural commitments, the purpose of 'democratic deliberation' (2013, 112) is to see if such conflicts could be resolved through the exchange of different points of view. Might the bans' defenders be persuaded to modify or even repeal the relevant laws? Might their critics be persuaded to reform or even abandon the cultural norm which conflicts with them?

To begin with, then, could the defenders of burqa bans be persuaded to change their views? Could they be convinced that such laws are not needed, or even that they are discriminatory?[12] In this chapter, I have focused on the French government's argument that the ban is necessary to advance a conception of social solidarity referred to as 'living together'. In my view, powerful criticisms have been made of this argument. Sune Lægaard, for example, raises three important objections to it. First, the aim of living together is unacceptably vague: 'it is . . . simply unclear what the conditions of living together are' (Lægaard 2015, 210), and thus the justification for the ban which refers to this aim fails.[13] Second, as I argued earlier, since '[t]here is no right to see the faces of others in the Convention' (2015, 211), the ban cannot be said to serve one of the legitimate aims for restricting rights identified in Article 9, namely to protect 'the rights and freedoms of others'. Third, the ban cannot be shown to be a proportionate means to achieve its (ill-defined) ends (2015, 212–18). Hence Lægaard concludes that 'living together' does not name a clear and coherent goal, the pursuit of which enjoys 'a justification sufficient to limit a human right' (2015, 207).[14] My contention is that the deficiencies of the 'living together' argument mean that the reduction of some individuals' opportunities relative to others cannot be justified by reference to this notion either.

If defenders of burqa bans were convinced of this or any other critique, then they should agree that the relevant laws should be repealed, and their adverse effects on equality of opportunity thus ended. But let us assume that burqa bans' supporters remain convinced that they are justified. In this case, it might still be possible to persuade them that such bans should be modified in some way so that the cost of compliance with them—in terms of diminished opportunities—is reduced or even eliminated.

In the case of some laws, rules, and regulations, it may be possible to change their *scope* in various ways. Here the literature on religious accommodation, and in particular on religious exemptions, is particularly pertinent (e.g., Bou-Habib 2006; Seglow 2017; Shorten 2010). If there is a general law in place which serves an important public purpose, but which disproportionately burdens a particular group, then it may be appropriate to grant members of that group an exemption from it. With reference to the Canadian Mounties, for example, Brian Barry argues that, since 'it is not justifiable to keep out a turbaned Sikh', an exemption should be granted; but the headgear rule should not be 'dropped altogether' because 'it could plausibly be said that the morale and standing of the force would be undermined' (Barry 2002, 217).

Could what Barry calls a 'rule-and-exemption approach' (Barry 2001, 33) work in this case? If the rule in question is a ban specifically on burqas, then of course it would be impossible to retain the rule and grant an exemption for this type of face covering! If, however, the rule prohibits the concealment of the face in public places, then it would be logically possible to grant an exemption for the burqa, while continuing to impose the rule on other sorts of face-coverings. What would the various interested parties make of such a modification? Certainly, it would be welcomed by those Muslim women who wish to wear the burqa. But it seems very unlikely that the defenders of the rule would agree to it. Since they believe that all facial concealment causes significant harm to social solidarity, they would argue that this exemption would cause such harm.

In the case of other laws, rules, and regulations, it may be possible to change their *content*, so that compliance with them is less demanding. For example, a law against the wearing of religious symbols in schools could be modified so that it only prohibited symbols above a certain size. In the present case, it is possible to imagine a more narrowly construed ban which only requires Muslim women to show their faces in particular locations and at particular times – for instance, when entering banks, passing through airport security, posing for official photographs (e.g., passports), and giving evidence in court (Miller 2013, 110).

As I have explained, in this chapter I am focusing on the 'living to-gether' argument for burqa bans. Other arguments have been made, in-cluding the claim that such bans are necessary for public safety (Elliot-Williams 2016, 347; Yusuf 2014, 279, 292). If the bans' defenders relied on this argument alone, then a more tightly formulated ban might be accept-able to them. If, however, the bans' defenders claim that they are neces-sary to maintain social solidarity, then, once again, they could not agree to this proposed modification since it would permit burqas to be worn most of the time in most public places. In short, it is difficult to see how burqa bans might be modified in a way which reduces the burdens that they place on some individuals, but which at the same time assures their advocates that they can still fulfil what they regard as their purpose.

To turn now to the other side of the argument, could those Muslim women who wish to veil in public places be persuaded to reinterpret their religious commitment in order to make compliance with burqa bans less burdensome for them? At this point in the process, Miller suggests that it is necessary to 'step inside' a culture in order to evaluate the importance of the particular commitments which are associated with it (2013, 113–14). In practice, stepping inside a culture is more of a matter of listening carefully to those who are already inside: 'Of course we cannot step inside the culture in a literal sense. So our liberalism has to make room for political dialogue in which groups are able to explain the signif-icance of particular requirements and prohibitions' (2013, 114). In partic-ular, Miller thinks that it is appropriate to ask members of the 'cultural minority' why they believe that a particular norm exists, how important that norm is for the group, and whether it could be understood in a way which makes it less costly to comply with.

With regard to the first of these questions, Muslim women might 'reasonably be asked to produce evidence about the status of the code' in which the relevant cultural commitment is to be found. Here, of course, several verses of the Quran are pertinent. The Surah al-Nur declares: 'Say to the believing women that: they should . . . not display their beauty except what is apparent, and they should place their khumur [scarf, veil, head covering] over their bosoms' (24:31). And in the Surah al-Ahzaab we read: 'O Prophet! Say to your wives, your daughters, and the women of the believers that: they should let down upon themselves their jalabib [plural of jilbab, loose tunic]' (33:59). Although the precise signification of these verses is a matter of considerable dispute, we can certainly say that there is some textual evidence which may support the view that there is an obligation to veil.[15]

So far as the second question about the significance of compliance with the norm is concerned, SAS herself provides an answer in her testimony to the European Court. Here she says that, as a result of the implementation of law 2010-1192,

> I now feel like a prisoner in my own Republic, as I no longer feel able to leave my house unless it is essential. I leave the house less frequently as a result. I wear my veil with even less frequency when out in public as a result. Indeed, I also feel immense guilt that I am forced to no longer remain faithful to my core religious values. [16]

It is clear that SAS experiences the burqa ban as a very significant burden, since it renders her unable to enter public places while at the same time being true to what she calls her 'core religious values'. In support of SAS's testimony, a report by the Open Society Justice Initiative, entitled *After the Ban*, examined the experiences of thirty-five women. It contended that respondents 'who continue to wear their niqab explained that, to them, not covering their faces would mean disowning their religion or abandoning part of their religious identity' (2013, 2).

The cost of the French ban to those who wish to veil in public can also be expressed more explicitly in terms of opportunities. Urban theorists, sociologists of the city, and others describe the public realm in highly evocative ways. For Lyn Lofland, for instance, it is

> a realm of immense social value which offers, among other benefits, a rich environment for learning, a site for needed respites and refreshments, a locus of communication, an opportunity for the practice of politics, a stage for the enactment of social arrangements and social conflict, and assistance in the creation of cosmopolitans. (Lofland 2007)

To focus on those aspects of the public realm of particular relevance in the current context, we can say that the opportunity to have unfettered access to this realm opens up a range of other important opportunities. I would suggest that this first opportunity is *instrumental* when access to public space is necessary to take up other opportunities such as education or employment, and that it is *intrinsic* in so far as being able to appear in public in a manner of one's own choosing is regarded as an important good in itself. [17] While there is much more that could be said about the nature and importance of these various opportunities, these brief remarks should be enough to demonstrate the importance of open access to public space. From this perspective, then, the difficulty that SAS and others in her position face is that, in order to be able to take advantage of these opportunities, they must pay a high price which others do not have to pay.

If we turn to the third of Miller's questions, Muslim women might be asked if they could alter their understanding of their commitment to veil in order to make it less burdensome for them. Might, for example, alternative forms of clothing – which cover the hair and neck but not the face, say – be acceptable (Miller 2013, 110)? It is, after all, much more common for Muslim women to wear a hijab or khimar than a burqa or niqab. As Bhikhu Parekh puts it: 'In some cases a cultural inability can be overcome with relative ease by suitably re-interpreting the relevant cultural norm or practice' (Parekh 2000, 241). However, just as it was difficult to see how advocates of burqa bans might come to accept the case for the repeal or reform of those bans, so it is difficult to see how those Muslim women who believe that they have at least a commitment and possibly a duty to veil in public might be persuaded to reinterpret or change their belief just in order to make it less burdensome to them. In light of the strength of SAS's testimony, and that of others in the same situation, it seems unlikely that asking the questions Miller proposes would change their minds.

4. DISTRIBUTION OF COSTS

If there is a genuine conflict between a general law and a particular cultural commitment, and if a process of democratic deliberation fails to persuade either the law's defenders or those holding this commitment to change their views, then Miller suggests that in these circumstances 'the question straightforwardly becomes one of the distribution of costs' (2013, 110). Earlier on, I suggested three ways in which this might work out in practice. If the rule is fully retained, then any goal it is said to advance will still be advanced, but those who are burdened by it will continue to enjoy fewer opportunities than others. If the rule is repealed, those whom it had benefitted must bear the cost, but ceteris paribus individuals' opportunities will become more equal. If the rule is modified in some way, so that those had been burdened are partially or fully exempt from it, then more a complex distribution of costs between the various relevant parties may result.

How would each of these options work out in the particular case with which I am concerned? If a burqa ban was retained in an unmodified form, then its supporters would argue that a necessary condition of 'living together' would be protected. On the other hand, Muslim women who wish to veil in public would continue to experience a very significant burden, not experienced by others, if they wanted to make use of the opportunities available in public space. By contrast, if a burqa ban was repealed, then, if the argument about 'living together' is valid, social solidarity would be harmed. On the other hand, the repeal of the ban would mean that Muslim women who wish to veil would then be able to take advantage of the opportunities available in public spaces without having to endure a cost which others do not have to endure.

How costs would be distributed if a modification was made to a burqa ban would depend on the nature of that modification. If a general ban on the covering of the face in public included an exemption for burqas, then this would completely lift the burden on women who wish to wear the burqa. If a ban only required faces to be uncovered at particular locations such as airport security, then, on the plausible assumption that no Muslim women would find this requirement costly, this rule would significantly ease the burden on them. On the other side of the debate, anyone supporting a ban since they were concerned exclusively with issues of public safety could agree to the second modification. By contrast, those endorsing the argument from 'living together' would argue that both of these modifications would undermine that important objective.

With these options in mind, determining how the costs should be distributed between the various affected parties requires us to ask two questions. First, how important a purpose does the law in question advance? Second, how significant a burden does it impose on some of those subjected to it?

To begin with the second question, I would argue that burqa bans impose very significant costs on those women who wish to veil in public, presenting them with a stark choice between complying with what they regard as their religious commitment and taking up the valuable opportunities which would be available to them in public space. Much of the discussion about equality of opportunity focuses quite rightly on the spheres of education and employment, and so it is worth pointing out that taking up virtually every opportunity of this kind requires people to enter and to pass through public spaces. In addition, the ability to appear in public in the manner of one's own choosing is a highly significant opportunity in itself. Thus, although only some Muslim women wish to veil, the effects of burqa bans on them are severe.[18]

To turn to the first question, I would argue that 'living together' is too ill-defined a conception of social solidarity to justify the costs of the burqa bans it is said to require. In other words, I think that the supporters of such bans have failed to show that they are necessary to deliver the significant benefits which they think justify their detrimental effects on opportunities. Furthermore, I would argue that, even if there was *some* truth to the claim that face-veiling damaged social solidarity, so few Muslim women wish to veil that permitting them to do so would have an insignificant effect on such solidarity. One news report on Austria's burqa ban points out that the 'law is expected to affect just 150 women – that's 0.03% of the Austrian Muslim population and 0.002% of the entire population.'[19] Although the corresponding numbers are of course higher in other states such as France and Belgium, I would nevertheless suggest that the practical effect on social solidarity of a few hundred or thousand women not showing their faces would be negligible. Finally, I would argue that in practice burqa bans are counterproductive since they set back rather than facilitate the aim of 'living together' by compelling some

Muslim women to remain isolated at home rather than interacting with others in public space.[20]

Putting my answers to these two questions together, it should be clear that I think that the right way to distribute costs in the case of burqa bans is to take the second option mentioned above. The repeal of existing burqa bans, and the refusal to allow new bans to come into effect, is justified since the very real costs to those adversely affected by them strongly outweighs nebulous claims about the benefits they are supposed to deliver.

5. CONCLUDING REMARKS

In this chapter, I have considered how burqa bans may be judged from the perspective of equality of opportunity, rather than from the more usual perspective of rights. To be more precise, I have asked whether such bans should be lifted since they undermine equality of opportunity or whether they should be retained in spite of their effect on such equality. In seeking to answer this question, I have drawn inspiration in particular from Miller's essay on 'Liberalism, Equal Opportunities and Cultural Commitments'. I have, however, extensively reworked his own analysis in order better to support my own particular aims. This has involved restructuring his own presentation, and placing greater emphasis on some parts of it than on others.

The result has been the development of a three-stage procedure for determining how to resolve clashes between general laws and cultural commitments. At the first stage, it is necessary to ask whether what appears to be a serious conflict between a general law and a cultural commitment can simply be dissolved by showing that the former does not serve an important purpose or that the latter is in some way harmful. If the conflict cannot be dissolved, then, at the second stage, it may be possible through a process of democratic deliberation to persuade either the law's defenders or those with the cultural commitment to change their minds. Finally, at the third stage, if such a deliberative process fails, it is necessary to determine how costs should be distributed between the various parties concerned.

In the specific case of burqa bans, I argued, at the first stage, that someone committed to equality of opportunity could not simply dismiss the claim that face-veiling is a necessary condition of 'living together'. But I also suggested that the claim that face-veiling causes others direct harm could not be sustained. Then, at the second stage, I looked in greater detail at the argument that burqa bans are necessary for 'living together', as well as at the counterargument that they cause severe inequalities of opportunity. Finally, at the third stage, I suggested that the idea of 'living together' is too vague a notion to justify the creation of such inequalities. In this case, I concluded, burqa bans should be repealed, and if their repeal creates any costs, these should be borne by all of those who were meant to benefit from them.

REFERENCES

Abizadeh, Arash. 2002. 'Does Liberal Democracy Presuppose a Cultural Nation? Four Arguments'. *American Political Science Review* 96 (3): 495–509.

Arendt, Hannah. 1958. *The Human Condition*. Chicago: University of Chicago Press.

Barry, Brian. 2001. *Culture and Equality*. Cambridge: Polity Press.

———. 2002. 'Second Thoughts—And Some First Thoughts Revived'. In *Multiculturalism Reconsidered*, edited by Paul Kelly, 204–38. Cambridge: Polity Press.

Bou-Habib, Paul. 2006. 'A Theory of Religious Accommodation'. *Journal of Applied Philosophy* 23 (1): 109–26.

Chiodelli, Francesco, and Stefano Moroni. 2014. 'Typology of Spaces and Topology of Toleration: City, Pluralism, Ownership'. *Journal of Urban Affairs* 36 (2): 167–81.

Edwards, Susan. 2014. 'No Burqas We're French! The Wide Margin of Appreciation and the ECtHR Burqa Ruling'. *Denning Law Journal* 26 (2): 246–60.

Elliot-Williams, Gabrielle. 2016. 'Protection of the Right to Manifest Religion or Belief Under the European Convention on Human Rights in SAS v France'. *Oxford Journal of Law and Religion* 5 (2): 344–51.

European Court of Human Rights. 2011. 'Grand Chamber, Case of Lautsi and Others v. Italy (Application no. 30814/06), Judgment, Strasbourg, 18 March 2011'. https://udoc.echr.coe.int/webservices/content/pdf/001-104040?TID=etmfltkqsp.

———. 2014. 'Grand Chamber, Case of *S.A.S v. France* (Application no. 43835/11), Judgment, Strasbourg, 1 July 2014'. https://hudoc.echr.coe.int/sites/eng/pages/search.aspx?i=001-145466.

Feinberg, Joel. 1987. *The Moral Limits of the Criminal Law Volume 1: Harm to Others* . Oxford: Oxford University Press.

Hibbert, Neil. 2008. 'Citizenship and the Welfare State: A Critique of David Miller's Theory of Nationality'. *Canadian Journal of Political Science* 41 (1): 169–86.

Hunter-Henin, Myriam. 2015. 'Living Together in an Age of Religious Diversity: Lessons from Baby Loup and SAS'. *Oxford Journal of Law and Religion* 4 (1): 94–118.

Kelly, Paul, ed. 2002. *Multiculturalism Reconsidered: 'Culture and Equality' and Its Critics*. Cambridge: Polity Press.

Laborde, Cécile. 2012. 'State Paternalism and Religious Dress Code'. *International Journal of Constitutional Law* 10 (2): 398–410.

Lægaard, Sune. 2015. 'Burqa Ban, Freedom of Religion and "Living Together"'. *Human Rights Review* 16 (3): 203–19.

Lofland, Lyn. 2007. 'Public Realm'. In the *Blackwell Encyclopedia of Sociology*, edited by George Ritzer. Oxford: Blackwell.

Miller, David. 2013. 'Liberalism, Equal Opportunities and Cultural Commitments'. In *Justice for Earthlings: Essays in Political Philosophy*, 93–114. Cambridge: Cambridge University Press.

Open Society Justice Initiative. 2013. *After the Ban: The Experiences of 35 Women of the Full-Face Veil in France*. https://www.opensocietyfoundations.org/sites/default/files/after-the-ban-experience-full-face-veil-france-20140210.pdf.

Parekh, Bhikhu. 2000. 'Barry and the Dangers of Liberalism'. In *Multiculturalism Reconsidered*, edited by Paul Kelly, 133–50. Cambridge: Polity Press.

Quong, Jonathan. 2006. 'Cultural Exemptions, Expensive Tastes, and Equal Opportunities'. *Journal of Applied Philosophy* 23 (1): 53–71.

Seglow, Jonathan. 2017. 'Religious Accommodation: Responsibility, Integrity and Self-Respect'. In *Religion in Liberal Political Philosophy*, edited by Cécile Laborde and Aurelia Bardon, 177–90. Oxford: Oxford University Press.

Shorten, Andrew. 2010. 'Cultural Exemptions, Equality and Basic Interests'. *Ethnicities* 10 (1): 100–26.
Yusuf, Hakeem. 2014. 'S.A.S v France: Supporting "Living Together" or Forced Assimilation?' *International Human Rights Law Review* 3 (2): 277–302.

NOTES

1. The Swiss canton of Tessin introduced such a ban 'in public places' in July 2016; see http://www.telegraph.co.uk/news/2016/07/07/burka-ban-for-muslims-enforced-in-switzerland-with-fines-of-up-t/. In September 2017, the German Bundesrat passed a partial ban on burqas for car drivers; see https://www.dw.com/en/german-bundesrat-approves-burqa-ban-for-drivers-beefs-up-road-race-sanctions/a-40642060.   Austria's Anti-Face-Covering Act of October 2017 'provides that in public places or in public buildings, facial features may not be hidden or concealed by clothes or other objects in such a way that they are no longer recognizable'; see http://bmeia2014.int.t3.world-direct.at/en/travel-stay/entry-and-residence-in-austria/anti-face-veiling-act/.

2. In the European Court of Human Rights, this battle has been fought out between those challenging bans who have focused on the first paragraph of Article 9, which specifies that the right to religion may be enjoyed 'in public or private' and may be 'manifest' in various ways, and those supporting bans who have focused instead on the second paragraph, which suggests that this right may be restricted 'in the interests of public safety, for the protection of public order, health or morals, or for the protection of the rights and freedoms of others'.

3. It has been argued that burqa bans also violate rights to association, expression, privacy, and nondiscrimination. See, for example, SAS v. France (2014).

4. This essay was first published in Kelly (2002), and republished in Miller (2013). I shall refer to the latter version here.

5. See also Jonathan Quong's example of a liberal Protestant and an Orthodox Jew: both wish to become police officers, but, since that job requires working on the Sabbath, only the former can (Quong 2006). I return to this case briefly later on.

6. It may be noted that, considering the same case, Barry reaches a different conclusion, suggesting that its 'particular circumstances make the balance-of-advantage argument for an exemption rather powerful' (Barry 2001, 49).

7. With this wording, I seek to sidestep a well-known point of disputation about opportunities. On what can be called the 'objective' account, Jamila has exactly the same opportunity to enter public space as Janice, but may choose not to avail herself of this opportunity (Barry 2001, 37). On what can be called the 'subjective' account, Jamila lacks the same opportunity as Janice, because, in light of her cultural commitments, entering public space is not an opportunity for her (Parekh 2000, 241). On my entirely unoriginal account, the difference between these two women's situations is that Jamila – but not Janice – carries a burden which impedes her religious conduct and makes it more costly to perform (Bou-Habib 2006, 110–11).

8. As Barry puts it: 'If there is no objectively good reason for having the law that put a cultural or religious minority at a disadvantage, its members can rightly complain of injustice'; as he says, unjust laws place 'more or less onerous burdens . . . on adherents of some religions' but do not serve 'legitimate public goals' or have a 'legitimate public objective' (Barry 2002, 213).

9. Although the French government did make other arguments in support of the ban, I shall concentrate on the 'living together' argument for the reasons Lægaard gives in his commentary on this case (Lægaard 2015, 206).

10. See http://www.hartlepoolmail.co.uk/news/local/sunderland-muslim-woman-s-veil-ripped-from-face-during-alleged-race-hate-attack-in-her-home-city-1-7996760.

11. Alternatively, Neil Hibbert argues that 'principled social unity – a principled sense of membership in a normative community as central to members' self-understanding – is necessary for the legitimacy and stability of its corresponding institu-

tions', but he then denies that nationality can supply such a sense of unity (Hibbert 2008, 184).

12. According to Barry, unjust laws 'are either defended by saying explicitly that some religion(s) should be privileged or by putting forward manifestly trumped up reasons for having a law whose real purpose is discriminatory' (Barry 2002, 213).

13. For similar criticisms, see Edwards (2014, 256); Elliot-Williams (2016, 345); Hunter-Henin (2015, 97).

14. Lægaard has pointed out to me that strictly speaking his critique only concerns the version of the argument about living together which is supposed to work within the framework of Article 9 of the ECHR. He notes that there might be a more general moral argument that would not be constrained by this rights framework. But he does not say anything about such an argument, and nor do I in this chapter.

15. To get a sense of the debate within Islam regarding the interpretation of these verses, here are just a couple of commentaries on them. An article on the website *Islamic Pamphlets* suggests that 'Islamic texts make it very clear that the hijab is compulsory for Muslim women to observe'. It goes on to note that 'Islamic scholars have agreed that both the burqa and niqab are part of Islam, but have differed as to whether they are also compulsory or optional acts of virtue' (http://islamicpamphlets.com/the-burqa-niqab-uncovering-the-facts). An article in The National news website reports the contrasting view of a 'leading cleric at Egypt's prestigious Al Azhar Mosque' who has 'applauded France's ban on the face veil worn by some devout Muslim women' (https://www.thenational.ae/world/africa/egyptian-cleric-praises-france-s-ban-on-niqab-1.536968). Finally, in an article in the *Huffington Post*, Junaid Jahangir presents the views of 'the few Muslim male scholars who support the permissibility of not wearing the headscarf' (https://www.huffingtonpost.ca/junaid-jahangir/islam-wearing-hijab_b_14046520.html).

16. Witness Statement of the Applicant, Annex 1 to Final Observations, 1-2, *S.A.S. v. France*, Eur. Ct. H. R. (App. No. 43835/11). SAS's remarks also suggest that the ban fails in its own terms, since it sets back the cause of social integration, marginalizing those whom it purports to include. I return to this point later.

17. One way of developing this last point would be by drawing on Hannah Arendt's account of the public realm (1958).

18. Although I put this argument aside in this chapter, I also think that such bans violate the right to religion.

19. See https://qz.com/1090885/austria-just-slapped-a-burqa-ban-on-the-150-women-who-dare-to-wear-one/.

20. Speaking of cultural nationalists in general, Abizadeh argues that 'state-sponsored nationalist projects of cultural assimilation, speciously justified by reference to some supposed need for homogeneity, have increasingly proven to be not just ineffective, but positively counterproductive to the goal of integration' (Abizadeh 2002, 508). With regard to burqa bans in particular, see Elliot-Williams (2016, 350) and Yusuf (2014, 283, 296).

TEN

What Is Wrong with the Swiss Minaret Ban?

Esma Baycan and Matteo Gianni

The issue of Muslim integration in Switzerland has received a great deal of attention internationally since the vote for the popular initiative 'against the minarets'. The initiative, which aimed at forbidding the building of minarets in Switzerland – even though only four minarets existed in the country at the time at which the vote took place – was presented by the initiators as respecting the right of Muslims to practice their religion, yet provided a clear symbolic message and legal limitation to what the Swiss People's Party (henceforth *SPP*) termed the *Islamization* of Swiss public space. In November 2009, 57.5 percent of Swiss voters accepted the ban, providing a direct democratic legitimation to a decision that, according to several observers, involves the unfair treatment of Muslims (Vatter 2011).

The Swiss controversy began with a Turkish cultural association's application for a construction permit for a minaret to its Islamic community centre in 2005 in *Wangen bei Olten*. When faced with residents' opposition, the controversy ultimately went before the *Federal Supreme Court*, which approved the construction permit. Right-wing political parties, especially the *SPP*, successfully launched a referendum and added a clause to the Swiss Constitution that banned the construction of new minarets. This form of popular consultation is called a 'federal initiative' in the Swiss political system; it allows citizens to 'initiate' changes to the constitution. It is a demanding process that requires one hundred thousand signatures – to be collected in eighteen months – in order to be launched, as well as a double majority of citizens and cantons to succeed. *Normatively*, the proposed initiative should not breach *jus cogens* principles.[1]

There is a consensus among normative political philosophers who have written on the topic that the ban is unjust, and we agree on this; yet exactly why it is so is much more controversial. The main culprits are breaches of democratic requirements (e.g., Miller 2016) and equal citizenship (e.g., Zellentin 2014; Thompson 2018; Laborde forthcoming). In this chapter, we extend the equal citizenship argument by supplying a contextual explanation for what is wrong with the Swiss minaret ban. Like others, we argue that it is not only the ban itself that is unjust, but also – and more importantly – some aspects of the democratic process that led thereto. In particular, we argue that, given the role of and the values embedded in direct democracy in the Swiss polity, Muslims suffer of a lack of recognition as autonomous and political subjects, and that this calls into question the ban's legitimacy. In our view, the contextual normativity inherent to direct democracy, that is, the values underpinning and legitimating direct democracy as a just modality of adopting political decisions, entails recognizing the equal status of *all* as autonomous citizens and political agents, if democratic decisions are to be legitimate. These preconditions were not satisfied in the overall Swiss political setting leading to the ban. Therefore, we expand the meaning of equal citizenship at the level of its implementation in the Swiss context in order to capture political injustices inherent in the way that direct democracy produced the ban by popular vote.

In this chapter, we aim to complement and extend Cécile Laborde's argument against the ban, which emphasizes the exclusion of Muslim citizens from equal *national* belonging. We argue that if we take seriously the normativity that is embedded in the Swiss direct democratic context (Carens 2004), especially in its ability to determine the substance of *national* belonging, then the symbolic exclusion of Muslims from *political* belonging is more relevant than the former with regard to democratic justice. Section 1 defines basic notions and presents some arguments that were circulated in Swiss society during the referendum campaign. Section 2 will present extant arguments in normative political philosophy about the ban. Section 3 expands our argument, which can be summarized as follows: the double absence of recognition of Muslims as (i) equal autonomous subjects and (ii) as political agents calls into question the legitimacy of the direct democratic process that led to the ban, making it unjust by the standards implicit within democratic practices in Switzerland.

1. CONTEXTUAL ARGUMENTS

This section systematically presents the political arguments for and against the ban and how they relate to the Swiss context; prior to that we clarify what the ban concretely implies *formally* as well as *contextually* with respect to the background political process.

The federal initiative succeeded in adding a clause to Article 72 of the Swiss Constitution, an article entitled 'Church and State'. Previously, this article had only two clauses: (1) Cantons are competent to determine the nature of the relationship between Church and state; (2) Within the scope of their powers, both cantons and federal authorities take measures to preserve public peace between the members of different religious communities. With the constitutional amendment, a new clause was added: (3) The construction of minarets is prohibited. The *formal* subject of this clause is straightforward: it does not require the removal of minarets already constructed in Switzerland; it is also independent of prayer calls, given that prayer calls never existed in Switzerland as a practice; it prohibits neither the construction of new mosques, nor the banishment of the collective worship of Islam. Yet, from within the Swiss political context, there has been an ongoing *political process* running in the background, expanding this limited *formal* subject into a broader *contextual* one that problematizes not only the construction of new minarets, but also the *public visibility of Islam* in Switzerland. Indeed, the most commonly spread argument for the ban concern the fact of stopping what defenders of the ban qualify as the *Islamization* trend in Switzerland. This includes the wearing of headscarves, Islamic burial customs, burka/burkini wearing, and the domination of Muslim women. Defenders of the ban have politicized all such issues, before and after the vote (a decade later, such matters are still relevant, and are often debated in their intersection with citizenship-related questions, i.e., naturalization and integration). Thus, the campaign against minarets, orchestrated by populist political actors, aimed at agenda-setting Islam and Muslims in the public debate, possesses a temporal character that extends into the pre- and post-vote dynamics.[2] Meanwhile, opponents of the minaret ban contested it through different political arguments.[3] One of these was often mentioned implicitly, in different ways, namely what we call the *recognition* argument. According to this, the political process led people to *question the political belonging* of Muslim residents/citizens to Switzerland, and this was detrimental to equal citizenship. To give an idea of the background context, it is important to mention that the campaign aggressively represented Muslims as a threat to democracy: as 'radical fundamentalist foreign elements threatening Switzerland'.[4] An emblematic campaign poster, a common feature of many Swiss walls, featured a drawing of a Muslim woman in niqab alongside some minarets on a Swiss flag represented in a way 'reminiscent of missiles'. The *SPP* did not hesitate to publish another version of the poster with the minarets protruding through Swiss flag. It is against this background that many different actors repeatedly voiced the recognition argument, such as the Swiss authorities, Christian religious associations, Muslim and other minority organizations.

The Swiss authorities, while not known for being very active in intervening in the political process, were nonetheless against the ban. The Federal Council recommended that Swiss people oppose the ban as it 'infringes guaranteed international human rights and contradicts the core values of the Swiss Federal Constitution. Such a ban would endanger peace between religions and would not help to prevent the spread of fundamentalist Islamic beliefs' (Swiss Federal Council 2008). After the vote, the head of the Federal Department of Justice and Police, Eveline Widmer-Schlumpf, stated that the ban on minaret construction should be understood not as 'a rejection of the Muslim community, religion or culture. Of that the Federal Council gives its assurance' (Swiss Federal Council 2009). The Federal Council's malaise is well expressed by this quote, which captures the worries that were present before the vote and concern the implications that the ban would have had on the equal belonging of Muslims in the Swiss nation.

The reaction described above resonated with Muslim organizations' and representatives' concerns in Switzerland. Farhad Afshar, the president of the Coordination of Islamic Organizations in Switzerland asserted: 'Most painful for us is not the minaret ban, but the symbol sent by this vote . . . Muslims do *not feel accepted* [our emphasis] as a religious community' (Cumming-Bruce and Erlanger 2009). Similarly, during an interview conducted prior to the vote, Youssef Ibram, an imam at Geneva's main mosque and the Islamic Cultural Foundation, was reported to have said that 'whatever the outcome of the vote, Muslims would lose out from a campaign that had played on fears of Islam and exposed deepseated opposition to their community among many Swiss' (Cumming-Bruce and Erlanger 2009). These statements clearly put an emphasis on the campaign's process and imply that irrespective of the outcome of the vote, the campaign had already succeeded in calling the national belonging of Muslims in Switzerland into question.

Opponents of the ban also drew attention to the aggressive nature of the process *targeting* Muslims in Switzerland. The former president of the Swiss Federal Supreme Court, Giusep Nay, stated that: 'The Muslim minority is being attacked. [. . .] This is an exclusion campaign hindering all kinds of on-going integration efforts' (Euronews 2009). In a similar manner, the president of The Federation of Islamic Organizations in Zürich, Taner Hatipoğlu, emphasized the risk of Swiss Muslims' marginalization (Euronews 2009). This aggressive targeting was also contested by minority organizations. For example, the Swiss Association for the Minorities, the Swiss Federation of Israeli Communities, and the Platform of Liberal Jews of Switzerland all argued that social cohesion in Switzerland is safeguarded by respecting Switzerland's linguistic, cultural, and religious diversity. According to them, the campaign favours the discrimination and exclusion of citizens of Muslim religion, given that it obliges them to give up one of their religious symbols, while there is *no discussion* of a restriction for other communities.

To conclude, a number of different political actors agreed that the public debate which occurred before the vote failed to recognize Muslims as equal political agents. Muslims were repeatedly depicted as lacking a commitment to democratic culture, and for that reason were symbolically excluded from national belonging. In the following section, we show that, with the partial exception of Miller, arguments proposed by political philosophers against the ban broadly resonate with this interpretation. Nonetheless, we argue, in the last section, that focusing on the denial of equal citizenship through the symbolic exclusion of Muslims from national belonging almost exclusively, they underestimate a more relevant form of political misrecognition. This is the fact that Muslims are not only symbolically excluded from national belonging, but also from the *political* belonging as autonomous actors who have a fair chance to have a political voice when supporting their conception of the good in the Swiss polity. As we will show, such a misrecognition calls into question the contextual legitimacy of direct democracy in the production of legitimate outcomes.

2. PHILOSOPHICAL ARGUMENTS

Political philosophers who have written about the Swiss vote mostly agree that the minaret ban is unjust. Nevertheless, they disagree about exactly why this is so. There are two main kinds of arguments contesting the ban: the first concerns breaches of democratic requirements such as revisability and subsidiarity (Miller 2016), while the second concerns equal citizenship (Zellentin 2014; Thompson 2018; Laborde forthcoming). This section provides a systematic overview of these arguments, focusing, in particular, on arguments about equal citizenship. According to our reading, arguments such as Miller's are about inclusion within a 'national community', while the other arguments are about inclusion into a 'nation understood as a political community'. The difference is that while in the former view it is enough that minorities be recognized as belonging to the nation, the latter view requires that they also be recognized as full and equal members of the political community.

According to David Miller (2016), the decision to ban the construction of minarets is objectionable in two respects. First, the substance of the decision is objectionable, since although Miller believes that it is generally permissible for historical majorities to shape public spaces in order to reflect their own culture, this can at most justify selective restrictions on minaret building, and not a general prohibition (Miller 2016, 454). Second, Miller also objects to the procedure by which the decision was reached. Not only did it fail to respect the principle of subsidiarity, which states that decisions about the character of public space ought to be taken at the local level, but it also violated the principle of revisability, since it took the form of a constitutional amendment and thereby removed the issue from future democratic contestation (Miller 2016, 453).

Strikingly, Miller rejects two additional arguments against the ban. First, in accordance with his minimalist understanding of human rights (Miller 2007, chap. 7; Baycan 2014), he insists that the ban did not violate a human right to freedom of religion, because the construction of minarets is not an essential religious practice (Miller 2016, 445). Second, he also argues that the ban did not violate the principle of equal treatment, because that principle does not apply to contested public spaces. Instead, in accordance with his commitment to liberal nationalism, he argues that majority precedence in public spaces is both permissible and compatible with equal citizenship.[5]

For Miller, it is permissible for liberal states to promote their national cultures in public spaces. He allows that immigrants ought to be free to contest particular constructions of the national identity and to propose revisions. However, he thinks that they have no right to insist that their culture also be promoted, since by migrating they waived their rights to their own 'societal culture' (Miller 2016, 449). Moreover, if they fail to persuade the majority about the need to revise the national culture, then Miller insists that they have no grounds for complaining that their equal status has been undermined (Miller 2016, 452). However, in our view, this is plausible only if citizenship is understood as a *formal* set of equal individual rights. Citizenship has broader implications if it is instead understood as a practice in which we form, revise, and intersubjectively define the content of the popular will. In particular, being unable to participate on an equal footing to the (re)framing of national identity, or not being considered as having the relevant democratic skills to participate to such a process, arguably means that one is not regarded as an equal and full member of the political community.[6] We will return to this point below.

Alexa Zellentin argues that the Swiss minaret ban is unjust because it does not respect the equal and fair value of political rights, which in turn is detrimental to equal citizenship. Departing from Rawlsian premises, she argues that cultural differences – and not just economic ones – can threaten the fair value of equal political participation rights (Zellentin 2014, 50). In her view, citizens are equals to the extent that they are 'equally entitled to participate in shaping society' (Zellentin 2014, 48). Equal standing requires both that citizens have equal rights and that these rights have 'fair value' for all citizens (Zellentin 2014, 49–50). The Swiss ban harms both of the components of equal citizenship, and is, therefore, unjust with regard to equal standing. The fair value of political rights demands a roughly equal position for making *formal* use of the rights (Zellentin 2014, 48). Under the circumstances of postmigration cultural diversity, this demand is undermined, given that the culturally diverse citizens are unfairly burdened most especially when a historically dominant majority fails to recognize cultural minorities' belonging as members with equal standing (Zellentin 2014, 50). From these premises, Zellentin concludes that the ban made '*the already unfair situation worse*' (our emphasis) (Zellentin 2014, 52 n. 8), given that such an outcome sent two different messages both to voters and to Muslims. To the former, it reassured them that nonrecognition of Muslims citizens' belonging and religious visibility is legitimate; to the latter, it affirmed that their political input is unwelcome, which in turn cannot but lead Muslims to question 'their standing and self-respect as free and equal citizens' (Zellentin 2014, 52 fn. 8).

While we agree with Zellentin that equal citizenship requires the equal standing and self-respect of citizens of migration background, we think that she underestimates the political implications of a lack of equal standing in a *direct democratic context*. Equal standing and self-respect are required to allow Muslims in the national community and assess whether they are equal citizens in relational terms to majority nationals. However, they seem to be too abstract to fully capture what can go wrong when the content of a national identity is defined through direct democratic procedures whose outcome are not submitted to judicial review. In such settings, and given the unequal distribution of political and symbolic resources among majority nationals and citizens of, or assigned to, cultural-religious minorities, what is particularly relevant is *political equal standing*, namely the recognition of minority citizens as full members of the political community and as fully autonomous political agents. This is true even if they are predominantly considered as not fully belonging to the nation or foreigners (as is the case in Switzerland). As we argue later, in a society such as Switzerland, marked by majority/minority tensions, and where direct democracy can be used to enforce a particular national identity at the expense of some people's equal political standing, this latter becomes more relevant to equal citizenship than equal national standing.

Cécile Laborde (forthcoming) goes a step further in this direction. She argues that the minaret ban is unjustified as it is an instance of arbitrary majority domination over Muslims. This is due to the use of *religion* as an *assigned identity*. It is assigned, because, as a matter of fact, very few Muslims demand minarets. She opposes Miller, not only because for her majority national precedence is incompatible with equal citizenship, but also because she believes that people ought to have a degree of discursive control over how their identities are constructed. In contrast, the direct democratic campaign dominated Muslims, both by denying them this

minimum civic standing and by excluding them from the imaginary community of citizens and of the national community. The civic standing of
Muslims was undermined by assigning a negative identity to them and
by depriving them of control over that identity. By turning Muslims into
irreducible aliens, the referendum's outcome gave to this majority domination *a permanency* (forthcoming).

There are two aspects of Laborde's perspective that we tackle in our
attempt to reconstruct the relevant injustices inherent to the ban. The first
is the need to broaden the meaning of the ban and of the overall process
of the politicization of Muslims in order to better assess the wrongs with
regard to equal citizenship. As mentioned previously, when the process
of constructing Muslims as figures of alterity is understood as larger than
the particular direct democratic campaign itself – something that Laborde
does not do – then the contextual meaning of the ban concerns the *visibility of Islam*, namely Muslims' visible presence in the public space, rather
than *the Islamization of Switzerland*, namely a voluntarist political strategy
to impose rigorist Islam in Swiss society, as Laborde argues. This latter
meaning stems from the proponents' way of framing the debate promoting the ban and we are convinced that she cannot avoid reiterating the
Islamization view, unwillingly and by using a reductive interpretation of
the reasons advocated to support it. She does so by emphasizing that
what the ban rejected was not Muslims or Islam but Islamism, understood as a radical and antiliberal-democratic ideology dismissed by most
Muslims. However, when the contextual meaning is understood as concerning the *visibility of Islam*, the ban's meaning includes aspects other
than minaret construction and results in the targeting of Muslims much
more directly in almost all forms of their religious visibility. In fact, the
frame mobilized by the supporters of the ban inevitably disregards the
possibility of recognizing that Muslims may just be being themselves/be
seen as themselves without intending to *Islamize their surroundings*.

Secondly, and more importantly for our argument, Laborde considers
religion functioning as a category of assigned identity as problematic. This is
because such an assignation calls into question the minimal political
standing which includes, at least, a degree of discursive control over how
one's identity is construed and assigned by others (forthcoming). Therefore, she argues, Muslims have been unfairly treated by the minaret ban,
not as Muslims, but as citizens. In her view, Muslims did not suffer from
a lack of recognition, but from the fact of being considered too different to
belong to the national community (what she calls an excess of misrecognition). This is a very interesting point, which strongly resonates with
what we also see as morally wrong in the ban, namely the marginalization of Muslims in the political community of citizens. Nonetheless, we
believe that Laborde underestimates what happened in Switzerland and
the extent to which the unfair treatment of Muslims – and the social

representations justifying it – has significant implications for the lack of recognition of Muslims' equal citizenship.

We argue that the unfair treatment Laborde is writing about can be better captured by analysing the nature of the lack of recognition experienced by Muslims. We take equal recognition as a central aspect of equal citizenship.[7] This is because the latter implies at least (1) respecting the autonomy of all individuals, namely their inner capacity to determine their conception of the 'good life'; (2) granting the members of minorities the symbolic and institutional resources to participate as equals in democratic decision making; and (3) granting some opportunities or legal protections to minorities to avoid or to be protected against majority decisions that go against (1) and (2). Theories of recognition provide several reasons to question the legitimacy of the process that led to the ban of minarets. For instance, regarding the belief that Muslims' religious particularities are unworthy of being socially visible, Anna Galeotti has argued that '[i]f a social difference is denied public visibility and legitimacy in the polity, [then] the group associated with it inevitably bears social stigma' (Galeotti 1993, 597). Stigma is a social condition that affects equal citizenship for the members of the group. In a similar way, Axel Honneth (1996) identifies the lack of equal rights and of social esteem as clear cases of misrecognition, implying that as such Muslims suffer a condition of status subordination (Fraser 2005). Although such theories present different insights into the moral or ethical worth of recognition, all share a common element: equal citizenship is not fulfilled if citizenship rights are not supplemented with the recognition of all in their capacity as equal participants and as equal autonomous moral actors in a given polity.

According to Laborde, the main form of misrecognition raised by the minaret ban is that it led Swiss national identity to be limited to its external borders to prevent Muslims from joining – by imagining it per definition as a European-Secular-Christian identity (forthcoming). In our view, such a misrecognition results in a more grievous structural injustice in the Swiss case. It resides in the fact that the systematic politicization of Islam and of Muslims in Switzerland is made possible by a lack of recognition of them as equal actors in the political community. A more fine-grained consideration of the context, and of the process, shows that this lack of recognition is not only unjust because it goes against an abstract theory of recognition; but that it also violates some of Switzerland's own central values of public philosophy, namely democracy and citizenship.

More specifically, as we will argue in the next section, in the case of Muslims, the content of the religious identity that the majority has assigned to them has important political implications that affect the recognition of their status as equal political subjects, and therefore as citizens. They are indeed not only excluded from national belonging, but also – and more importantly for the sake of equal citizenship – from equal political belonging, considered as fair opportunities provided to them to have a say in the political definition of the content of national belonging. We maintain that the identity assignation which affects Muslims is based on two distinctive failures of recognition, which can be summarized as the refusal to recognize Muslims as 'equally autonomous individuals' with 'equal political agency'. Both of these recognition failures call equal citizenship into question. This is not only problematic at the ideal level of democratic justice; it is also problematic with regard to the Swiss contextual understanding of what counts as a legitimate process of constructing the popular will, of enforcing it, and of managing cultural-religious pluralism in the country.

Switzerland is *a sui generis* polity in many respects, but this is especially true regarding the peculiarly *radical* trade-off it strikes between democracy and justice. The fact that democracy and justice may come into conflict is nothing new, as the democratic procedures may produce unjust decisions either because: 'democratic majorities [. . .] can act in good faith but be mistaken about what justice requires, or they can vote selfishly, with no regard for the interests of minorities' (Valentini 2013, 180). Overall, as Laura Valentini mentions, the general solution to striking a justice-enhancing trade-off adopted by liberal democracies is 'giving the most fundamental requirements of justice the status of constitutional rights, thus removing them from the democratic process' (2013, 180). This is where Switzerland is actually quite radical in its trade-off: it is the only country in which the popular initiatives do not require any form of judicial review (El Wakil, Baudoui, and Gianni 2016). This comes from some specificities of Swiss political culture, namely the fact that citizens are understood to be able to freely determine their will and to search for compromises when needed (given the ethno-cultural and linguistic pluralism on which the country is historically built). The fact that citizens are allowed through direct democracy to revise the constitution (besides imperative law) well illustrated the idea that, as citizens are autonomous and free enough to determine their political will, the decisions taken by them are considered as being procedurally legitimate, whatever the outcome may be. Therefore, concerning the issue of minarets and given the significant value of direct democracy to Swiss national and political identity, it would have been very difficult for institutions (such as the national assembly) to override the initiative and avoid the popular vote. Although, as mentioned in section 1, fears about the legitimacy of the ban had been voiced during the campaign, the saliency of the Swiss specific injunction of 'letting the People decide' prevailed among political actors. But, is this enough to say that the vote, as well as its result, are legitimate with regard to the procedural normative standards implicit within democratic practices in Switzerland?

3. DIRECT DEMOCRATIC PROCESS AND ITS INJUSTICES

The banning of minarets in Switzerland was the result of a popular vote. Is there something about the procedural characteristics of the democratic process that can be apprehended by a more fine-grained contextual approach (Carens 2004) and that might expand the qualification of the moral wrongs produced thereby? We contend that this is the case. The campaign to ban minarets took place in a context that had previously been marked by strong negative representations of values and behaviours of Muslims, and especially of their presumed unwillingness to integrate into the nation and the democratic polity more generally. In our view, such a misrecognition involves a lack of respect for some important contextual preconditions that allow Switzerland's direct democratic process to produce minimally legitimate outcomes. These preconditions include the necessity of protecting minority groups against majority decisions, respecting their autonomy, and including them in political processes that aim to accommodate conflicts between divergent interests or conceptions of the good. Indeed, the focus on the direct democratic process allows us to apprehend two forms of a lack of recognition that affect the practice of equal citizenship in the Swiss case. We call them a lack of *recognition of equal autonomy* and a lack of *recognition of political agency*. These two forms of recognition are intrinsically relational and, therefore, are dependent on existing social conditions and power relations. We argue that assigning an essentialized religious identity to Muslims fails to recognize both their capacity for autonomy and their actual political opportunities to influence and shape the norms that govern them. Before addressing these aspects, let us first introduce some elements of the Swiss direct democratic system.

Swiss Direct Democratic Process: Normativity and Functioning

Direct democracy is a fundamental pillar of the Swiss political system and of its political culture (Kriesi 1998). Normatively, Swiss citizens recognize it as being the ultimate procedure by which to provide legitimacy to collective decisions (in the case of disagreements between political actors or in civil society). This ideal is based on a thick conception of citizenship (Barber 1988), one grounded on a positive conception of freedom, and on the idea that – some constitutional constraints notwithstanding – the ultimate legitimacy of any decision requires acceptance by the people. Nonetheless, besides imperative law, the expression of popular sovereignty is partly limited by at least two features. First, the protection of ethno-linguistic minorities. Indeed, a double majority (citizens and cantons) is required for constitutional amendments, in order to protect small cantons against the more demographically powerful ones. Second, Swiss institutions have implemented what is called 'consensus de-

mocracy' (Lijphart 1999, 31) in order to avoid an excess of direct democracy, which would hamper governance—that is, the need to find compromises among the political elites through a long, extra-parliamentary, decision-making process. This means that all of the relevant political actors
who are affected by the proposal of a new law often discuss it at length,
even outside the parliament, in order to find the most consensual expression thereof and in order to avoid the commencement of a referendum.
Indeed, this structuring principle of Swiss democracy is based on the
view that the individuals affected should have a say in the construction
of the contents of the laws that concern them directly (Barber 1988).

However, direct democracy is not only a legitimating principle, it is
also a device available to political parties and civil society's actors by
which to organize their political strategies. It functions as a modality of
agenda-setting topics that are considered as sufficiently relevant to call
for a political decision. In this perspective, the launching of federal initiatives does not necessarily aim to win a vote, but more often to structure
the political debate around certain issues that will continue to arise even
after the vote itself. Indeed, the Swiss direct democratic process has a
temporality that both precedes and that goes beyond the vote itself. Although the success rate of actually winning the vote is very low – one out
of ten on average, actors use the instrument of federal initiative to keep
issues salient and to reaffirm their political programs. This is particularly
the case with regard to the issue of foreigners, which has historically been
a key topic in the Swiss public debate. In fact, direct democracy has been
regularly used to define the politics of belonging, namely to perform and
reiterate the symbolic exclusion of some groups from common belonging – for example, the Jews in 1891, foreigners in general in the 1960s and
1970s, refugees, and now Muslims (Vatter 2011). Nevertheless, although
such topics ineluctably raise racist or xenophobic implications, the idea
that 'the People decides' is endorsed by political actors as a legitimate
way to adjudicate collective decisions in Swiss political culture.

As mentioned previously, bearing in mind the normative values that
legitimize it, and the political role played by direct democracy in Switzerland, it would be implausible to argue that the vote should not have
taken place because it violated the principles of equal citizenship or equal
belonging. However, this does not mean that there are not contextual
reasons to explain why the vote should have been avoided, or why the
easily foreseeable wrongs that arose during the campaign should have
been thwarted. This is because, given the constant politicization of the
Muslim question in recent years (Gianni 2016b), actors knew that the
minimal preconditions needed to ensure that the public debate did not
reinforce the symbolic exclusion of Muslims were not present when the
initiative was launched and when the National Assembly decided to formally allow the vote. In fact, that Muslims were affected by a lack of
symbolic recognition as full participants and as fully belonging to Swiss

society was hardly a novelty. The politicization of Muslims in Switzerland is the product of a programmatic organization, one orchestrated by political actors involved in the agenda-setting of Islam and Muslims as a problem. The contents of this politicization proceed from a structure of negative representations that are continuously performed by those same actors who are setting an agenda that suits their interests.

A Double Lack of Recognition of Muslims: Equal Autonomy and Political Agency

In our view, and referring to Laborde's terminology, the arbitrary domination over Muslims results mainly from the lack of two forms of recognition, namely of *equal autonomy* and of *political agency*. We take autonomy to mean 'the real and effective capacity to develop and pursue one's own conception of a worthwhile life' (Anderson and Honneth 2005, 130). Analogously, political agency is the capacity to have a say and equal standing in the political definition of common values and norms. Although they are related, the two aspects remain distinct, given that autonomy does not necessarily entail that political agency has been performed.

We argue that some 'socially supportive conditions' (Anderson and Honneth 2005) to ensure equal autonomy are not present in the Swiss context. Muslims had already been symbolically excluded from the boundaries of the Swiss imagined-identity long before the vote on minarets. Since 2004, when citizens rejected a proposal to facilitate the procedure to obtain Swiss citizenship for the third generation of immigrants, Muslims have been constructed as figures of alterity, namely as subjects who cannot belong to the Swiss nation if they are unwilling to assimilate – which also involves being less *visible* in the public space. This politicization, via identity assignation, has led to the crystallization of the figure of the 'generalized Muslim' (Van den Brink 2007). Public controversies prominently portrayed 'him' as possessing given and fixed cultural-religious attributes, as deeply opposed to the ethos of democracy and gender equality, as carrying with him a threat of violence and, more generally, as being a problem for the democratic ethos because of his religious radicalism. Such a 'generalized Muslim' is represented as an actor who is devoid of moral autonomy with regard to democracy, given that he is heteronomously driven by religious values and, therefore, is maladjusted to democratic interactions or practices. For instance, claims articulated by Muslims about the need to reinterpret the content of some Swiss civil laws in order to provide better ways of accommodating their religious practices, have systematically been represented as a dangerous contestation of non-negotiable secular democratic values. Muslims are represented as lacking the democratic culture needed to participate in the determination of collective norms on an equal footing. Indeed, such an 'assigned identity', in

Laborde's terms, not only excludes Muslims from common belonging, but also from the Swiss conception of citizenship. Their supposed over-religiosity entails their lack of autonomy, namely the capacity to partially revise their religious conception of the good and to endorse democratic values.

Of course, research has shown that this is not the case empirically (Gianni, Giugni, and Michel 2015); however, symbolically, the disavowal of their autonomy calls into question the intrinsic value of their practices of citizenship because, according to Swiss contextual values, citizenship is precisely the expression of one's autonomy and freedom. The assignation of this negative identity has not been produced through the campaign on minarets; it is rather the opposite: the campaign is the performative result of the processual construction and reiteration of such an essentialised identity that took place almost a decade previously. Unsurprisingly, the ban on minarets has not stopped the politicization of Muslims' presence in the national community. Other issues pertaining to their religious practices – for example, the banning of the burka, Islamic headscarf, cemeteries reserved for Muslims, calls for the strengthening of integration policies' requirements, respect for secular institutions, respect of gender equality – have all been (and continue to be) debated since the vote. Indeed, the vote did not produce, but instead crystallized, previous representations of Muslims that call their autonomy into question.[8] Therefore, a central aspect of the Swiss contextual understanding of democratic legitimacy, namely that members of the political community are conceived of as autonomous, and that their autonomy should at least minimally be protected in order to respect democratic principles, is partially denied to Muslims, thus calling into question their actual standing as equal citizens.

The lack of recognition of Muslims' political agency follows on from their lack of recognized autonomy. By political agency, we refer to the actions undertaken by free and equal citizens in participating in, supporting, or contesting the norms, values, or power relations that structure the polity. In Switzerland, to have political agency means at least two things: to have the ability (recognized and supported by institutions) to resist and reject injurious identity assignations that occur in public debate, and to be recognized as a social and political actor who is allowed to participate in compromise-building procedures (necessary to avoid the imposition of majority decisions). Neither of these conditions are satisfied for Muslims in Switzerland. Muslims' political voices have been rendered inaudible by negative representations regarding their intrinsic autonomy, namely their capability to endorse democratic values while pursuing their conception of the good. Therefore, Muslims are *depoliticized* as political actors. Put otherwise, the injunction to unilaterally assimilate to democratic norms, in order to belong to Swiss society and polity, entails their *depoliticization as citizens*. With regard to equal citizenship taken as a normative principle, we consider that the injustice inherent to depoliticization is more fundamental than the exclusion from national identity. If the exercise of Muslim political agency – in claiming issues that pertain to their religious practices, for instance – is automatically categorized as incompatible with democratic values, then their political voice is disregarded as a legitimate component of the process of definition of common norms and of the contents of national identity. Instead of being democratically and deliberatively legitimated (or eventually modified) by the participation of (all) affected individuals, such common norms are enforced by the majority as though they were nonnegotiable, *pre-* or *extra-political;* therefore, they are treated as if they should *neither be the object nor the result* of a democratic deliberation with Muslims. When a conflict between Muslims and public authorities does occur, the institutional response is mostly based on law or formal decisions, but does not open up to the setting of political devices intended to build postconventional identities based on an intersubjective recognition of all actors concerned (Williams 1995). Such a view contradicts some of the basic contextual values that legitimize Swiss direct democracy.

In Swiss political culture, the idea of reaching an agreement or a compromise between opposing political forces is an important requirement to legitimize collective decisions. It is an historical specificity of the functioning of Swiss democracy and a central part of Switzerland's paradigmatic success in accommodating the country's original multicultural setting (Linder 1994). Indeed, as a consensus democracy, the Swiss polity is built around a very large set of formal and informal political procedures that seek to foster agreement between actors that belong to territorialized cultural and linguistic groups. However, the situation is almost the opposite concerning nonterritorialized minority groups. In the case of Muslims, and given the negative representations spread throughout society, almost nothing has been done by political institutions in order to provide them with political opportunities to be part of the process of defining the terms of their inclusion in society. For instance, Muslim associations have not been systematically contacted by the federal state to try to promote a strategy by which to counter negative representations or to find common agreements – as has been done in some cantons. Very few associations have obtained public recognition from the state to be associations of general interest (namely pursuing objectives that go beyond ethnic groups or religious communities, but considered of social utility for all the population; Christian associations generally obtain such a status). The state is also reluctant to enforce article 261 of the penal code that punishes hate speech towards religious, ethnic, or racial minorities.

Indeed, Swiss political elites have decided that direct democratic value (according to which the people have the last word) was superior to the values of respecting Muslims' capability for autonomy and of the political accommodation of conflicts through their inclusion in the decision-making process. This choice is mainly driven by political reasons: (1) the reluctance of political parties to be seen as unpopular (or illegitimate) if they deny the exercise of democratic, popular sovereignty on this issue; (2) the reluctance of political actors to go against the negative views about Muslims spread throughout the population in order to hold onto their electorate. In sum, neither the recognition of autonomy, nor the empowerment of political agency have been a clear goal for specific public policies. These contextual choices have triggered and perpetuated a process in which Muslims are unfairly treated and in such a way that calls into question the legitimacy of the campaign and the vote, as well as its outcome. Through the popular initiative on minarets, the direct democracy allowed majority citizens to determine the content of national identity. However, the side effects of such a process go far beyond the content of national identity: they result in the symbolic and political confinement of Muslims in a position of 'second-class' citizens, as lacking basic competences to be full participants to the democratic process. Instead of being a procedure providing all citizens with an equal and fair way to take a collective decision respecting the equal standing of all – what equal citizenship should be – the Swiss democratic process, not limited by judicial review, has contributed to the creation of unequal citizens.

In conclusion, in our view, the moral wrong of the minaret ban mainly concerns the fact that the iteration of negative identity assignations to Muslims has taken place in a context marked by the lack of recognition of their *equally being full citizens* – understood as providing an autonomous subject with the political opportunity to strive for their conception of the good. In order to recognize Muslims as being part of the Swiss community, and allowing for a minimally legitimate democratic process, the public debate should have been more strictly regulated (by the state and by political actors) in order to avoid the crystallization of negative representations. This would not necessarily have changed the outcome of the vote, but it would have provided a minimal institutional recognition that Muslims belong to both society and the political community and that, like every other citizen, they have to be protected against injurious categorizations that undermine their equal footing with the members of the majority in terms of their autonomy and political agency. Institutions and political actors have not made significant steps, neither formally nor symbolically, to provide Muslims with such a double recognition, which is necessary for a contextual legitimation to the direct democratic outcomes. In so doing, they have undermined the preconditions that provide legitimacy to Swiss direct democracy's outcomes, whatever these outcomes may be.

4. CONCLUSION

In this chapter, we have argued that the injustice inherent in the ban of minarets is twofold. On the one hand, as argued by Cécile Laborde, it affects the principle of equal citizenship needed to sustain democratic justice; on the other, it results from the disrespect of some crucial preconditions providing legitimacy to the contextual normativity embedded in the Swiss conception of direct democracy. As shown in section 2, several political philosophers, with whom we agree, argue that the ban is unjust. In our view, for instance, in focusing on a single religious minority and restricting the civil rights of its members, it entails a form of discrimination. However, we believe that such a conclusion is insufficient to fully make sense of the injustice at stake. The latter also emanates from some characteristics of the broad process that led to the ban and whose temporality largely precedes and follows the 2009 vote. We have shown how the assignation to Muslims of a negative and essentialized religious identity, through a contextual specification of Laborde's arguments, not only excludes them from national belonging, but also, and more importantly for us, from the opportunity to be considered as full citizens in the political community. Such a politically unfair treatment cannot be captured by referring only to a formal principle of equal citizenship; a contextual analysis of the case is needed to uncover it. Our analysis shows that the lack of recognition suffered by Muslims ultimately calls the legitimacy of the minaret ban into question, regarding the specific values that inform the direct democratic ethos in Switzerland. If this is true, then the minaret ban is much more than a case of majority precedence in the religious composition of the public space; it clearly shows injustices that fix Swiss Muslims in a second-class position regarding the worth of their citizenship. Given that such an injustice is democratically sanctioned by popular vote, it is much more relevant, in our view, to once again take up the challenge of coming up with a fair accommodation of cultural-religious groups in multicultural societies marked by a strong majority's power over minorities.

ACKNOWLEDGEMENTS

The National Center of Competence in Research (NCCR) supported this research—'On the Move' funded by the Swiss National Science Foundation. Esma Baycan presented previous versions of the argument during InCite Rencontres de la Citoyenneté at the University of Geneva in Spring 2017, NCCR Research Days in Fall 2017, and Religion in Liberal Politics Panel MANCEPT Workshops in Fall 2018. The authors are grateful to all of the participants at these events, and specifically to Helder De Schutter, Stefanie Kurt, Peter Scholten, Aurélia Bardon, Elise Rouméas and Noémi

Michel. Gratitude is also due to the editors of the current volume, Jonathan Seglow and Andrew Shorten, to Ian O'Flynn and the anonymous reviewers who provided very helpful criticisms on different versions of the chapter.

REFERENCES

Anderson, Joel, and Axel Honneth. 2005. 'Autonomy, Vulnerability, Recognition, and Justice'. In *Autonomy and the Challenges to Liberalism*, edited by John Christman and Joel Anderson, 127–49. Cambridge: Cambridge University Press.

Barber, Benjamin. 1988. 'Participation and Swiss Democracy'. *Government and Opposition* 23 (1): 31–50.

Baycan, Esma. 2014. 'Review Essay: Justice for Earthlings, David Miller'. *Ethical Perspectives* 3:429–39.

Carens, Joseph. 2004. 'A Contextual Approach to Political Theory.' *Ethical Theory and Moral Practice* 7 (2):117–32.

Cumming-Bruce, Nick, and Steven Erlanger. 2009. 'Swiss Ban Building of Minarets on Mosques'. *New York Times*, 29 November. https://www.nytimes.com/2009/11/30/world/europe/30swiss.html.

El Wakil, A., R. Baudoui, and M. Gianni. 2016. 'Etat d'exception, Démocratie Directe, Exception Démocratique : Le Cas Suisse'. *En Jeu* 7:105–16.

Euronews. 2009. 'Minaret Debate Angers Swiss Muslims'. *Euronews*, 19 November. https://www.euronews.com/2009/11/19/minaret-debate-angers-swiss-muslims.

Federal Statistical Office. 2012. Ständige Wohnbevölkerung ab 15 Jahren nach Religions - und Konfessionszugehörigkeit in den Sprachregionen (revidierte Daten vom 11.10.2012). http://www.bfs.admin.ch/bfs/portal/de/index/news/04/01.Document.159819.zip.

Fraser, Nancy. 2005. *Qu'est-ce que la justice sociale? reconnaissance et redistribution*. Paris: Éd. la Découverte.

Galeotti, Anna Elisabetta. 1993. 'Citizenship and Equality: The Place for Toleration'. *Political Theory* 21 (4): 585–605.

Gianni, Matteo. 2016a. 'La régulation de l'Islam et l'intégration des musulmans en Suisse: Une relation paradoxale ?' In *Réguler le religieux dans les sociétés libérales ?*, edited by Amélie Barras, François Dermange, and Sarah Nicolet, 45–62. Genève: Labor et Fides.

———. 2016b. 'Muslims' Integration as a Way to Defuse the Muslim Question? Insights from the Swiss Case', *Critical Research on Religion* 34 (1): 21–36.

Gianni, Matteo, Marco Giugni, and Noémi Michel. 2015. *Musulmans en Suisse. Profils et intégration*. Lausanne: Presses polytechniques et universitaires romandes.

Gladney, Dru. 2009. 'Non à l'initiative Anti-Minarets'. Amnesty International Switzerland. March. https://www.amnesty.ch/fr/pays/europe-asie-centrale/suisse/docs/2009/non-initiative-minarets/initiative-anti-minarets.

Honneth, Axel. 1996. *The Struggle for Recognition: The Moral Grammar of Social Conflicts*. Cambridge, MA: MIT Press.

Kriesi, Hanspeter. 1998. *Le Système Politique Suisse*. Second edition. Collection Politique Comparée. Paris: Economica.

Laborde, Cécile. forthcoming. 'Miller's Minarets. Religion, Culture, Domination'. In *Political Philosophy, Here and Now. Essays in Honour of David Miller*. Oxford: Oxford University Press.

Lægaard, Sune. 2015. 'Multiculturalism and Contextualism: How Is Context Relevant for Political Theory?' *European Journal of Political Theory* 14 (3): 259–76.

Langer, Lorenz. 2010. 'Panacea or Pathetic Fallacy—The Swiss Born on Minarets'. *Vanderbilt Journal of Transnational Law* 43 (4): 863–951.

LeNews. 2017. 'Swiss Feel Threatened by Islam, According to Survey'. 30 August.

Lijphart, Arend. 1999. *Patterns of Democracy: Government Forms and Performance in Thirty-Six Countries*. New Haven, CT: Yale University Press.
Linder, Wolf. 1994. *Swiss Democracy: Possible Solutions to Conflict in Multicultural Societies*. Basingstoke: Palgrave Macmillan.
Miller, David. 2007. *National Responsibility and Global Justice*. Oxford: Oxford University Press.
———. 2016. 'Majorities and Minarets: Religious Freedom and Public Space'. *British Journal of Political Science* 46 (2): 437–56.
Mills, Charles W. (Charles Wade). 2005. 'Ideal Theory as Ideology'. *Hypatia* 20 (3): 165–84.
Modood, Tariq, and Simon Thompson. 2017. 'Revisiting Contextualism in Political Theory: Putting Principles into Context'. *Res Publica* 24 (3): 339–57.
Swiss Federal Council. 2008. 'Press Release: Opinion on the Popular Initiative against the Construction of Minarets'. 27 August. https://www.bj.admin.ch/bj/en/home/aktuell/news/2008/ref_2008-08-27.html.
———. 2009. 'Press Release of the Federal Council'. 29 November. https://www.admin.ch/gov/en/start/documentation/media-releases.msg-id-30430.html.
Rescher, Nicholas. 2000. *Process Philosophy: A Survey of Basic Issues*. Pittsburgh: University of Pittsburgh Press.
Taylor, Charles. 1994. 'The Politics of Recognition'. In *Multiculturalism: Examining the Politics of Recognition*, edited and introduced by Amy Gutmann, 25–74. Princeton, NJ: Princeton University Press.
Thompson, Simon. 2018. 'The Expression of Religious Identities and the Control of Public Space'. *Ethnicities* 19 (2): 231–50.
Valentini, Laura. 2013. 'Justice, Disagreement and Democracy'. *British Journal of Political Science* 43 (1): 177–99.
van den Brink, Bert. 2007. 'Imagining Civic Relations in the Moment of Their Breakdown: A Crisis of Civic Integrity in the Netherlands'. In *Multiculturalism and Political Theory*, edited by Anthony S. Laden and David Owen, 350–72. Cambridge: Cambridge University Press.
Vatter, Adrian. 2011. *Vom Schächt- zum Minarettverbot. Religiöse Minderheiten in der direkten Demokratie*. Zürich: NZZ Verlag.
Williams, Melissa. 1995. 'Justice toward Groups: Political not Juridical'. *Political Theory* 23 (1): 67–91.
Zellentin, Alexa. 2014. 'Freedom, Equality, Minarets'. *Res Publica* 20 (1): 45–63.

NOTES

1. The *jus cogens*, established to safeguard the 'core' principles of human rights, protects some fundamental principles of international law: crimes against the humanity or human trafficking, for instance.
2. It is, therefore, possible to distinguish an *ex-ante* and an *ex-post* instantiation of the same process. During the rejected vote on *facilitated naturalization for foreigners* in 2004, the SPP mainly argued that: 'if the vote was accepted, Switzerland would risk to become a majority Muslim state by 2040'. Similarly, an upcoming vote banning the face-covering – the *de facto* burqa ban – will continue to keep the political stamina alive with an *ex-post* instantiation about ten years later.
3. Other arguments oppose the ban in order to: protect Switzerland's international reputation; guarantee different liberties protected by the Swiss Constitution; efficiently fight against religious fundamentalism; and refute the defense of banning minarets as a replication of the limits put on Christian religious practices in Islamic countries. See Gladney (2009).
4. The presence of Muslims in Switzerland is a very recent phenomenon: the Muslim population increased by almost twenty times between 1970 and 2000 (from about 16,000 to 311,000), amounting to 4.3 per cent of the residents. According to the most

recent estimations in 2010, the Muslim population has increased to 440,000, or 5.5 per cent of the overall population. Muslims living in Switzerland are mainly foreigners, although the proportion of Muslims holding a Swiss passport is increasing: while only 11.7 per cent of them were Swiss citizens in 2000, estimates based on more recent data suggest that 31 per cent or more of the Muslim population are Swiss citizens (Federal Statistical Office 2012).

5. Simon Thompson (2018) has suggested that Miller has three arguments for majority precedence when it comes to shaping public space, namely contribution, expression, and alienation (Thompson 2018, 5–12). However, Thompson argues that, by the standards of Miller's own theory, at least some of the claims on public space that come from minorities should be recognized (Thompson 2018, 7).

6. We thank the anonymous reviewer for having emphasized this aspect.

7. According to Charles Taylor: 'equal recognition is not just the appropriate mode for a healthy democratic society. Its refusal can inflict damage on those who are denied it [. . .]. The projection of an inferior or demeaning image on another can actually distort and oppress, to the extent that the image is internalized' (1994, 36).

8. According to a survey presented in August 2017 by the *Sonntags Blick*, 38 per cent of the 1,003 people surveyed said that they feel threatened by Muslims in Switzerland. This percentage is more than double the 16 recorded in a similar survey in 2004 (LeNews 2017). It is important to note that nothing particular happened in Switzerland during this time span – terrorist attack, etc.

Index

About the Contributors

Andrea Baumeister is Senior Lecturer in the Division of History and Politics at the University of Stirling. Her main research interests lie within the area of liberal political philosophy, with a focus on questions of legitimacy, democratic participation, and citizenship in contemporary pluralist liberal democracies.

Christoph Baumgartner is Associate Professor of Ethics in the Department of Philosophy and Religious Studies at Utrecht University. Principal topics of his research are religion in the public sphere, religious diversity, freedom of religion and freedom of expression, blasphemy, tolerance, citizenship, and secularity and (post)secularism.

Esma Baycan is working on ethics and politics of immigration; nationalism in its post- and substate forms; as well as global justice, at KU Leuven and the University of Geneva. She is particularly interested in articulating competing research paradigms framing the debate in ethics of immigration.

Paul Billingham is Associate Professor of Political Theory in the Department of Politics and International Relations at the University of Oxford, and a Fellow of Magdalen College. His research focuses on debates within political liberalism and concerning the place of religion in public life. His work has been published in various journals in moral, political, and legal philosophy, including *Politics, Philosophy & Economics, Journal of Moral Philosophy, Law and Philosophy*, and *Oxford Journal of Law and Religion*.

Matteo Gianni is Associate Professor in the Department of Political Science and at the Institute of Citizenship Studies of the University of Geneva. He is member of the NCCR—*On the move* at the University of Neuchâtel. His research focus on the normative theory of citizenship and multiculturalism, and the political integration of Muslims in Switzerland and Europe.

Sune Lægaard is Associate Professor of Philosophy in the Department of Communication and Arts at Roskilde University, Denmark. He works on various issues related to multiculturalism, including policies of recognition, toleration, freedom of religion and free speech, secularism and on methodological issues in political theory. He is editor-in-chief of the journal *Res Publica* (published by Springer).

Nick Martin is Lecturer in Political Theory in the Department of Politics at the University of Liverpool. He is currently working on two research projects: (1) the justification and regulation of exemptions; and (2) the political ethics of adoption. He has previously published research on liberal neutrality and charitable organizations.

Élise Rouméas is a Research Associate in the Department of Politics and International Relations at the University of Oxford and an associate member of Nuffield College. Her current research explores various procedural and institutional responses to religious diversity. She focuses on specific contexts (e.g., the workplace) or situations (e.g., internal dissent) and advocates for concrete conflict resolution tools or regulative frameworks.

Sebastián Rudas is a Postdoctoral Researcher in Political Philosophy at the University of São Paulo. His research focuses on political secularism and the rights of indigenous peoples in Latin American democracies. His publications in this field include 'Against Moralized Secularism' in *Les ateliers de l'éthique/The Ethics Forum* and 'Laicidad y Anticlericalismo' in *Ideas y Valores*.

Jonathan Seglow is Reader (Associate Professor) in Political Theory at Royal Holloway, University of London. He is the author of *Defending Associative Duties* and has recently published on freedom of speech, and religious accommodation and establishment, among other areas.

Andrew Shorten is Senior Lecturer in Political Theory at the University of Limerick. He is author of *Contemporary Political Theory* as well as articles and book chapters on religious accommodation, linguistic justice, federalism and multiculturalism. He is currently working on a book about multiculturalism.

Simon Thompson is Associate Professor in Political Theory at the University of the West of England, Bristol, UK. He is author of *The Political Theory of Recognition* (2006) and coeditor of *Global Justice and the Politics of Recognition* (2013), *The Politics of Misrecognition* (2012), *Politics and the Emotions* (2012), *Emotions, Politics and Society* (2006) and *Richard Rorty: Critical Dialogues* (2001).

www.ingramcontent.com/pod-product-compliance
Lightning Source LLC
Chambersburg PA
CBHW021816270326
41932CB00007B/211